The Metaverse and Smart Cities
Urban Environments in the Age of Digital Connectivity

Smart Cities

The Metaverse and Smart Cities

Urban Environments in the Age of Digital Connectivity

Zaheer Allam
Deakin University, Geelong, VIC, Australia

Zarrin Allam
University of Western Australia, Perth, WA, Australia

ELSEVIER

Elsevier
Radarweg 29, PO Box 211, 1000 AE Amsterdam, Netherlands
125 London Wall, London EC2Y 5AS, United Kingdom
50 Hampshire Street, 5th Floor, Cambridge, MA 02139, United States

Copyright © 2024 Elsevier Inc. All rights are reserved, including those for text and data mining, AI training, and similar technologies.

Publisher's note: Elsevier takes a neutral position with respect to territorial disputes or jurisdictional claims in its published content, including in maps and institutional affiliations.

No part of this publication may be reproduced or transmitted in any form or by any means, electronic or mechanical, including photocopying, recording, or any information storage and retrieval system, without permission in writing from the publisher. Details on how to seek permission, further information about the Publisher's permissions policies and our arrangements with organizations such as the Copyright Clearance Center and the Copyright Licensing Agency, can be found at our website: www.elsevier.com/permissions.

This book and the individual contributions contained in it are protected under copyright by the Publisher (other than as may be noted herein).

Notices
Knowledge and best practice in this field are constantly changing. As new research and experience broaden our understanding, changes in research methods, professional practices, or medical treatment may become necessary.

Practitioners and researchers must always rely on their own experience and knowledge in evaluating and using any information, methods, compounds, or experiments described herein. In using such information or methods they should be mindful of their own safety and the safety of others, including parties for whom they have a professional responsibility.

To the fullest extent of the law, neither the Publisher nor the authors, contributors, or editors, assume any liability for any injury and/or damage to persons or property as a matter of products liability, negligence or otherwise, or from any use or operation of any methods, products, instructions, or ideas contained in the material herein.

ISBN: 978-0-443-22351-8

> For information on all Elsevier publications
> visit our website at https://www.elsevier.com/books-and-journals

Publisher: Mica Haley
Acquisitions Editor: Kathryn Eryilmaz
Editorial Project Manager: Shivangi Mishra
Production Project Manager: Selvaraj Raviraj
Cover Designer: Greg Harris

Typeset by STRAIVE, India

Working together to grow libraries in developing countries

www.elsevier.com • www.bookaid.org

Contents

1. **Introduction to the metaverse**

Introduction	1
History of the metaverse	2
On the perceived importance of the metaverse	3
From the internet to the metaverse	5
The metaverse and its foundational elements	6
Use cases of the metaverse	8
The metaverse economy	10
Fears and critisms of the metaverse	11
Challenges and imperatives	12
How does the metaverse link to smart cities?	13
References	14

2. **The history and evolution of the metaverse**

Introduction	19
The origins of the metaverse concept	22
The first steps: Early virtual worlds and gaming environments	24
The rise of massively multiplayer online games (MMOGS)	26
The metaverse in science fiction and pop culture	28
The emergence of virtual reality and augmented reality	29
The metaverse in the 21st century	31
References	33

3. **The metaverse and smart cities**

Introduction	37
Overview of smart cities	40
Understanding the metaverse	43
Intersecting the metaverse and smart cities	45
Case studies and examples	46
Ethical, legal, and social implications	48
Future directions	50
References	51

4. The metaverse and sustainable cities

Introduction	55
Sustainable cities: Challenges and opportunities	57
Case studies of the metaverse in sustainable cities	60
Copenhagen: Virtual collaboration for climate adaptation	60
Singapore: Smart nation initiative and virtual Singapore	61
Barcelona: Superblocks and the metaverse	61
Amsterdam: Circular economy and the metaverse	62
Lessons learned and implications for future applications	62
Benefits and challenges of using the metaverse in sustainable cities	63
As a tool for promoting sustainability	63
Challenges and limitations of using the metaverse	63
Potential risks and unintended consequences	64
Ethical considerations	64
Recommendations for addressing challenges and maximizing benefits	64
Future directions and implications for research	65
Conclusions	67
References	67

5. The metaverse and future cities

Introduction	73
Metaverse-enabled smart infrastructure for future cities	75
Metaverse-enabled urban experience and engagement	77
Metaverse-enabled work and education in future cities	80
Challenges and limitations of metaverse-enabled future cities	82
Conclusions and future directions for metaverse-enabled future cities	85
References	87

6. The impact of the metaverse on urban life

Introduction	93
Challenges of urban life	95
Accessibility	95
Congestion	96
Social isolation	97
Potential applications of the metaverse in urban life	99
Examples of metaverse applications in urban life	101
Benefits and challenges of using the metaverse in urban life	103
Potential benefits of the metaverse in urban life	103
Challenges and limitations of the metaverse in urban life	104
Addressing challenges in the metaverse	105
Informing the design and implementation of the metaverse in urban settings	105

Case studies of metaverse in urban life 106
    Virtual Helsinki: Urban planning and cultural events 106
Ethical and social implications of the metaverse in urban life 108
Opportunities for collaboration and cocreation in metaverse
    and urban life 110
Conclusion 111
References 112

7. **The metaverse and urban planning**

Introduction 117
Opportunities and benefits of using the metaverse in urban
    planning 119
Applications of the metaverse in urban planning 122
Challenges and limitations of using the metaverse in urban
    planning 124
Potential developments in using the metaverse in urban
    planning 127
Case studies of metaverse use in urban planning 129
Conclusion and future outlook 130
References 131

8. **The metaverse and real estate development**

Introduction to metaverse in real estate development 135
Traditional real estate development: Challenges and
    limitations 136
The metaverse and virtual real estate 139
The metaverse and real estate visualization 142
Smart technologies in real estate management 144
The benefits and challenges of metaverse in real estate 145
Case studies 147
    Decentraland 147
    Sotheby's international realty 148
    WeWork 149
    Cryptovoxels 149
    Microsoft 150
Conclusion and future outlook 150
References 151

9. **The social implications of the metaverse in cities**

Challenges of social interactions in urban environments 155
Enhancing community building and social connections 157
Augmented reality for cultural experiences and diversity 158
Smart technologies for efficient social service delivery 160
Privacy considerations in the metaverse 162
Inclusivity and accessibility in the metaverse 164

	Cultural sensitivity in virtual environments	165
	Discussions and conclusions	167
	References	168
10.	**The economic implications of the metaverse in cities**	
	Economic challenges in traditional urban settings	173
	Economic opportunities of the metaverse in cities	175
	Urban economic planning and development with the metaverse	178
	Implications of the metaverse for urban employment and skills	180
	Equity and inclusivity considerations in metaverse-based economies	182
	Ethical and legal implications of metaverse-based economies	183
	Discussions and conclusions	184
	References	186
11.	**The environmental implications of the metaverse**	
	Energy efficiency and resource management	191
	Environmental monitoring and analysis	194
	Sustainable transportation and mobility	196
	Waste management and circular economy	198
	Green spaces and urban biodiversity	200
	Sustainable lifestyles and behaviors	202
	Ethical considerations and future challenges	203
	References	205
12.	**Reflections and prospects: The metaverse and cities**	
	Introduction	209
	Future developments in the metaverse	210
	Challenges and limitations of the metaverse	213
	The future of the metaverse and cities	215
	Recommendations for policy and decision-makers	216
	Final thoughts and closing remarks	218
	References	219
Index		223

Chapter 1

Introduction to the metaverse

Introduction

The advent of the metaverse, a revolutionary iteration of the industry revolution (industry 4.0), holds the promise of a new adventure for human experience and connection. As technology advances and new innovations emerges, the metaverse becomes ever more poised to transform the way humans coexist, work, enjoy their recreation, respond to urban challenges like climate change, and interact (Henz, 2022). The melding of VR and augmented reality (AR) at the forefront of this revolution suggests that the boundaries between the physical and virtual dimensions may soon be indistinct (Lee et al., 2021).

Smart city technology is an essential component of the metaverse, lending the virtual world an opportunity to integrate cutting-edge advancements, such as IoT, AI, Crowd Computing, Big Data, and latest mobile connectivity technologies, to enhance the quality of life for its inhabitants (Allam, 2019). The metaverse will serve as an ideal arena for the implementation and optimization of smart city technology on an unparalleled scale (Allam et al., 2022).

The metaverse is argued to hold the potential to revolutionize smart cities application in multiple ways. For instance, it expected to offer a new and unmatched opportunities for urban planning and design, allowing architects and urban planners to experiment and perfect their designs in a virtual environment before actualizing them in the physical world (Lv et al., 2022). It may also present new avenues for citizen to participation and engage with the urban managements, and those in positions of authority, allowing them to become more involved in city planning and decision-making processes in a manner that is simply not feasible in the physical world (Allam et al., 2022).

Moreover, the metaverse can also generate novel economic opportunities within the smart cities. For instance, it promises to avail opportunities to host virtual marketplaces, allowing residents to engage in trade and commerce within a virtual environment (Cheng et al., 2022). Furthermore, it has the potential to revolutionize how cultural assets and heritage, plus tourist products are consumed by locals and virtual visitors from all over the world (Hemmati, 2022).

However, the metaverse also brings with it a range of challenges: both ethical and legal. For example, there are concerns over privacy and security especially of data and private information in the virtual realm (Allam, 2020) as well as the need to establish a clear set of regulations and guidelines for virtual commerce, trading activities, and tourism (Rosenberg, 2022). Bridging the digital divide will also be a crucial step in ensuring that all residents have equal access to the benefits of the metaverse.

Those drawbacks notwithstanding, the metaverse holds immeasurable promises and prospects for the future of our interactions and the urban landscape. In particular, as technology advances, the potential of metaverse prompt sweeping and far-reaching changes to the way we live and work grows stronger.

History of the metaverse

The first instances of a metaverse can be traced back to the 1960s and 1970s, when computer scientists and science fiction writers first began to imagine a virtual world where people could interact with each other and with a computer-generated environment. The term "metaverse" was first used in Neal Stephenson's 1992 science fiction novel Snow Crash (Stephenson, 2003), where he described a virtual world inhabited by both people and artificial intelligence. This early vision of the metaverse was heavily influenced by the computer and science fiction cultures of the time, and it was seen as a possible future for humanity.

The concept of metaverse was born in the late 1990s and early 2000s as widespread adoption of the internet became inevitable (Mystakidis, 2022). This was pointed by the exponential rise on online communities and virtual worlds, such as Second Life, World of Warcraft (McArthur et al., 2010), and others, as people began to imagine the potential of a virtual world where they could increase their interactions with others and with a computer-generated environment. And true to this, it is reported that now, Second Life has over 65 million users by 2021 (Greener, 2022), while World of Warcraft had an estimated user base of 12 million people (Bassey, 2020). It is worthwhile to note that these early virtual worlds were limited in scope and capabilities. However, the opened opportunities and provided glimpses of what a metaverse could be, especially after other supportive technologies such as mobile connectivity (such as 5G and 6G) continue to materialize (Allam & Jones, 2021).

In the early 2000s, after the fourth industrial revolution, the development of VR technology, such as the VR Forge (2001), Oculus Rift (2012), the HTC Vive (2016) (Borrego et al., 2018), and others accelerated the actualization of the idea of the metaverse. As such, for the first time, people could experience a virtual world in a fully immersive way. However, it is noted that this new wave of virtual worlds was more sophisticated and had more advanced capabilities, but the available technologies were still in infancy stage to warrant advanced capabilities.

Over the past few years, the concept of the metaverse has gained even more momentum, with major tech companies, such as Facebook (projected to have invested over $19.2 billion by end of 2023) (Adepetun, 2022) and Google (which invested approximately $39.8 billion already) (Investing.com, 2022) investing heavily in the development of VR and augmented reality technologies. The recent advancements in these technologies have made it possible to create virtual worlds that are more realistic and immersive than ever before. Additionally, the growth of blockchain technology and the rise of decentralized networks have created new opportunities for the metaverse (Gadekallu et al., 2022), allowing people to own virtual assets and engage in virtual commerce in a secure and decentralized way.

The current state of the metaverse is still in its early stages, but it has the potential to become a major part of our lives in the future. Many experts believe that the metaverse will eventually become a central hub for social interactions, commerce, entertainment, and even education. The metaverse has the potential to bring people from all over the world together in a virtual environment, breaking down the barriers of distance, and creating new opportunities for interaction and collaboration.

On the perceived importance of the metaverse

First, the metaverse is considered critical because it increases the capabilities to create new and more immersive experiences for people. With the use of VR and AG technologies, the metaverse has the advances the level of immersion in ways not possible in the physical realm (as depicted in Fig. 1.1 below). For instance, the metaverse version by Meta promises to revolutionize the traditional work environment by helping them recreate digital twin of the same such that remote working becomes just is the case in real life (Weishaupt, 2022). Further, with prospects of social interactions becoming rare each day due to a

FIG. 1.1 An individual using VR headset during virtual collaboration (XR Expo, 2020).

myriad of factors like work commitment, geographical distances, and health concerns, the metaverse is expected to open new frontiers where people can interact in more immersive ways (Alfaisal et al., 2022). That is, it will make it possible for people to play games, have adventures, create new products, and transact, among other this, in the virtual realm in more interactive ways (Dwivedi et al., 2022).

In addition, the metaverse has the potential to bring people from diverse backgrounds together in a virtual environment, thus overcoming the barriers of distance and creating new opportunities for interaction and collaboration. With the ability to create virtual identities and interact with others in a virtual world, people may be able to connect with others who they would not have been able to meet in the physical world. This has the potential to create new communities and social networks that can span across countries and continents (Zhao et al., 2022).

The metaverse also has important implications for the future of work and commerce (Roy, 2021). With the ability to create virtual storefronts and conduct virtual transactions, the metaverse has the potential to revolutionize the way we do business. This could lead to new opportunities for entrepreneurs and small businesses, as well as new ways for consumers to purchase products and services (Cheah & Shimul, 2023). Additionally, the metaverse could provide new opportunities for remote work, allowing people to work and collaborate with others from diverse location globally. This would be particularly important as the risks of COVID-19 are still live, and people are seeking ways they can reduce interactions while they remain productive (Allam & Jones, 2021; Park et al., 2022). Further, with the ability to create own unique avatar, the metaverse increases the potential to overcome work-related challenges like racism, gender bias, and other prejudices that continue to haunt the global societies (Dwivedi et al., 2022).

Another reason why the metaverse is considered as an indispensable tool is its potential to create new forms of expression and creativity. With the ability to create and manipulate virtual environments and objects, people may be able to express themselves in new and innovative ways (Allam et al., 2022). This could lead to the creation of new forms of art, music, and storytelling and provide new opportunities for people to showcase their creativity and imagination (Qi, 2022). This further opens new frontiers for self-employment especially the youthful generations, which as of 2022 represented the highest number of unemployed demographics (Purdy, 2022).

The metaverse also has important implications for privacy and security. With the rise of decentralized networks and blockchain technology, the metaverse has the potential to provide a secure and private environment for people to interact and conduct transactions (Aks et al., 2022; Falchuk et al., 2018). This has the potential to create new opportunities for online privacy and security, as well as provide a platform for people to engage in online activities without fear of being monitored or having their personal information or data captured and used especially by the profit-oriented corporations. As technology continues to advance and our society becomes more interconnected, the metaverse is likely to play an increasingly important role in our lives.

From the internet to the metaverse

The internet first started as a way for researchers to share information and data, but it quickly evolved into a platform for communication and information sharing for the general public. The advent of the World Wide Web in the 1990s made it easier for people to access information and connect with others online (Antonucci et al., 2017). With the growth of e-commerce and social media, the internet has become an integral part of our daily lives, providing access to information, communication, and commerce. For instance, social media platforms are allowing people to interact in new ways. A reference case could be 2021, where over 4.26 billion people interacted via different social media platforms (Dixon, 2023). In business, the activities continue to expand courtesy of the internet. For instance, in 2020, during the height of COVID-19, it is reported that e-commerce transactions of about $791.7 billion were made in the United States (Weedmark, 2021) alone. Globally, the transactions reached a high of $26.7 trillion same year, which was a 4% increase from the 2019 record (UNCTAD, 2021).

However, the internet as it exists today is still limited in terms of its ability to provide immersive experiences in diverse frontiers. While it is possible to access information, interact, and communicate with other people on the digital platforms, the internet has yet to fully replicate the experience of being in a physical environment and interacting with others in real time. This then renders the concept of metaverse superior, taking the internet to the next level by providing a virtual realm that is truly immersive and interactive.

The development of VR and AR technologies has made it possible to create a metaverse that is both immersive and interactive. This provides the users with capabilities to not only experience VRs, but also interact with them (example in Fig. 1.2), and with their peers in real time (Bibri et al., 2022; Koohang et al., 2023). With the ability to create virtual identities (e.g., workplaces, offices, and homes) and engage in virtual activities, the metaverse has the potential to provide a new level of experience and engagement that was not possible with the internet as it exists today.

In addition, the metaverse is transforming our relationship with information and experiences by providing access to unimaginable dimensions. With the ability to avail diverse, virtual environments, the metaverse can provide access to simulations (like the case of digital twins) and experiences that would otherwise be relatively dangerous, costly, time consuming, and sometimes impossible to perform in the physical world (Mitsuhara & Shishibori, 2022). It also increases the possibility to improve on areas like emergency response,

FIG. 1.2 Senior couple enjoying VR 3D games at home (Getty Images, 2022).

conservation, and research that would improve best practices in the health sectors, tourism industry, and energy production among other frontiers.

Furthermore, the metaverse is also changing the way we consume and interact with media. With the ability to create virtual environments, the metaverse has the potential to provide new forms of entertainment and media that are more immersive and interactive. This could lead to new forms of storytelling, gaming, and other forms of entertainment that are more engaging and interactive than what is possible with traditional media (Qi, 2022).

The metaverse and its foundational elements

> Metaverse: Virtual world that provides a digital environment in which users can interact with each other and digital objects in real-time.

The term metaverse refers to a virtual world that provides a digital environment in which users can interact with each other and digital objects in real time. This digital ecosystem is built upon a combination of cutting-edge technologies including three-dimensional (3D) graphics, real-time collaboration software, VRs, mobile connectivity, and blockchain-based decentralized finance tools. At its core, the metaverse is a new kind of online platform that leverages advanced digital technologies to create an immersive VR that is more interactive, engaging, and responsive than any previous online platform. While the concept of a metaverse has been around for decades, recent technological advances have made it possible to build these environments with high levels of detail, interactivity, and responsiveness. For instance, the 5G technology is now providing low latency, high speeds, and greater capacities than the previous mobile connectivity technologies, thus shaping the experiences in metaverse (Rahman et al., 2021).

The metaverse is being viewed as a potentially game-changing technology with significant implications for the way people live, work, and play in the future. It is widely believed that the metaverse will ultimately become a place where people can connect with each other and the digital world in entirely new ways, offering prospects of new and advanced opportunities in sectors like tourism, health, education, entertainment, urban planning, and financial sectors among others.

However, despite the potential of the metaverse, there is currently little agreement on how it will ultimately take shape. Lauren Lubetsky, senior manager at Bain & Company, speaking at the 2022 MIT Platform Strategy Summit, outlined three possible scenarios for the future of the metaverse (Brown, 2022):

- Niche applications: In this scenario, the metaverse remains a domain of niche applications, used primarily for entertainment and gaming but stopping well short of becoming an all-encompassing VR.
- Competing ecosystems: In this scenario, the metaverse is controlled by large competing ecosystems such as Apple and Android metaworlds, with limited interoperability between them.
- Dynamic, open, and interoperable space: In this scenario, the metaverse becomes a dynamic, open, and interoperable space, much like the internet but in 3D.

Several factors will determine which of these scenarios will play out, including the degree of interoperability among virtual worlds, data portability, governance, and user interfaces (Mystakidis, 2022). The development of the metaverse will also be influenced by advances in 3D graphics, virtual and augmented reality technology, and the ability to create and run simulations in real time (Dwivedi et al., 2022).

The metaverse is built on a combination of various technical components. At its core, the metaverse requires 3D graphics to provide users with an immersive experience, real-time collaboration software to enable users to interact with each other and the digital world, and blockchain-based decentralized finance tools to provide a secure, decentralized infrastructure for conducting transactions (Gadekallu et al., 2022).

The 3D graphics component of the metaverse is critical to the overall user experience (an example of 3D graphic for the metaverse in captured in Fig. 1.3 below), providing them with a high level of detail and interactivity. Advanced graphics technologies such as ray tracing and global illumination are used to create highly detailed and realistic environments, while physics engines are used to simulate real-world physics, enabling users to interact with the virtual environment in a more natural way (Zhao et al., 2022). The real-time collaboration software component of the metaverse is what enables users to interact with each other and the digital world in real time. This technology is built

8 The metaverse and smart cities

FIG. 1.3 3D metaverse palm tree (And Machines, 2022).

on the concept of networked virtual environments and allows multiple participant to engage in the same virtual environment simultaneously, sharing a common experience (Koohang et al., 2023).

Finally, the blockchain-based decentralized finance tools that underpin the metaverse provide a secure and decentralized infrastructure for conducting transactions, reducing the risk of fraud and enabling new forms of commerce (Roy, 2021). This infrastructure also enables the creation of new forms of decentralized digital assets that can be traded, bought, and sold within the metaverse (Trunfio & Rossi, 2022).

Use cases of the metaverse

The online gaming industry, with its decades of experience in creating immersive virtual worlds, is the first mainstream use of the metaverse. The massive audiences of Roblox, Epic Games, and Decentraland are evidence of this (McKinsey, 2022), as players flock to these virtual worlds to play games, build virtual worlds, and invest in virtual real estate (Frank, 2022). In the workplace, enterprises are experimenting with metaverse applications to support remote work, with an initial focus on workplace training. For instance, hospitals are already using VR and AR technologies to train medical professionals for common procedures, such as the AR surgical system Medivis (Venkatesan et al., 2021).

A digital twin is a virtual representation of a physical object, process, or system that exists in the digital realm.

Digital twin avatars are another application of the metaverse in the workplace. These AI-powered holograms or holographic images can be assigned tasks and used for remote work and collaboration (Caggianese et al., 2020), allowing a CEO, for example, to engage with multiple stakeholder groups at once. The metaverse is also being used to enhance remote work experiences by setting up 3D rooms where employees can collaborate in real time, adding an element of realism to virtual meetings (Pickering et al., 2006).

The metaverse has the potential to transform education as well. Virtual classrooms and training sessions can provide an interactive and engaging learning experience, giving students access to resources and experts from around the world (Alfaisal et al., 2022). The metaverse can break down barriers to education, allowing for new forms of collaboration and innovation in learning.

In addition to the cases mentioned in the previous paragraph, the metaverse has numerous other potential applications in diverse industries. For instance, it can be used in the tourism second to create new consumer-centric products like virtual tourism where people would have the latitude to visit and explore diverse destinations across the globe, including remote locations from anywhere, including their homes (Hemmati, 2022). The metaverse, as expressed by Meta, can also be used to promote and allow people enjoy entertainment activities such as virtual events and concerts, letting users participate and experience live performances in a real, immersive virtual environment (Hemmati, 2022). The retail industry can also benefit from the metaverse, allowing customers to explore, interact with entrepreneurs, and even shop in virtual stores. Further, it will be possible for potential clients to choose and try on clothing in virtual fitting rooms (Marr, 2022), thus reducing unnecessary need for physical presence. The metaverse can also be used for virtual real estate tours, just like in the case of 360 degrees video technology, allowing potential buyers to explore properties in detail before proceeding with the purchase process. In the healthcare industry, the metaverse can be used for telemedicine, providing virtual consultations and reducing the need for in-person visits.

Additionally, the metaverse can be utilized in the healthcare sector as a tool for therapy and rehabilitation. For instance, it could be used for virtual rehabilitation, allowing patients to complete physical therapy exercises in a simulated environment without the need to visit physical clinic (Bhattacharya et al., 2022). In the entertainment industry, the metaverse can be used for virtual movie theaters, allowing people to watch films together. This would increase the potential for producers and actors to increase their productivity, as well as earn extra revenues from their works. For gamers, the platform is expected to increase their experience by providing and serving as virtual escape rooms (Mystakidis, 2022).

The metaverse has numerous potential applications and is poised to transform a range of industries. From gaming and entertainment to health care and enterprise, the metaverse has the potential to revolutionize the way we work, play, and interact with each other. As the metaverse continues to evolve and mature, it will open new opportunities for innovation, creativity, and collaboration and have a profound impact on our lives and society as a whole.

The metaverse economy

The rise of the internet brought about a new digital economy, introducing new business models, jobs, and career paths. Similarly, the metaverse, a virtual world offering immersive 3D experiences, is expected to revolutionize the way we interact, transact, and engage in various activities. As the metaverse economy continues to gain momentum, it is poised to become a significant contributor to the global economy, driving growth, and innovation (UNCTAD, 2021).

One of the pioneers of the metaverse economy is IMVU, an avatar-based social network with over 10 million monthly active users as of July 2022 (DMR, 2023). The platform offers an ecosystem where thousands of creators design and sell virtual products, such as outfits, furniture, cosmetics, music, stickers, and pets, generating an annual revenue of around $25million and $50 million (Similar web, 2023).

> Meshers: Individual who creates software tools or algorithms that are used to generate meshes from 3d models or point clouds.

In addition to the creators, the metaverse also creates new opportunities for "meshers," who design basic 3D templates that can be tailored and sold as virtual products (Purdy, 2022). A successful mesh design can be replicated and sold multiple times, potentially earning a significant income for the developer.

> Holoporting: a technology that enables real-time, three-dimensional (3D) teleportation or transmission of individuals or objects to a different location through the use of holographic displays.

Another platform, Decentraland, enables users to purchase, sell, and construct businesses on virtual land, earning the digital currency called "Mana." This platform is creating virtual real estate opportunities and contributing to the growth of the metaverse economy (Bruner, 2022). As the metaverse continues to grow, we can expect to see the emergence of metaverse-native enterprises and businesses that are solely developed and operated within the virtual world. The metaverse will also create new job opportunities, such as avatar conversation designers, holoporting travel agents, metaverse digital wealth managers, etc. (Bruner, 2022).

The metaverse economy holds enormous potential for growth and innovation, and its market capitalization is projected to continue growing in the years to come, especially as connectivity technologies such as 5G and anticipated 6G become ubiquitous. Currently, metaverse market valuation is estimated to be above $47.5 billion, with projections that it would reach a high of $678.8 billion by 2030 (Thomas, 2022).

The metaverse is a rapidly growing field that holds enormous potential for growth and innovation, making it an exciting and intriguing field to watch. Whether you are an entrepreneur, worker, or simply interested in the future of technology and the digital economy, the metaverse is a field that is worth keeping an eye on.

Fears and critisms of the metaverse

While the metaverse has been argued to be a promising new frontier for human experience and interaction, there have been genuine concerned about the potential negative consequences that might emerge. This section thus seeks to explore several of those criticisms and fears around the metaverse including some of the potential downsides of this new technology.

One of the major criticisms of the metaverse is that it exacerbates social isolation and prompt disconnection from reality, especially among addicts of the platform. That is, as people spend more and more time in virtual dimension, they may start to prioritize their online lives over their real-world relationships, which could have serious consequences for their mental, physical, and emotional well-being (Benrimoh et al., 2022). In addition, people may become addicted to the instant gratification and social validation that they receive in the metaverse, which could further isolate them from the real world and lead to problems such as depression, anxiety, and other mental health issues as expressed by Dwivedi et al. (2022).

Another real concern surrounding the metaverse is the probability for it to create and fuel social disorder. To put this into perspective, the metaverse is a shared virtual space, which means that people from diverse parts of the world will have the capacity to interact. As this, this could lead to several negative consequences, such as cyberbullying, online harassment, and other forms of digital aggression including terrorism (Debuire, 2022). Furthermore, the anonymity that people can enjoy in the metaverse could embolden them to engage in harmful or illegal activities, such as hacking, identity theft, and other forms of cybercrime (Pooyandeh et al., 2022).

Another concern about the metaverse is the potential for it to perpetuate and promote existing social inequalities and biases in the society. Just as real-world systems of oppression and inequality can be replicated in the digital world, so too can the metaverse reproduce these same systems of injustice. For example, people with disabilities (especially the visually impaired and the deaf) may find it more difficult to access and participate in the metaverse, while people of color and other marginalized communities may face discrimination and marginalization within the virtual world (Park & Kim, 2022). This is true also for the low-income demographic that may not have the means and financial capacities to afford the basic requirements (VR tools and gadgets) to allow them login into the virtual world (Taylor & Soneji, 2022).

Finally, there are concerns about the commercialization and monetization of the metaverse. Many companies are eager to capitalize on the growing interest in VR, and the metaverse represents a new frontier for digital commerce (Filipova, 2023). However, this could lead to a situation where people are effectively locked out of certain parts of the metaverse unless they can afford to pay for access. This could exacerbate existing inequalities and create a two-tiered system where only those who can afford to pay and buy necessary tools and gadgets for access are able to fully experience and participate in the virtual world (Bojic, 2022).

The metaverse is an intricate and fast evolving technology that has been argued to hold potential to transform human experience and interaction from the traditionally known norms. This notwithstanding, the probable downsides of this new technology require serious considerations and informed solutions. By considering the concerns and fears around the metaverse, we can ensure that this new frontier is accessible, equitable, and safe for everyone.

Challenges and imperatives

Despite the potential benefits of a fully functioning metaverse, there are significant challenges that must be addressed to ensure the vision leapfrogs from the infancy stage. These challenges include the formidable computing power and infrastructure requirements that are current not available (Gadekallu et al., 2022), the lack of unified virtual worlds (Xi et al., 2022), and the numerous regulatory and HR compliance issues. To overcome these challenges, business leaders, policymakers, and HR leaders must take a proactive approach to the development and adoption of the metaverse.

One of the main imperatives for a successful metaverse is to prioritize the portability of skills. With the potential for workers to engage in virtual work environments, there is a need for skills and qualifications to be transferable across virtual worlds and real-world life. This can be achieved by creating certified standards for skills acquired in the metaverse, with appropriate accreditation of training providers. This will ensure that workers have the necessary skills and qualifications to be competitive in the metaverse, and that their experience is recognized by future employers.

Another important imperative is to be truly hybrid. With the recent shift to remote work during the pandemic (Allam & Jones, 2021), many enterprises were caught off guard, with outdated policies, lack of infrastructure, and a strict demarcation between consumer and business technologies. To avoid these mistakes in the metaverse, companies must adopt integrated working models that allow employees to move seamlessly between physical, online, and virtual working styles. This will require the use of consumer technologies native to the metaverse, such as avatars, VR headsets, and hand-track controllers, as well as emerging technologies such as virtual locomotion technologies and neural signal decoding (Huynh-The et al., 2023).

A third imperative is to engage with the younger generation. With many young people growing up in a gaming, 3D, socially connected environment, companies should look to them as they design their workplace metaverses. Reverse intergenerational learning, where members of the younger generation coach and train their older colleagues, could greatly assist the spread of metaverse-based working among the overall workforces (Purdy, 2022).

In order to facilitate its successes and wide acceptability, companies must keep the metaverse open. The technology has emerged as an open, decentralized movement, driven by millions of developers, gamers, designers, and emerging investors. To fully harness the power of this movement for their workers, companies must guard against efforts to control or dominate it and actively endeavor to extend and open it up even further for more users to participate. This can be achieved through open-source standards, software, and seamless connections between different virtual worlds. However, if they allow the metaverse to be dominated by major technology companies and profit-oriented corporations that will lock-out potential grass-roots innovation and start-ups that could potentially create a fairer and more competitive environment to encourage innovation.

How does the metaverse link to smart cities?

The metaverse represents a significant step forward in the development of smart cities, offering new opportunities for urban planning and design, as well as the creation of more sustainable and efficient cities (Hemmati, 2022). In this chapter, we will explore how the metaverse fits into the narrative of smart cities and how it has the potential to transform the way we live, work, and interact in our urban environments.

Smart cities are urban planning concept that encapsulates cities that use technology and data to improve the livability status of the residents. The goal of smart cities is to create more efficient, sustainable, and livable cities through the use of technology and data (Albert, 2019; Allam, 2018; Allam & Newman, 2018; Bibri & Krogstie, 2020). In this case, the metaverse offers new opportunities for the development of smart cities by providing a virtual platform for urban planning and design, to not only collaborate, share their works, but also perform simulations.

In the metaverse, virtual cities can be designed, tested, and refined in a controlled environment before being implemented in the physical world; hence reducing costs, increasing their acceptability, and getting best solution for major urban challenges such as climate change. This allows for the creation of more efficient and sustainable cities, with a reduced risk of unintended consequences. For example, the metaverse can be used to simulate the impact of new transportation systems, new solar energy power plants or the effect of different land use policies, giving city planners, and policymakers the ability to make informed decisions (Chamoso et al., 2016; Klebanov et al., 2018; Zhang et al., 2021).

Furthermore, the metaverse provides new opportunities for public engagement and participation in the development of smart cities (Dwivedi et al., 2022). In a virtual environment, a sizeable number of citizens can participate in virtual meetings, provide feedbacks on proposed developments, and take part in virtual tours of proposed developments. This increased level of public engagement can help ensure that the development of smart cities would capitalize and give priority to the needs and desires of the residents who will be living and working in these environments (Allam & Jones, 2021). It also ensures that the prospects of having abandoned public projects that come about as a result of little or no acceptance by the locals are eliminated (Damoah et al., 2020).

In addition to its potential for urban planning and design, the metaverse also has the potential to transform the way urban residents live and work within their environment. Virtual spaces provide a platform for successful remote working, reducing the need for daily commutes and overreliance on automobiles; thus, helping to mitigate traffic congestion and air pollution (Giovanis, 2018). Such would also help reduce incidences of rural-urban migration as people would not necessary life in urban areas.

The metaverse also has the capability promote access to public services and experiences that are currently limited by geography. For example, virtual environments could be used to provide remote access to healthcare services, government services education tourism adventures, and cultural events. This would be particularly important in targeting underserved communities, minority groups and areas and sites requiring conservation, rehabilitation, and even rejuvenation.

In conclusion, the metaverse represents a new frontier in the development of smart cities, offering new opportunities for urban planning, design, and simulation, and adoption of best practices in areas like energy production.

References

Adepetun, A. (21 December 2022). *Facebook plans $19.2b metaverse investment next year*. Retrieved from https://guardian.ng/business-services/facebook-plans-19-2b-metaverse-investment-next-year/.

Aks, S. M. Y., Karmila, M., Givan, B., Hendratna, G., Setiawan, H. S., Putra, A. S., et al. (2022). A review of blockchain for security data privacy with metaverse. In *Paper presented at the 2022 international conference on ICT for smart society (ICISS) (10-11 August 2022)*.

Albert, S. (21 April 2019). *Smart cities: The promises and failures of utopia technological planning*. Retrieved from https://theconversation.com/smart-cities-the-promises-and-failures-of-utopian-technological-planning-114405.

Alfaisal, R., Hashim, H., & Azizan, U. H. (2022). Metaverse system adoption in education: A systematic literature review. *Journal of Computers in Education*, *1*. https://doi.org/10.1007/s40692-022-00256-6.

Allam, Z. (2018). Contextualising the smart city for sustainability and inclusivity. *New Design Ideas*, *2*(2), 124–127.

Allam, Z. (2019). *Cities and the digital revolution: Aligning technology and humanity*. Springer Nature.

Allam, Z. (2020). Privatization and privacy in the digital city. In *Cities and the digital revolution* (pp. 85–106). Cham: Palgrave Pivot.

Allam, Z., & Jones, D. S. (2021). Future (post-COVID) digital, smart and sustainable cities in the wake of 6G: Digital twins, immersive realities and new urban economies. *Land Use Policy*, *101*, 105201.

Allam, Z., & Newman, P. (2018). Redefining the smart city: Culture, metabolism and governance. *Smart Cities*, *1*(1). https://doi.org/10.3390/smartcities1010002.

Allam, Z., Sharifi, A., Bibri, S. E., Jones, D. S., & Krogstie, J. (2022). The metaverse as a virtual form of smart cities: Opportunities and challenges for environmental, economic, and social sustainability in urban futures. *Smart Cities*, *5*(3), 771–801. https://doi.org/10.3390/smartcities5030040.

And Machines. (2022). *3D metaverse palm tree*. Retrieved from https://unsplash.com/photos/hKxsoF4aubY.

Antonucci, T. C., Ajrouch, K. J., & Manalel, J. A. (2017). Social relations and technology: Continuity, context, and change. *Innovation in Aging*, *1*(3), igx029. https://doi.org/10.1093/geroni/igx029.

Bassey, A. (2020). *Online gaming: A successful life? The influence of gaming on development*. Norway: University of South-Eastern Norway.

Benrimoh, D., Chheda, F. D., & Margolese, H. C. (2022). The best predictor of the future-the metaverse, mental health, and lessons learned from current technologies. *JMIR Mental Health*, *9*(10), e40410. https://doi.org/10.2196/40410.

Bhattacharya, S., Varshney, S., & Tripathi, S. (2022). Harnessing public health with "metaverse" technology. *Frontiers in Public Health*, *10*, 1030574. https://doi.org/10.3389/fpubh.2022.1030574.

Bibri, S., & Krogstie, J. (2020). Data-driven smart sustainable cities of the future: A novel model of urbanism and its core dimensions, strategies, and solutions. *Journal of Futures Studies*, *25*(2), 77–94. https://doi.org/10.6531/JFS.202012_25(2).0009.

Bibri, S. E., Allam, Z., & Krogstie, J. (2022). The metaverse as a virtual form of data-driven smart urbanism: Platformization and its underlying processes, institutional dimensions, and disruptive impacts. *Computational Urban Science*, *2*, 24. https://doi.org/10.1007/s43762-022-00051-0.

Bojic, L. (2022). Metaverse through the prism of power and addiction: What will happen when the virtual world becomes more attractive than reality? *European Journal of Futures Research*, *10*(1), 22. https://doi.org/10.1186/s40309-022-00208-4.

Borrego, A., Latorre, J., Alcañiz, M., & Llorens, R. (2018). Comparison of oculus rift and HTC Vive: Feasibility for virtual reality-based exploration, navigation, exergaming, and rehabilitation. *Games for Health Journal*, *7*(3), 151–156. https://doi.org/10.1089/g4h.2017.0114.

Brown, S. (4 October 2022). *2022 MIT platform report: Embracin data, preparing for Web3*. Retrieved from https://mitsloan.mit.edu/ideas-made-to-matter/2022-mit-platform-report-embracing-data-preparing-web3.

Bruner, R. (20 January 2022). *Why investors are paying real money for virtual land*. Metaverse. Retrieved from https://time.com/6140467/metaverse-real-estate/.

Caggianese, G., De Pietro, G., Esposito, M., Gallo, L., Minutolo, A., & Neroni, P. (2020). Discovering Leonardo with artificial intelligence and holograms: A user study. *Pattern Recognition Letters*, *131*, 361–367. https://doi.org/10.1016/j.patrec.2020.01.006.

Chamoso, P., De Paz, J. F., Rodríguez, S., & Bajo, J. (2016). *Smart cities simulation environment for intelligent algorithms evaluation*. Cham: Paper presented at the International Symposium on Ambient Intelligence.

Cheah, I., & Shimul, A. S. (2023). Marketing in the metaverse: Moving forward—What's next? *Journal of Global Scholars of Marketing Science*, *33*(1), 1–10. https://doi.org/10.1080/21639159.2022.2163908.

Cheng, X., Zhang, S., Fu, S., Liu, W., Guan, C., Mou, J., et al. (2022). Exploring the metaverse in the digital economy: An overview and research framework. *Journal of Electronic Business & Digital Economics*, *1*(1/2), 206–224. https://doi.org/10.1108/JEBDE-09-2022-0036.

Damoah, I. S., Mouzughi, Y., & Kumi, D. K. (2020). The effects of government construction projects abandonment: Stakeholders' perspective. *International Journal of Construction Management*, *20*(5), 462–479. https://doi.org/10.1080/15623599.2018.1486172.

Debuire, D. (12 April 2022). *Terrorist use of the metaverse: New opportunities and new challenges*. Retrieved from https://thesecuritydistillery.org/all-articles/terrorism-and-the-metaverse-new-opportunities-and-new-challenges.

Dixon, S. (24 January 2023). *Number of global social network users 2017-2027*. Retrieved from https://www.statista.com/statistics/278414/number-of-worldwide-social-network-users/#:∼:text=In%202021%2C%20over%204.26%20billionalmost%20six%20billion%20in%202027.

DMR. (8 January 2023). *IMVU statistics and facts*. Retrieved from https://expandedramblings.com/index.php/imvu-statistics-and-facts/.

Dwivedi, Y. K., Hughes, L., Baabdullah, A. M., Ribeiro-Navarrete, S., Giannakis, M., Al-Debei, M. M., et al. (2022). Metaverse beyond the hype: Multidisciplinary perspectives on emerging challenges, opportunities, and agenda for research, practice and policy. *International Journal of Information Management*, *66*, 102542. https://doi.org/10.1016/j.ijinfomgt.2022.102542.

Falchuk, B., Loeb, S., & Neff, R. (2018). The social metaverse: Battle for privacy. *IEEE Technology and Society Magazine*, *37*(2), 52–61. https://doi.org/10.1109/MTS.2018.2826060.

Filipova, I. (2023). Creating the metaverse: Consequences for economy, society, and law (2023). *Journal of Digital Technologies and Law*, *1*(1), 1.

Frank, R. (1 February 2022). *Metaverse real estate sales top $500 million, and are projected to double this year*. Retrieved from https://www.cnbc.com/2022/02/01/metaverse-real-estate-sales-top-500-million-metametric-solutions-says.html.

Gadekallu, T., Huynh-The, T., Wang, W., Yenduri, G., Ranaweera, P., Pham, V., et al. (2022). *Blockchain for the metaverse: A review*.

Getty Images. (8 October 2022). *Couple senior enjoy playing VR 3D games at home*. Retrieved from https://unsplash.com/photos/rW8mGeXEMt0.

Giovanis, E. (2018). The relationship between teleworking, traffic and air pollution. *Atmospheric Pollution Research*, *9*, 1–14. https://doi.org/10.1016/j.apr.2017.06.004.

Greener, R. (12 January 2022). *Second life storefront user traffic jumps 35 percent in 2021*. Retrieved from https://www.xrtoday.com/virtual-reality/second-life-user-traffic-jumps-35-percent-in-2021/#:∼:text=Since%20its%20inception%2C%20Second%20Lifeactive%20users%20on%20its%20platform.

Hemmati, M. (2022). The metaverse: An urban revolution effect of the metaverse on the perceptions of urban audience. *Tourism and Culture*, *2*(7), 53–60.

Henz, P. (2022). The societal impact of the metaverse. *Discover Artificial Intelligence*, *2*(1), 19. https://doi.org/10.1007/s44163-022-00032-6.

Huynh-The, T., Pham, Q.-V., Pham, X.-Q., Nguyen, T. T., Han, Z., & Kim, D.-S. (2023). Artificial intelligence for the metaverse: A survey. *Engineering Applications of Artificial Intelligence, 117*, 105581. https://doi.org/10.1016/j.engappai.2022.105581.

Investing.com. (4 September 2022). *Big tech metaverses: All you need to know about meta, Microsoft, Google, and Apple*. Retrieved from https://www.investing.com/news/cryptocurrency-news/big-tech-metaverses-all-you-need-to-know-about-meta-microsoft-google-and-apple-2885578.

Klebanov, B., Nemtinov, A., & Zvereva, O. (2018). Simulation as an effective instrument for strategic planning and transformation of smart cities. *International Multidisciplinary Scientific GeoConference: SGEM, 18*(2.1), 685–692.

Koohang, A., Nord, J. H., Ooi, K.-B., Tan, G. W.-H., Al-Emran, M., Aw, E. C.-X., et al. (2023). Shaping the metaverse into reality: A holistic multidisciplinary understanding of opportunities, challenges, and avenues for future investigation. *Journal of Computer Information Systems*. https://doi.org/10.1080/08874417.2023.2165197. 1-31.

Lee, L.-H., Braud, T., Zhou, P., Wang, L., Xu, D., Lin, Z., et al. (2021). All one needs to know about metaverse: A complete survey on technological singularity, virtual ecosystem, and research agenda. *Journal of Latex Class Files, 14*(8). https://doi.org/10.13140/RG.2.2.11200.05124/8.

Lv, Z., Shang, W.-L., & Guizani, M. (2022). Impact of digital twins and metaverse on cities: History, current situation, and application perspectives. *Applied Sciences, 12*(24). https://doi.org/10.3390/app122412820.

Marr, B. (1 July 2022). *The metaverse, digital dressing rooms and the future of the fashion retail*. Retrieved from https://www.forbes.com/sites/bernardmarr/2022/07/01/the-metaverse-digital-dressing-rooms-and-the-future-of-fashion-retail/?sh=4cfd06816b90.

McArthur, V., Teather, R., & Stuerzlinger, W. (2010). Comparing 3D content creation interfaces in two virtual worlds: World of warcraft and second life. *Journal of Gaming & Virtual Worlds, 2*, 239–258. https://doi.org/10.1386/jgvw.2.3.239_1.

McKinsey. (24 May 2022). *Marketing in the metaverse: An opportunity for innovation and experimentation*. Retrieved from https://www.mckinsey.com/capabilities/growth-marketing-and-sales/our-insights/marketing-in-the-metaverse-an-opportunity-for-innovation-and-experimentation.

Mitsuhara, H., & Shishibori, M. (2022). *Toward evacuation training in metaverse: Transforming normal time into emergency time* (pp. 97–124).

Mystakidis, S. (2022). Metaverse. *Encyclopedia, 2*(1), 486–497. https://doi.org/10.3390/encyclopedia2010031.

Park, S. M., & Kim, Y. G. (2022). A metaverse: Taxonomy, components, applications, and open challenges. *IEEE Access, 10*, 4209–4251. https://doi.org/10.1109/ACCESS.2021.3140175.

Park, J. Y., Lee, K., & Chung, D. R. (2022). Public interest in the digital transformation accelerated by the COVID-19 pandemic and perception of its future impact. *The Korean Journal of Internal Medicine, 37*(6), 1223–1233. https://doi.org/10.3904/kjim.2022.129.

Pickering, C., Miller, J., Wynn, E., & House, C. (2006). 3D global virtual teaming environment. In *Paper presented at the fourth international conference on creating, connecting and collaborating through computing, Berkeley, CA*.

Pooyandeh, M., Han, K.-J., & Sohn, I. (2022). Cybersecurity in the AI-based metaverse: A survey. *Applied Sciences, 12*(24), 12993. Retrieved from https://www.mdpi.com/2076-3417/12/24/12993.

Purdy, M. (5 April 2022). *How the metaverse could change work*. Retrieved from https://hbr.org/2022/04/how-the-metaverse-could-change-work.

Qi, W. (2022). The investment value of metaverse in the media and entertainment industry. *BCP Business & Management, 34*, 279–283. https://doi.org/10.54691/bcpbm.v34i.3026.

Rahman, A., Arabi, S., & Rab, R. (2021). Feasibility and challenges of 5G network deployment in least developed countries (LDC). *Wireless Sensor Network, 13*, 1–16. https://doi.org/10.4236/wsn.2021.131001.

Rosenberg, L. (2022). Regulation of the metaverse: A roadmap. In *Paper presented at the 6th international conference on virtual and augmented reality simulations (ICVARS 2022), Brisbane, Australia*.

Roy, A. (2 December 2021). *Doing business in the metaverse: Opportunity or threat?*. Retrieved from https://www.xrtoday.com/virtual-reality/doing-business-in-the-metaverse-opportunity-or-threat/.

Similar web. (January 2023). *IMVU*. Retrieved from https://www.similarweb.com/website/imvu.com/#overview.

Stephenson, N. (2003). *Snow crash: A novel*. New York, NY: Random House Publishing Group.

Taylor, S., & Soneji, S. (2022). Bioinformatics and the metaverse: Are we ready? *Frontiers in Bioinformatics, 2*, 863676. https://doi.org/10.3389/fbinf.2022.863676.

Thomas, A. (23 August 2022). *Metaverse market size worldwide* (pp. 2021–2030). Retrieved from https://www.statista.com/statistics/1295784/metaverse-market-size/.

Trunfio, M., & Rossi, S. (2022). Advances in metaverse investigation: Streams of research and future agenda. *Virtual Worlds, 1*(2), 103–129. Retrieved from https://www.mdpi.com/2813-2084/1/2/7.

UNCTAD. (3 May 2021). *Global e-commerce jumps to $26.7 trillion, COVID-19 boosts online sales*. Retrieved from https://unctad.org/news/global-e-commerce-jumps-267-trillion-covid-19-boosts-online-sales.

Venkatesan, M., Mohan, H., Ryan, J. R., Schürch, C. M., Nolan, G. P., Frakes, D. H., et al. (2021). Virtual and augmented reality for biomedical applications. *Cell Reports Medicine, 2*(7), 100348. https://doi.org/10.1016/j.xcrm.2021.100348.

Weedmark, D. (30 April 2021). *How do businesses use the internet?*. Retrieved from https://smallbusiness.chron.com/businesses-use-internet-752.html.

Weishaupt, F. (11 January 2022). *The metaverse: A new kind of workplace*. Retrieved from https://www.trainingjournal.com/articles/opinion/metaverse-new-kind-workplace.

Xi, N., Chen, J., Gama, F., Riar, M., & Hamari, J. (2022). The challenges of entering the metaverse: An experiment on the effect of extended reality on workload. *Information Systems Frontiers*. https://doi.org/10.1007/s10796-022-10244-x.

XR Expo. (18 June 2020). *XR expo 2019: Exhibition for virtual reality (VR), augmented reality (AR), mixed reality (MR) and extended reality (XR)*. Retrieved from https://unsplash.com/photos/ipDhOQ5gtEk.

Zhang, X., Shen, J., Saini, P. K., Lovati, M., Han, M., Huang, P., et al. (2021). Digital twin for accelerating sustainability in positive energy district: A review of simulation tools and applications. *Frontiers in Sustainable Cities, 3*(35). https://doi.org/10.3389/frsc.2021.663269.

Zhao, Y., Jiang, J., Chen, Y., Liu, R., Yang, Y., Xue, X., et al. (2022). Metaverse: Perspectives from graphics, interactions and visualization. *Visual Informatics, 6*(1), 56–67. https://doi.org/10.1016/j.visinf.2022.03.002.

Chapter 2

The history and evolution of the metaverse

Introduction

The concept of the metaverse has been gradually gaining substantial popularity over the past few decades and is now considered a potential game-changer in the digital landscape. The metaverse refers to a virtual world where users interact with each other and the virtual environment almost like in the physical world (Allam, Sharifi, et al., 2022). However, the interaction here is mostly through avatars, which offers new and exciting form of digital interaction. The idea of the metaverse was first explained in Neal Stephenson's 1992 novel dubbed Snow Crash (Stephenson, 2003). However, the nature of metaverse introduced in the novel depicted a negative form of digital environment which is substantially different from the metaverse being pursued. That notwithstanding, Stephenson's idea has been developed and explored by different groups of people such as artists, researchers, and developers each motived by diverse objectives. However, the efforts seem to be converging into the creation of virtual worlds such as Second Life and The Metaverse Roadmap.

The basis for the evolution of the metaverse has been the ultimate advancements in diverse technologies and the surging demand for immersive virtual experiences. At the core of spreading the popularity of metaverse to a wider audience has been the emergence and advancement of the internet, cloud computing technologies, and the high-speed internet. Such have leading to an increase in the number of users and available applications and services. The development of virtual and augmented reality technologies has also allowed for a more immersive experience for users, making the metaverse even more appealing.

The metaverse is argued to have the potential to transform the way people live, interact, travel, enjoy their recreation, work and pursue their interests, particularly in the context of smart cities. In smart cities, the concept of metaverse is being pursued with the aim of exploring how it can enhance city life and improve the livability status of citizens (Allam, Sharifi, et al., 2022). Among possible ways the metaverse is expected to impact the residents is by providing a platform that allows them to participate and contribute toward city decision-making processes, especially in regard to access city services. In addition, despite the notable urban flaws that discourages maximum human interactions, the metaverse could provide a platform for citizens to interact, create new social networks, and promote cultural heritage.

Second life is a virtual world and online game that allows individuals to create and customize their virtual avatars, interact with other users, explore virtual landscapes et cetera.

World of warcraft (wow) is a massively multiplayer online role-playing game (MMORPG) developed and published by blizzard entertainment.

In the course of exploring this concept of metaverse, the history and its evolution are critical as they help in providing insight into the potential it holds for shaping the future of smart cities, as well as the hurdles that have derailed its ultimate success. With the information and clear understanding of the history, researchers, policymakers, practitioners, and diverse stakeholders are kept abreast of its developments and potential impacts (both negative and positive) on society, hence, allowing them to make concrete decisions.

Whereas some people may take the idea of metaverse as just a futuristic mirage, it is already a reality, with some people already fully immersed in it. For instance, as noted in the first chapter, virtual worlds such as Second Life, World of Warcraft, and The Metaverse Roadmap have been in existence for over a decade. Further, in the recent years, as the concept gain more traction, it has been observed that the number of users and available applications and services is growing at a rapid pace. For instance, it is argued that there are over 400 million users, and the number is expected to reach over 1.5 billion people by 2024 (Clement, 2022a). The metaverse offers a new and exciting form of digital interaction that is increasingly accessible to a wider audience, courtesy of growing list of VR and AR and associated technologies.

One of the selling points of the metaverse is that it allows users to experience improved immersive and interactive experience compared to traditional forms of digital interaction (Bibri et al., 2022). In some virtual worlds such as gaming, entertainment, and work environment, immersive experiences are achieved through the use of avatars, which give users an upper hand in choosing how they interact with each other and the environment in a way that feels more real and engaging. Avatars also provide the users the advantages of being anonymous, thus enabling them to explore and express their identity in new and creative ways (Cheong, 2022).

In the work realm, the metaverse has been transforming and is expected to initiate even more innovative approaches of how people work, especially post COVID-19. For example, virtual meetings and virtual conferences are becoming the norm, and could become more domestic in the future, allowing individuals to participate in business and professional activities from anywhere in the world. For instance, it is not surprising that even sensitive businesses, such as court businesses, are being conducted virtually (Rossner & Tait, 2021). In other dimensions such as engineering, planning, computer science, and others, the metaverse is expected to provide an unmatched platform for remote collaboration, enabling teams to work together on projects in real time, regardless of geographical, time, and other limitations.

On the social scenes, there is enthusiasm that the metaverse will prompt much needed revolution especially on how individuals socialize, interact, communicate, and share valuable time. According to the proponent of this new technology, it provides a novel platform for users to form new relationships and social connections. It also increases their abilities to participate in activities and events together regardless of their physical locations (Meta, 2021). This could lead to the creation of new virtual communities and cultures, which could be an important factor in shaping the future of society, especially as existing cultures are under constant threat from emerging trends.

In addition to the above, it is impossible not to recognize how the metaverse is expected to transform how humans access and use information (Bibri et al., 2022). On this, it is worth noting that information and data being produced and shared on different platforms are increasing in astronomical ways, courtesy of advancement in technologies. For instance, it is reported that over 2.5 quintillion bytes of data are created and shared each day (Bulao, 2023). With such information, the metaverse could provide opportunities for the creation of virtual libraries and archives, making information more accessible and easier to find. This would also be important in overcoming the data storage challenge that has become a bane in most organizations and establishments. The concept of the metaverse is not just limited to the digital world. It also extends into the physical world, thus allowing capabilities to create a hybrid environment that comprises both the virtual and physical experiences. For example, with the AR, VR, and digital twins technologies, it is possible to seamlessly integrate objects in both realities, thus creating a more immersive experience for users.

Moreover, the metaverse has been found to prompt the creation of new business ventures, such as virtual real estate, avatars, and virtual tourism products that increase the revenue streams for companies, including start-ups (Xi et al., 2022). When monetized, through virtual currencies and transactions, virtual products and services can lead to expand the revenue sources for proprietary owners. However, unlike in the physical world, the virtual realm has unlimited scope for business opportunities, thus able to accommodate limitless business ideas. Additionally, companies could use the metaverse as a platform to reach and engage with customers, creating new marketing and advertising opportunities. For instance, in the recent past, Qatar Airways has launched its own form of metaverse dubbed QVerse, allowing its clients to navigate the check-in area and other areas of the airline (Trade Arabia, 2022).

Despite the aforementioned positive benefits, it is worth acknowledging that the metaverse also raises a number of valid social and ethical issues that warrant speedy attention. For example, the technology could perpetuate and accelerate existing social and economic inequalities if it is not designed and developed with inclusivity in mind. Additionally, it prompts genuine concerns on privacy and security, as user data and personal information could be vulnerable to misuse and abuse (Xi et al., 2022). Therefore, it is imperative for policymakers, developers, and researchers to consider the implications of those drawbacks and to work toward creating a more inclusive, secure, and equitable virtual world.

The origins of the metaverse concept

> Virtual Realities are immersive digital environments that simulate realistic sensory experiences, primarily through the use of computer-generated visuals, sounds, and interactive elements.

Virtual realities and the prospects of experiencing a virtual world have been capturing the imagination of scientists, inventors, and writers for many decades. This acclamation could be affirmed by a review of Jules Verne's works, which inspired a generation of visionaries, to the science fiction works of the 1980s and 1990s (Faraboschi et al., 2022). His idea of a parallel digital universe has been a popular topic of discussion among enthusiasts. Today, with much progress in diverse technologies, the metaverse is considered a possible and promising concept in the digital world, and major corporations are increasing their efforts to bring it into reality.

The background of the concept of a virtual world can be tracked back to the writings and literal works of several key figures who explored its philosophical and theoretical foundations. A notable such figure is Jules Verne, whose works, such as "Journey to the Center of the Earth" (1864) (Verne, 2015) and "From the Earth to the Moon" (1865) (Verne, 2006), inspired a generation of inventors and visionaries. Another classical work is by H.G. Wells who wrote the book "The Country of the Blind" (1904) (Wells, 1905), in which he described the idea of a machine that could simulate reality. This work is argued to have had a profound influence on the development of virtual reality.

The advent of the computers, however, catapulted the concept of VR into greater heights. For instance, it is during this eon (1960s and 1970s) that the first leap was made when computer graphics pioneer Ivan Sutherland and his students at MIT developed the first head-mounted display (HMD) (Sutherland, 1968). This enabled the users to see and interact with computer-generated graphics in real time. With this feat, the development of virtual reality technologies became feasible (Bown et al., 2017) and is still instrumental in today's quest for the metaverse.

During the period of 1980s and 1990s, there were much activities focusing on the development of the metaverse. It was then that fiction writers such as

Neal Stephenson's ["Snow Crash" (1992)] (Stephenson, 2003) and William Gibson's ["Neuromancer" (1984)] (Gibson, 1984) produced their works, all trying to imagine the metaverse, though in very diverse ways. The metaverse was depicted in fictional movies such as "eXistenZ" (Cronenberg, 1999), "Matrix Series" (Zhao et al., 2022), and "Ready Player One" (Hudson, 2018).

The natural theme in all those publications and movies was to showcase the possibility of human interacting in a realm beyond the physical. Beyond the works of fiction, the current form of metaverse, in addition to providing new opportunities for social interaction, is a game-changer in different aspect of human lives. For example, it is gradually being used as a platform for remote learning, where it allows students to attend virtual classes, interact with teachers and classmates, and participate in hands-on activities (as shown in Fig. 2.1 below), all from the comfort of their own homes (Zhang et al., 2022). This can greatly improve access to education, especially for individuals who face barriers such as distance, disability, and poverty. This user case is similar to the application of metaverse in the work environment, where the trends are for people to work remotely. Through the metaverse, it is becoming possible for individuals working in the same environment, or in a similar fields/disciplines to freely interact, attend virtual meetings, and collaborate on projects in real time (Trunfio & Rossi, 2022). These services in the metaverse are superior to online-based meetings and collaborations that are usually hindered by geographical locations and different time zones (Dwivedi et al., 2022). In the metaverse, such limitations usually do not exist as productivity and efficiency are greatly improved, as workers have greater flexibility, being able to balance work and personal commitments (Purdy, 2022).

In the entertainment realm, the metaverse promises unmatched potentials and transformations. Through its users are now able to participate in 3D virtual

FIG. 2.1 Students participating in virtual activities (Getty Images, 2023).

games, attend virtual concerts and performances, and explore new and exciting virtual environments. It is not surprising that filmmakers and entertainment studios and theme parks are now increasingly developing digital collectibles, meant to enhance the experience of their fun base. With the metaverse, the entertainment industry is now offering interactive movies, stories, and live sports, by providing a new platform for artists and performers to reach a wider audience and create new and innovative experiences for their clientele (Marr, 2022).

The many potential benefits of the metaverse, however, attract several challenges and risks that cannot be overlooked if the platform were to succeed. One of the main concerns is the potential to increase data collection by third parties; hence, exacerbating the privacy and security concerns that already haunts the deployment of technology-based applications such as smart cities. As such, possible solutions being proposed include ensuring security and privacy frameworks that are built in tandem with the development of other features of metaverse (Gupta et al., 2023).

At human capacity level, there are fears that the metaverse will accelerate existing social and economic inequalities and biases (Anderson & Rainie, 2022). Such challenges are associated with factors such as income levels, accessibility to basic amenities like the internet and relevant tools and gadgets that would allow people to connect to the digital infrastructure. Further, it is also argued that VR has the capacity to increase addiction to metaverse which increases physical disconnection with the real reality. The challenges of cybercrime are inescapable in the metaverse, as it has been argued that even the "bad guys" are joining the metaverse, with the aim of taking advantage of the vulnerable and unsuspecting users (Anderson & Rainie, 2022). Cases of harassment, racial discrimination, and fraud are also expected to abound in this new realm, especially since it is still in its infancy stage (Dwivedi et al., 2022).

Finally, there is the issue of regulation and governance of different issues in the metaverse. As the metaverse continues to evolve and grow, it is essential that a framework is established for the regulation of the virtual world, in order to ensure that it is safe, secure, and fair for all users. For instance, it would be put in place mechanism of regulating activities such as trade and other transaction to void cases of fraud, discrimination, exploitation, and other related ills. Governance and control would further come in handy in ensuring cases like sexual harassments, racial discrimination, and prejudice are prevented. Therefore, it will be necessary for a proactive collaboration between government, industry, and academic experts, in order to establish clear guidelines and regulations that protect the rights and interests of all users (Lubin, 2022).

The first steps: Early virtual worlds and gaming environments

The emergence and development of virtual worlds and 3D gaming environments are associated with the period beginning late 1960s and early 1970s

(Bown et al., 2017). As noted in the previous section, during this time, the first creation of interactive graphics programs and games was achieved. Its development was spearheaded by computer scientists and researchers who sought to develop computer-generated environments for scientific and military simulations, educational training, and entertainment purposes (Curtis, 1972). Following their success, a number of breakthroughs were achieved with the first true virtual world, *Maze War,* created in 1974 (Momtaz, 2022). This was succeeded by a number of other pioneering games such as *Adventure* (Crowther & Woods, 1976), *Colossal Cave Adventure* (Crowther, 1976), and *Zork* (LeBlanc & Blank, 1979). These early virtual worlds and games laid the foundation for the development of more complex and sophisticated virtual environments that mirror the current form of the metaverse.

The above feats were achieved during the period when technology development was not as expounded as it is today. However, after the fourth industrial revolution happened in the early 2000s, substantial developments started to emerge (Allam, 2019). Among these include the creation of Second Life, a ground-breaking virtual world and game, which was launched in 2003. This platform provided a substantially advanced multiplayer online game experience that allowed players to create and inhabit virtual worlds. It also allowed them to engage in various activities such as socializing, virtual trading, exploration of new dimensions, and a wide range of entertainment activities (Steinkuehler & Williams, 2006). Another influential virtual world was World of Warcraft, which was released in 2004 and quickly became a funs' favorite online games worldwide (Castronova, 2005). The breakthrough in these early virtual worlds and games formed a concrete foundation upon which development of more complex and sophisticated virtual environments, such as the metaverse has been founded.

In the context of the early virtual worlds, their key features and limitations could be understood in the view of their technological and social development. To begin with, these platforms were only as good as the availability of hardware and software at the time. Therefore, it would be inconsequential to criticize their graphics and environments, which in all fairness were relatively simple and limited. Another major obstacle that hindered full exploitation of the early virtual worlds and games is the challenge of storage of massive data that were begin produced. Therefore, it became daunting to build complex and sophisticated virtual environments (Messinger et al., 2009). Despite these limitations, early virtual worlds and games represented a major step forward in the development of virtual environments and had a profound impact on the development of the metaverse concept.

The impact of early virtual worlds on the metaverse concept can be understood by analyzing their role in promoting and advancing the diverse agendas and applications of virtual environments, especially in frontiers such as entertainment, work environment, education, health, and tourism among others. The initial environments can be argued to have helped in build a sense of community belonging among users. With the achievement of this agenda, it became potent to development more complex and sophisticated virtual environments as expressed by Steinkuehler and Williams (2006). Further, those initial platforms could also be attributed to gradual development of social virtual environments, such as the metaverse (Castronova, 2005).

The rise of massively multiplayer online games (MMOGS)

A number of factors could be attributed to the development of the metaverse. However, the contribution of Massively Multiplayer Online Games (MMOGs) can be singled out for being the most prominent and pronounced platform under which the concept promoted. The improvements and evolutions of MMOGs have been exceptional in shaping the nature, the form, and status of the new metaverse platforms being advanced by a wide range of corporations (Investing.com, 2022). For instance, the idea of using avatars and the use of VR and AR technologies in the metaverse have all been borrowed from the gaming world (Dwivedi et al., 2022). In right to this truth, in this section we will delve in literature about MMOGs and highlight pertinent issues such as its history and evolution. Further, the section will also discuss how those platforms have been instrumental in the gradual metamorphosis of the metaverse concept to its current form.

In definition, MMOGs could be referred to as online games that allow a substantial number of users and players to interact in a shared and unending, immersive, virtual world (Kazija, 2018; Lee et al., 2021). From the available literature, these games were first introduced in the late 1990s, with the first game under this genre being Zork, under the then-popular platform called Multiuser Dungeon (MUD) (Machin, 2015). Later, in 1992, the second game that opened the stage was called *Legends of Future Past*. Thereafter, numerous other games such as Ultima Online, EverQuest, Nexus, and others were launched (Machin, 2015). In comparison, it would be safe to argue that early MMOGs were relatively primitive compared to the sophisticated virtual worlds available today, but they nonetheless helped set the foundation for the development of the genre. Ever since, MMOGs have grown in popularity and complexity, with millions of hours spent on those platforms. For instance, it is reported that in September 2022 alone, a cumulative of over 53 million hours were spent on mobile-based MMOGs alone (Clement, 2023).

The selling point for MMOGs is their ability to allow players to interact and socialize with each other in real-time online. On this, it is worthwhile to note that the interactions can take diverse forms, ranging from simple chats to more complex social dynamics, such as player-run economies and political systems (Kazija, 2018). In short, these games offer players an environment that that could be termed as a digital twin of the physical environments where features such as cities, forests, oceans, subways, among others, abound (Cronenwett, 2002). The ability to simulate the physical realm has been noted as a key factor driving the popularity of MMOGs and has helped to drive the development of the metaverse concept.

After establishing that there is no doubt that MMOGs have been influential on the development of the metaverse concept, it is now worth highlighting some of the reasons that could be attributed to this. The first indicator is the ways in which MMOGs have advanced the concept of virtual worlds as a social platform (Kazija, 2018). Here, it is obvious that these gaming platforms are accessible by millions of people that are willing to spend significant amounts of time and money in digital realms, not only for the sake of playing games, but also with the aim of achieving other social objectives like trading, politicking, exploring, and enjoying different forms of entertainments (Kazija, 2018). In the course of all these activities, they contribute to the advancement of the concept of social interaction. On this, as expressed in Chapter 1, the concept of social interaction is one cornerstone and selling feature for the metaverse, hence affirming the major role MMOGs have played in influencing its profile.

Massively Multiplayer Online Games (MMOGS) are online video games that support a large number of players simultaneously in a persistent virtual world.

Secondly, MMOGs have been argued to be the backbone over which the development of advanced modern technologies, essential to the metaverse, has been built and promoted. For instance, MMOGs have been instrumental in the development of technologies such as VR, AR, as well as advanced rendering and simulation technologies (Nevelsteen, 2018). When these technologies are coupled with others such AI, Big Data, Crowd Computing, and mobile connectivity technologies, they helped to make the metaverse and the experience therein more immersive. In addition, the advanced model adopted in the gaming world of monetizing is expected to be adopted in the metaverse, as more virtual products such as virtual tourism, virtual real estate, and others continue to take shape. Therefore, it is safe to argue that those technologies are crucial to the development of the metaverse, as they allow for the creation of highly detailed virtual environments that can be fully immersive and responsive to player interactions.

Finally, it is important to note that different challenges have been overcome in the course of creating different MMOGs, where the experiences acquired provided valuable insights into the design and implementation of virtual worlds, under which the metaverse is hosted. However, there still linger some concerns, especially in regard to governance and control in the metaverse that though they may have not been present in the gaming poses real risks into how the metaverse may pan out. Therefore, they need to be addressed, and if probably, as early as the metaverse designs are implemented such that they do not outgrow the potential to mitigate them in future.

The metaverse in science fiction and pop culture

The influence of science fiction on the introducing and popularizing of the metaverse cannot be understated. This genre of art, whether in written form or in movies, has played a critical role in influencing how people view the future, technology, and their relationship with the world. At its core, science fiction has explored and exposed diverse aspects of the metaverse and depicted it in various forms. However, the bottom line is that regardless of the type of metaverse portrayed (whether negative or positive), it has provided a glimpse into what the future of our society, education system, workplaces, health sector, tourism, entertainment, and other frontiers might look like. These representations have not only prompted an imagination on the public on what the metaverse might be about, but they have also influenced the development of the technology itself.

One of the earliest depictions of the metaverse in science fiction genre dates back to the 1950s with classical example being the work of William Gibson captured in his novel *Neuromancer* (Gibson, 1984). Later on, in the 1982, a movie dubbed *Tron*, directed by Steven Lisberger, was released. The movie imagines a virtual world where people could interact and participate in various games (Rinzer, 2010). As suggested above, the novel by Neal Stephenson's novel "Snow Crash" (1992) is another classical work that clearly depicts the metaverse. The novel explores the idea of a virtual world where people can interact and engage in various activities, though with stringent controls and governance to void the risks associated with technological control. The depiction of the metaverse as a place of freedom, where people can interact and explore different dimensions devoid of the constraints of physical reality, as depicted in the examples cited here, has influenced the development of the urge for the development of immersive realities, currently made possible through innovations such as VR, AR, 360 degrees, digital twins, and others (Allam, Bibri, et al., 2022; Trunfio & Rossi, 2022).

One of the classical movies that clearly showcases how the metaverse could turn out to be a tool for negative control is the *Matrix trilogy* (Wachowski & Wachowski, 1999), which is a popular science fiction film series. In the movie, the metaverse is depicted as a dystopian place where populations are controlled and manipulated by machines. This representation has helped raise awareness about the potential dangers of VR and the need to consider the ethical implications of new technologies (Dwivedi et al., 2022). The representation of the metaverse as a possible tool for oppression has prompted further discussions about the impact of technology on the society, and it has sparked debates about the responsibilities of technology companies and governments in regulating the use of VR and AR technologies (Turkle, 2011).

Besides the exploring the dystopian characteristics that could become of the metaverse, there are other science fiction works that showcase similar aspects of the metaverse. For instance, in the video game *Second Life*

(McArthur et al., 2010) and the movie *Ready Player One* (Snowden, 2019), a positive picture of the metaverse is painted, where virtues such as human symbiotic interactions in digital realm are emphasized. This representation of the metaverse is important as it helps to weather down the fears that people might have of this new technology, hence hamper its acceptability or successful take off. Further, the representation helps elucidate the fact that the metaverse is just another dimension, just like the physical realm where people can continue with their normal activities, albeit without the physical limitations (Hertzfeld, 1999). The movie, "Ready Player One" further showcases the metaverse as a place where people can escape from the realities of the physical world. This would be important for people, who might be undergoing some form of mental or psychological challenges. While this idea is controversial, in the sense that it may depict the metaverse to be addictive and one that could trigger issues of mental and physical health of people, it is worth noting that the escape routes it provide can be a solution (copying therapy) to those suffering from some diverse forms of addictions such as drugs (Gutiérrez-Maldonado, 2022; Maples-Keller et al., 2017).

It is arguable that science fiction, as a genre, has had numerous impacts on influencing and popularizing the concept of metaverse. Whether positive or negative connotation of this technology has been painted in diverse fictional arts, the important factor is that they have truly helped shape the metaverse as it is now and continue to inspire its future form. In particular, they have helped increase the understanding of the need for control and proper governance of the metaverse to ensure it does not turn out to be dystopian.

The emergence of virtual reality and augmented reality

In the previous section, it has been rightly argued that the concept of virtual reality, introduced and subsequently popularized in science fictions, works. With fictional literal works on this idea being around for decades, it is not surprising that people across the globe were inspired enough, to the point of starting to experiment on the idea of entering the digital realm. At the center stage of these imaginations and experimentations was the use of VR headsets (depicted in Fig. 2.2), which in all fairness were popularized through movies and fictional books. For instance, an early work that showcases the importance of movies in introducing and popularizing the VR headset is in the form of movie titled, *The Lawnmower Man* (Snowden, 2019), which depicted a character entering into a virtual world via the use of head gears, which later became very popular in other creative arts.

In the real world, the development of VR technology has been relatively slow, but steady, courtesy of some factors like universal acceptability due to mixed user experience. Also, due to high costs of development of the gadgets that were prohibitive for a majority of potential customers, the production was also hampered by limited virtual content that the gadgets could be used for.

30 The metaverse and smart cities

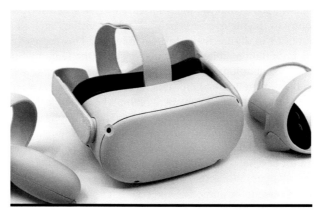

FIG. 2.2 VR headset (Mediamodifier, 2022).

Despite those challenges, the first VR headset dubbed *"the Sword of Damocles"* was created in 1968 by Ivan Sutherland for research purposes (Sutherland, 1968). However, it was after solving the aforementioned challenges in the late 1990s and early 2000s that VR technology started to become more advanced and accessible. The influx of VR headset during this period could be attributed to factors like increased improvements and affordability in computer hardware technologies, availability of 3D modeling and animation software, and increased interest in video games and advancement in internet connectivity among other factors (Bown et al., 2017). Among the most notable VR headsets and accessories that could be attributed to this period include the *Virtual Boy* (1995) by Nintendo (NIntendo, 2023), the *iGlasses* (1995) by Virtual I/O (Stanford Education, 1995), and the Oculus Rift (2013) by Oculus VR (Borrego et al., 2018).

To complement VR, AR technology was also developed, with the first known product, referred then as *Virtual Fixtures* being produced in 1992 at the USAF Armstrong Research Lab Louis Rosenberg (Arena et al., 2022). AR may be defined as the integration of digital information into the physical world (Allam, Sharifi, et al., 2022). The earliest form of AR by Louis Rosenberg was the heads-up display (HUD), which was used in military aircrafts, and in manufacturing and engineering works (Arena et al., 2022). However, today, AR technology is much advanced and has been integrated into diverse applications, such as smartphones and gaming devices to increase user experience. The scope of for AR has also increased and is now reliably being deployed in industries such as education, manufacturing, health care, tourism, retail and e-commerce, and entertainment among many others (Allam, Sharifi, et al., 2022; Arena et al., 2022).

The two technologies have had significant impacts in urban planning and with the same breadth are expected to continue influencing the development of metaverse urban concepts. In particular, their ability to enhance the creation of digital environments that mimic the physical world has allowed developers and other stakeholders to expand their imagination of the metaverse, hence making it a reality. For instance, it is through these technologies that people are able to interact, create innovative virtual products, explore the virtual environments, and learn and conduct virtual commercial transactions to name a few. Additionally, the development of VR and AR technologies has opened up new possibilities for metaverse applications, such as gaming, virtual tourism, and virtual real estates.

Key innovations and developments in VR and AR have led to the creation of more immersive and interactive digital environments such as simulations, mixed realities, new virtual worlds and environments, social media and communication platforms, and virtual marketplaces. For instance, when coupled with digital twins technology, it is becoming possible to conduct interactive, training simulations in industries such as manufacturing, health care, and education (Huynh-The et al., 2023). Further, the two technologies are being used in the energy sector to simulate and optimize various systems, hence helping in combating cases of climate change, bolster adoption of alternative mobility option, and creation of sustainable water systems et cetera (Ustundag & Cevikcan, 2018).

Following the increased attention on the metaverse, particularly after the devastating impacts of the COVID-19 pandemic (Allam, 2018, 2020a, 2020b, 2020c), the focus on producing even more powerful VR and AR technologies is now real. The intention is to increase their potential to complement the total immersive experiences that users are yearning. The advancement attention on these two technologies is also tied to the notable development in other technologies such as internet connectivity being spearheaded by improvement in mobile broadband connectivity upgrade to 5G, which is faster (approximately 1000% faster) and offers low latency than the 4G (Allam & Jones, 2021). This is expected to allow for quicker sharing of information, enhancing virtual streaming and exploration, gaming, and other activities that are synonymous with the metaverse, and made possible by the AR and VR technologies.

The metaverse in the 21st century

The current state of the metaverse can be characterized by analyzing the different corporations and companies that are spearheading their developments. Years back, this characterization was based on leading platforms and initiatives mostly dominated by gaming ventures such as Second Life (SL) (2003), World of Warcraft (WoW) (2004) (McArthur et al., 2010), and Roblox (2006) (Roblox, 2021), which developed at different time periods. These platforms became the pioneers in ensuring that users were experiencing rich and immersive virtual experiences. As a result, there were millions of users who subscribed to those virtual worlds, and the early market mover, led to these initial platforms still

32 The metaverse and smart cities

commanding some dominance. For instance, SL currently has over 64.7 million users and an in-game economy of over $500 million (Greener, 2022). On the other hand, WoW has over 5.5 million active players as of end of 2022 and is considered among some of the most popular online games in the world. On its part, Roblox has over 150 million active users, with over 58.8 million users logging in daily worldwide (Clement, 2022b).

The evolution of metaverse to its current and anticipated form has been due to astronomic growth and advancement in diverse technology and the unending increase in demand for immersive virtual experiences. Currently, after the devastating impacts of the pandemic, and the resulting changing social dynamics, where the calls for social distancing coupled with increased remote working, the demand for the metaverse can only continue to increase. Further, unlike in earlier days where interaction by users in the virtual realm was based on text and limited capabilities, today's technologies are increasingly advanced, thus making connectivity and sharing of data faster and safer (Bibri & Allam, 2022). The emergence of technologies such as blockchain has also increased the aura of metaverse by helping create the decentralized virtual worlds and enabling to increase the security and privacy of virtual transactions, data, and networks (Aks et al., 2022). The blockchain is thus helping overcome security concerns which have been cited as among key hindrance that may continue to derail the acceptability of the metaverse (Fig. 2.3 sums the power of blockchain technology).

Besides technology, economics and societal expectations are also playing critical roles in shaping the current and future metaverse. For instance, economics is playing a role in shaping and influencing the metaverse by driving the growth of virtual assets and virtual economies. A case in point is the way large corporations such as Meta (formerly Facebook), Microsoft, Apple, Google (Investing.com, 2022), Qatar Airways (Trade Arabia, 2022), and Seoul City

FIG. 2.3 An advert promoting use of blockchain technology in transactions (Bernardon, 2019).

(Park et al., 2022), among others have been keen to invest and be part of the metaverse. On its part, the society is playing a role in shaping the metaverse by driving the demand for virtual experiences and by influencing the cultural norms and values within virtual worlds.

References

Aks, S. M. Y., Karmila, M., Givan, B., Hendratna, G., Setiawan, H. S., Putra, A. S., Winarno, S. H., Kurniawan, T. A., Simorangkir, Y. N., Taufiq, R., Herawaty, M. T., & Asep. (2022). A review of blockchain for security data privacy with metaverse. In *2022 international conference on ICT for smart society (ICISS), (10-11 August 2022)*.

Allam, M. Z. (2018). *Redefining the smart city: Culture, metabolism and governance. Case Study of Port Louis, Mauritius* Curtin University.

Allam, Z. (2019). *Cities and the digital revolution: Aligning technology and humanity*. Springer Nature.

Allam, Z. (2020a). The first 50 days of COVID-19: A detailed chronological timeline and extensive review of literature documenting the pandemic. In *Surveying the Covid-19 pandemic its implications* (p. 1).

Allam, Z. (2020b). *Surveying the Covid-19 pandemic and its implications: Urban health, data technology and political economy*. Elsevier.

Allam, Z. (2020c). The third 50 days: A detailed chronological timeline and extensive review of literature documenting the COVID-19 pandemic from day 100 to day 150. In *Surveying the Covid-19 pandemic its implications* (p. 41).

Allam, Z., Bibri, S. E., Jones, D. S., Chabaud, D., & Moreno, C. J. S. (2022). Unpacking the '15-Minute City' via 6G, IoT, and digital twins: Towards a new narrative for increasing urban efficiency, resilience, and sustainability. *Sensors, 22*(4), 1369.

Allam, Z., & Jones, D. S. (2021). Future (post-COVID) digital, smart and sustainable cities in the wake of 6G: Digital twins, immersive realities and new urban economies. *Land Use Policy, 101*, 105201. https://doi.org/10.1016/j.landusepol.2020.105201.

Allam, Z., Sharifi, A., Bibri, S. E., Jones, D. S., & Krogstie, J. (2022). The metaverse as a virtual form of smart cities: Opportunities and challenges for environmental, economic, and social sustainability in urban futures. *Smart Cities, 5*(3), 771–801. https://www.mdpi.com/2624-6511/5/3/40.

Anderson, J., & Rainie, L. (2022). *The metaverse in 2040*. Pew Research Centre.

Arena, F., Collatta, M., Pau, G., & Termine, F. (2022). An overview of augmented reality. *Computers, 11*(2), 28. https://doi.org/10.3390/computers11020028.

Bernardon, P. (2 June 2019). *Nasdaq advertisement*. Unsplash. Retrieved 6th June 2023 from https://unsplash.com/photos/zt0HWquGXlQ.

Bibri, S. E., & Allam, Z. (2022). The metaverse as a virtual form of data-driven smart cities: The ethics of the hyper-connectivity, datafication, algorithmization, and platformization of urban society. *Computational Urban Science, 2*, 22. https://doi.org/10.1007/s43762-022-00050-1.

Bibri, S. E., Allam, Z., & Krogstie, J. (2022). The metaverse as a virtual form of data-driven smart urbanism: Platformization and its underlying processes, institutional dimensions, and disruptive impacts. *Computational Urban Science, 2*, 24. https://doi.org/10.1007/s43762-022-00051-0.

Borrego, A., Latorre, J., Alcañiz, M., & Llorens, R. (2018). Comparison of oculus rift and HTC Vive: Feasibility for virtual reality-based exploration, navigation, exergaming, and rehabilitation. *Games for Health Journal, 7*(3), 151–156. https://doi.org/10.1089/g4h.2017.0114.

Bown, J., White, E., & Boopalan, A. (2017). Chapter 12—Looking for the ultimate display: A brief history of virtual reality. In J. Gackenbach, & J. Bown (Eds.), *Boundaries of self and reality online* (pp. 239–259). Academic Press. https://doi.org/10.1016/B978-0-12-804157-4.00012-8.

Bulao, J. (7 February 2023). *How much data is created every day in 2023?*. Tech Jury. Retrieved 11th February 2023 from https://techjury.net/blog/how-much-data-is-created-every-day/#gref.

Castronova, E. (2005). *Synthetic worlds: The business and culture of online games*. University of Chicago Press.

Cheong, B. C. (2022). Avatars in the metaverse: Potential legal issues and remedies. *International Cybersecurity Law Review, 3*(2), 467–494. https://doi.org/10.1365/s43439-022-00056-9.

Clement, J. (2022a). *Metaverse—Statistics & facts*. Statista. (28 November 2022). Retrieved 11th February 2023 from https://www.statista.com/topics/8652/metaverse/#topicOverview.

Clement, J. (2022b). *Roblox games global DAU as of Q3 2022*. Statista. (17 November 2022). Retrieved 13th February 2022 from https://www.statista.com/statistics/1192573/daily-active-users-global-roblox/.

Clement, J. (11 January 2023). *Multiplayer online battle arena (MOBA) games—Statistics & facts*. Statista. Retrieved 12th February 2023 from https://www.statista.com/topics/2290/moba-gaming/#topicOverview.

Cronenberg, D. (1999). *eXistenZ [Dimension Films]*. Alliance Atlantis Communications, Canadian Television Fund, & Harold Greenberg Fund; Dimension Films.

Cronenwett, W. (2002). The metaverse: A fully-realized virtual world. *Journal of Interactive Technology and Smart Education, 1*(2), 95–104.

Crowther, W. (1976). Colossal cave adventure. *Communications of the ACM, 19*(12), 342–346.

Crowther, W., & Woods, B. (1976). Adventure. *Communications of the ACM, 19*(12), 357–361.

Curtis, P. A. (1972). Simulation of 3-dimension objects by computer. In *Proceedings of the 5th national conference on computer graphics and interactive techniques*.

Dwivedi, Y. K., Hughes, L., Baabdullah, A. M., Ribeiro-Navarrete, S., Giannakis, M., Al-Debei, M. M., Dennehy, D., Metri, B., Buhalis, D., Cheung, C. M. K., Conboy, K., Doyle, R., Dubey, R., Dutot, V., Felix, R., Goyal, D. P., Gustafsson, A., Hinsch, C., Jebabli, I., … Wamba, S. F. (2022). Metaverse beyond the hype: Multidisciplinary perspectives on emerging challenges, opportunities, and agenda for research, practice and policy. *International Journal of Information Management, 66*, 102542. https://doi.org/10.1016/j.ijinfomgt.2022.102542.

Faraboschi, P., Frachtenberg, E., Laplante, P., Milojicic, D., & Saracco, R. (2022). Virtual worlds (metaverse): From skepticism, to fear, to immersive opportunities. *Computer, 55*(10), 100–106. https://doi.org/10.1109/MC.2022.3192702.

Getty Images. (18 April 2023). *Happy schoolchildren wearing a virtual reality goggles at school in computer science class*. Unsplash. Retrieved 6th June 2023 from https://unsplash.com/photos/tt-ymlv8KB0.

Gibson, W. (1984). *Neuromancer*. Ace.

Greener, R. (12 January 2022). *Second life storefront user traffic jumps 35 percent in 2021*. XR Today. Retrieved 10th February 2023 from https://www.xrtoday.com/virtual-reality/second-life-user-traffic-jumps-35-percent-in-2021/#:~:text=Since%20its%20inception%2C%20Second%20Lifeactive%20users%20on%20its%20platform.

Gupta, A., Khan, H. U., Nazir, S., Shafiq, M., & Shabaz, M. (2023). Metaverse security: Issues, challenges and a viable ZTA model. *Electronics, 12*(2), 391. https://doi.org/10.3390/electronics12020391.

Gutiérrez-Maldonado, J. (2022). The use of virtual reality technology in the treatment of psychopathological disorders. *Journal of Clinical Medicine, 11*(18), 5358. https://doi.org/10.3390/jcm11185358.

Hertzfeld, M. (1999). The metaverse: Virtual reality on the internet. In *The Third International Conference on Collaborative Virtual Environments (CVE'99)*. UK: University of Nottingham.

Hudson, L. (19 April 2018). If you want to know how we ended up in a cyber dystopia, read ready player one. *The Verge*. Retrieved 29/10/2021 from https://www.theverge.com/2018/4/19/17250892/ready-player-one-book-facebook-internet-dystopia.

Huynh-The, T., Pham, Q.-V., Pham, X.-Q., Nguyen, T. T., Han, Z., & Kim, D.-S. (2023). Artificial intelligence for the metaverse: A survey. *Engineering Applications of Artificial Intelligence*, *117*, 105581. https://doi.org/10.1016/j.engappai.2022.105581.

Investing.com. (4 September 2022). Big tech metaverses: All you need to know about Meta, Microsoft, Google, and Apple. *Investing*. Retrieved 10th February 2023 from https://www.investing.com/news/cryptocurrency-news/big-tech-metaverses-all-you-need-to-know-about-meta-microsoft-google-and-apple-2885578.

Kazija, J. (2018). The evolution and impact of massively multiplayer online games (MMOGs). *Journal of Gaming and Virtual Worlds*, *10*(2), 123–138.

LeBlanc, D., & Blank, D. (1979). Zork. *Creative Computing*, *6*(4), 42–49.

Lee, Z. W. Y., Cheung, C. M. K., & Chan, T. K. H. (2021). Understanding massively multiplayer online role-playing game addiction: A hedonic management perspective. *Information Systems Journal*, *31*(1), 33–61. https://doi.org/10.1111/isj.12292.

Lubin, A. (26 April 2022). Governance in the metaverse. *DataSphere*. Retrieved 12th February 2023 from https://www.thedatasphere.org/news/governance-in-the-metaverse/.

Machin, C. (12 November 2015). A brief history of the MMO: From world of warcraft and final fantasy XIV. *CGMagazine*. Retrieved 12th February 2023 from https://www.cgmagonline.com/articles/features/a-brief-history-of-the-mmo/.

Maples-Keller, J. L., Bunnell, B. E., Kim, S.-J., & Rothbaum, B. O. (2017). The use of virtual reality technology in the treatment of anxiety and other psychiatric disorders. *Harvard Review of Psychiatry*, *25*(3), 103–113. https://doi.org/10.1097/HRP.0000000000000138.

Marr, B. (1 July 2022). The metaverse, digital dressing rooms and the future of the fashion retail. *Forbes*. Retrieved 10th February 2023 from https://www.forbes.com/sites/bernardmarr/2022/07/01/the-metaverse-digital-dressing-rooms-and-the-future-of-fashion-retail/?sh=4cfd06816b90.

McArthur, V., Teather, R., & Stuerzlinger, W. (2010). Comparing 3D content creation interfaces in two virtual worlds: World of warcraft and second life. *Journal of Gaming & Virtual Worlds*, *2*, 239–258. https://doi.org/10.1386/jgvw.2.3.239_1.

Mediamodifier. (13 July 2022). *A pair of white headphones*. Unsplash. Retrieved 6th June 2023 from https://unsplash.com/photos/wV_05P-t15Y.

Messinger, P., Stroulia, E., Lyons, K., Bone, M., Niu, R., Smirnov, K., & Perelgut, S. (2009). Virtual worlds—Past, present, and future: New directions in social computing. *Decision Support Systems*, *47*. https://doi.org/10.1016/j.dss.2009.02.014.

Meta. (28 October 2021). *Introducing Meta: A social technology company*. Meta. Retrieved 11th February 2023 from https://about.fb.com/news/2021/10/facebook-company-is-now-meta/.

Momtaz, P. P. (2022). Some very simple economics of Web3 and the metaverse. *FinTech*, *1*(3), 225–234.

Nevelsteen, K. J. L. (2018). Virtual world, defined from a technological perspective and applied to video games, mixed reality, and the metaverse. *Computer Animation and Virtual Worlds*, *29*(1), e1752. https://doi.org/10.1002/cav.1752.

NIntendo. (2023). *Virtual boy*. Nintendo. Retrieved 13th February 2023 from https://nintendo.fandom.com/wiki/Virtual_Boy.

Park, J. Y., Lee, K., & Chung, D. R. (2022). Public interest in the digital transformation accelerated by the COVID-19 pandemic and perception of its future impact. *The Korean Journal of Internal Medicine*, *37*(6), 1223–1233. https://doi.org/10.3904/kjim.2022.129.

Purdy, M. (5 April 2022). How the metaverse could change work. *Harvard Business Review*. Retrieved 10th February 2023 from https://hbr.org/2022/04/how-the-metaverse-could-change-work.

Rinzer, J. W. (2010). *The art of Tron: Legacy*. Chronicle Books.

Roblox. (18 November 2021). Nike is building its metaverse inside of 'Roblox'. *Engadget*. Retrieved 2nd December 2021 from https://www.engadget.com/nike-roblox-nikeland-metaverse-192234036.html.

Rossner, M., & Tait, D. (2021). Presence and participation in a virtual court. *Criminology & Criminal Justice*, *23*(1), 135–157. https://doi.org/10.1177/17488958211017372.

Snowden, A. (2019). From lawnmower man to ready player one: A cultural history of virtual reality. In C. Deprez, & K. Gough (Eds.), *New directions in mobile media and performance* (pp. 57–69). Routledge.

Stanford Education. (1995). *Virtual I/O's iglasses! head mounted display*. Stanford Education. Retrieved 13th February 2023 from https://graphics.stanford.edu/infrastructure/gamma-corrected/iglasses.html.

Steinkuehler, C., & Williams, D. (2006). Where everybody knows your (screen) name: Online games as "third places". *Journal of Computer-Mediated Communication*, *1*(4), 885–909. https://doi.org/10.1111/j.1083-6101.2006.00300.x.

Stephenson, N. (2003). *Snow crash: A novel*. Random House Publishing Group. https://books.google.co.ke/books?id=RMd3GpIFxcUC.

Sutherland, I. E. (1968). A head-mounted three dimensional display. In *Fall joint computer conference, part I U.S*.

Trade Arabia. (11 September 2022). *Qatar Airways website wins FTE award for VR experience*. Trade Arabia. Retrieved 11th February 2023 from https://tradearabia.com/news/TTN_400518.html.

Trunfio, M., & Rossi, S. (2022). Advances in metaverse investigation: Streams of research and future agenda. *Virtual Worlds*, *1*(2), 103–129. https://www.mdpi.com/2813-2084/1/2/7.

Turkle, S. (2011). *Alone together: Why we expect more from technology and less from each other*. Basic Books.

Ustundag, A., & Cevikcan, E. (2018). *Industry 4.0: Managing the digital transformation*. Springer International Publishing.

Verne, J. (2006). *From the earth to the moon*. Frawley Corporation.

Verne, J. (2015). *A journey to the centre of the earth*. Enhanced Media.

Wachowski, L., & Wachowski, L. (1999). *Matrix Trilogy*. W. B. Entertainment; Imports.

Wells, H. G. (1905). The country of the blind. *Strand Magazine*.

Xi, N., Chen, J., Gama, F., Riar, M., & Hamari, J. (2022). The challenges of entering the metaverse: An experiment on the effect of extended reality on workload. *Information Systems Frontiers*. https://doi.org/10.1007/s10796-022-10244-x.

Zhang, X., Chen, Y., Hu, L., & Wang, Y. (2022). The metaverse in education: Definition, framework, features, potential applications, challenges, and future research topics [Review]. *Frontiers in Psychology*, *13*. https://doi.org/10.3389/fpsyg.2022.1016300.

Zhao, Y., Jiang, J., Chen, Y., Liu, R., Yang, Y., Xue, X., & Chen, S. (2022). Metaverse: Perspectives from graphics, interactions and visualization. *Visual Informatics*, *6*(1), 56–67. https://doi.org/10.1016/j.visinf.2022.03.002.

Chapter 3

The metaverse and smart cities

Introduction

> Metaverse can be defined as a concept that envisions a shared, immersive, and persistent digital environment where people can interact with each other and with digital content in real time.

As the world becomes increasingly digital, it is unsurprising that there are notable technological transformations in all human spheres. In particular, there are fundamental changes in the way people live, work, and interact with each other. Two of the most notable developments in this regard are the metaverse and the smart cities concept (Dwivedi et al., 2022; Toppeta, 2010). In this chapter, the attention is focused on exploring the connections between these two concepts and their potential implications on the urban planning and design pursuits.

The term "metaverse" was first coined by Neal Stephenson in his science fiction novel titled "Snow Crash," (Stephenson, 2003). This novel describes a VR dimension where people are able to freely interact with each other and with the virtual objects within this "unique" environment. Since this novel, the concept of the metaverse has evolved and expanded greatly, where it now includes a collective virtual shared space that is created by the convergence of physical and VRs. The main agenda of designing this space is to provide an experience that simulates the real world, where users have the capacity to interact with diverse virtual objects as well as with human being in the platform (Faraboschi et al., 2022).

Despite its ranging popularity, it should be understood that the metaverse is still in its early stages of development. However, postpandemic, a wide range of companies and organizations are actively involved in activities geared toward creating virtual worlds that can be accessed through the internet. A good example to demonstrate this is a look at the video game *Fortnite* which is purported to be a form of metaverse due to its ability to host concerts, events, and social gatherings within its virtual environment.

38 The metaverse and smart cities

Smart cities on their part can be described as cities that actively leverage technology and data to improve the quality of life for their (Allam & Newman, 2018). Unlike other form of urban planning models that have emerged over the years, the goal of a smart city is to create a more efficient, sustainable, and livable urban environment. Such have not been the case in contemporary cities due to factors like climate change, rapidly increasing urban population, high rates of urbanization, and decreasing natural resources et cetera. To achieve the three key objectives, smart cities rely on a variety of smart devices powered by technologies such as Internet of Things (IoT), sensors, and artificial intelligence (Allam & Dhunny, 2019; Allam & Newman, 2018; Batty, 2018). With the devices, it becomes possible to gather and analyze wide range of data and draw insights about the city's infrastructure, services, and operations. The conclusions drawn are then used to improve the operations within the city, optimize resource allocation, and enhance the citizen experience in diverse sectors.

The traction on smart city discourse and operationalization became apparent after the fourth industrial revolution which emerged as from the early 2000s (Ghobakhloo, 2020). Since then, there are notable examples of smart cities around the world, which have emerged and continue to improve in their stature. One of these is Singapore (Fig. 3.1 showing a section of Singapore city) which has deployed diverse smart technologies such as an electronic road pricing system that uses sensors to monitor traffic flow and adjusts pricing based on demand (Allam, 2020b; Menon & Guttikunda, 2010). The city has also implemented a smart waste management system that uses sensors to monitor garbage levels and optimize waste collection routes. Another key city is Barcelona which is reported to be leading other European cities in embracing the use of technology to improve its functioning and the livability status of the residents (Mora & Bolici, 2016). Indeed, it is not surprising that the smart cities euphoria has further helped stimulated current discourse where some cities such as Paris

FIG. 3.1 Sustainable, smart city Singapore at night (Banse, 2017).

are on course to implement an even more advanced model of smart cities concept dubbed as the 15-Minute City concept (Allam, Bibri, et al., 2022; Allam, Nieuwenhuijsen, et al., 2022).

The relationship between the metaverse and smart cities can be construed to lie in the potential for a metaverse to enhance the functioning of smart cities. In particular, its ability to help mirror the real world and simulate the functioning of a smart city just like it would be in the physical realm. This capability provides urban planners and designers with a platform to test different scenarios for city planning and improve the design of a city in a more cost-effective manner. It would also allow them to share the design with residents, thus allowing them to offer their suggestions and ideas before the plan is finally implemented, hence increasing acceptability and sense of ownership by residents. A practical example could be in regard desired changes in the transportation section. Here, a virtual model of a city could be created in the metaverse and be used to test different traffic flow scenarios and optimize traffic signals and parking (Glazebrook & Newman, 2018). In the energy sector, the metaverse could be used to simulate consumption trends in a city, allowing planners to test different renewable energy sources and predict future demand (Zhang et al., 2021). The virtual world can also be used to simulate emergencies and help in crafting of response programs that could benefit first responders in their preparation for any eventualities.

In addition, a metaverse can provide citizens with immersive experiences of their city, allowing them to explore different neighborhoods, parks, and landmarks. This can improve the citizen experience and provide them with access to information about city services, public transportation, and other resources (Cheng et al., 2022). This is groundbreaking especially postpandemic where the new trends in different cities include working from home reduced human interaction (social distancing), e-learning, and online shopping (e-commerce) among other things. As such, the metaverse is anticipated to speed up the actualization of such trends, while making the improving the users' experience. The convergence of the metaverse and smart cities has the potential to revolutionize the way people plan, design, and experience cities. Of notable mention is the way the metaverse is expected provides different opportunities for people to optimize the functionalities of a city, improve access to its products, services, and information, and enhance the quality of life for citizens.

It is noteworthy to appreciate that despite the numerous aforementioned benefits of the connections between the metaverse and the smart cities concept, there are a number of hurdles that will need to be overcome. One of the main concerns is the potential for a digital divide driven by the glaring social inequality that exists in cities (Park & Kim, 2022). That is, the access to the metaverse will be skewed in favor of those with financial and technological knowhow. At the same time, a sizeable number of urban residents might be locked out of the metaverse due to their inability to secure critical equipment such as VR gadgets such VR glasses, headsets, and others. This could exacerbate existing social inequalities and create new forms of exclusions and alienations. It could also lead to other form of social ills such as digital addiction and overreliance on VR, hence negatively impacting on human-to-human interactions etc. (Pasca et al., 2021). Additionally, with more data being collected for the sake of the metaverse and the smart cities, there are existing concerns about privacy and security that can only continue to grow unless amicably addressed (Ceyhan, 2022).

To address these concerns, it will be imperative to approach the development of the metaverse and smart cities in a responsible and ethical manner. This will require sincere and truthful collaboration between policymakers, urban planners, and technology companies to ensure that the development of these technologies is inclusive, equitable, is grounded on solid, legal frameworks, and seeks to respect privacy and security of everyone.

Overview of smart cities

Smart cities and the metaverse are two emerging concepts that are becoming increasingly intertwined in modern urban planning endeavors. To put this in context, it is worth understanding the basic tenets under which the concept of smart cities is anchored and how such are contributing to the realization of the metaverse. In particular, it is critical to expressly highlight that the convergent point of the two concepts is on the improvement of people's experience. That is, for the smart cities, the ultimate objective is to improve the lives of their citizens, while the metaverse provides a virtual platform where users can interact with both humans and with digital objects (Ball, 2020). In right of this background, this section delves further to expose the relationship between these two concepts. It will also explore the diverse characteristics of smart cities, the key challenges and opportunities in smart city development, and the examples of smart city initiatives.

HVAC: the technology and systems used to control indoor environmental conditions, including temperature, humidity, and air quality, in residential, commercial, and industrial buildings.

Smart cities are grounded on use of diverse technologies, aimed at increasing efficiency, improving performance and streamlining operations, service delivery (Bibri et al., 2022; Bibri & Krogstie, 2020). The ultimate objective is to enhance their livability status, and in the current dispensation, improve their resilience against phenomenon such as climate change. The applicable technologies can take many forms, including sensors that monitor different aspects such as traffic and air quality. Sensors could also be deployed to monitor smart grids and by extension HVAC installations with the aim of optimizing energy usage and promoting optimal resource consumption. Further, sensors are very critical in data collections for the sake of analytics, which in turn helps

FIG. 3.2 A smart heat control device mounted on a wall (LeFebvre, 2018).

urban planners and manager make concrete and informed decisions. Other technologies pertinent to smart cities include IoT smart devices such as camera, smart meters like the one shown in Fig. 3.2 below, etc.

> Smart cities are urban areas that leverage advanced technologies and data-driven approaches to enhance the quality of life, sustainability, efficiency, and overall functioning of the city.

One of the indisputable characteristics of smart cities is the focus on data. The data is generated, collected, and analyzed from a wide range of sources, such as the installed technologies, from government records and from social media platform (Bibri, 2021). Afterward, the data is analyzed and the subsequent results are used to draw insights into how different facets within the city are functioning. For instance, the conclusion made after the analytical processes are used to optimize city services, such as transportation, waste management, energy production, and utilization and to improve public safety.

Another characteristic of smart cities is the increased reliance on digital technologies to improve citizen communications, engagement, interactions, and access to a wide range of services. For instance, many smart cities have implemented mobile apps that allow citizens to report issues such as potholes, broken streetlights, and security concerns to name a few. These apps make it easier for citizens to interact with their city government and have their concerns addressed. A classical case to affirm this could be drawn from South Korea, where mobile apps were intensively used during the height of COVID-19 pandemic to trace, track, and ensure containment measures were strictly adhered to. As a result, the country, especially in cities like Seoul, managed to keep the number of infections at bay (Heo et al., 2020).

While smart cities are associated with numerous and priceless benefits, they are marred by a number of challenges. One of the biggest challenges is privacy and security of both the human and the installed infrastructure. On human beings, the idea of being monitored, or individual data being exposed to third parties have remained a bane to smart cities with a sizeable number of residents being reluctant to embrace this planning model. For instance, in the recent past, there has been a spirited conspiracy theory against the 15-Minute City planning model with the claim that it is a tool by those in leadership and governments to constrain human freedom, especially of movement (Parry, 2023). Whereas such theories have been discounted and proven to be only misguided conspiracies, they help to affirm the fears and apprehension that residents have when the technology deem to "touch" on their data. Further, noting that most of the smart technologies are outsourced from third parties, whom in this case comprises of profit-driven large corporations, it is worth securing the privacy and security of both the residents and the smart city infrastructure (Allam, 2020a). Doing so would give impetus to the acceptability of the digitalization process and further encourage urban residents to cooperate including in providing data and relevant information.

Another challenge is ensuring that smart city technologies are ubiquitous and accessible to all citizens. This is important as programs such as smart cities may contribute significantly to the widening of the inequality gap in the society, as those who do not have access to technology may be left behind. It is important to ensure that smart city initiatives are inclusive and that all citizens have access to the benefits that they offer. For instance, it would be critical to ensure technologies such as 5G are distributed in such a way that they cover and reach all urban residents (Allam & Jones, 2021).

Those challenges and many others should, however, not be excused to overshadow the numerous opportunities that accompanies smart city development. One opportunity is the potential to help address and reduce the environmental footprints of cities (Paiva et al., 2021). On this, there is sufficient evidence that showcases that cities are the main source of global emissions (contributing approximately 70% of total emissions), despite them occupying only a small percentage of the habitable landmass (Dasgupta et al., 2022). With smart city technologies, it is possible to optimize energy consumption, improve air quality, and promote waste management. Another opportunity is the potential to improve the efficiency and effectiveness of city services delivery. By collecting and analyzing data, smart cities can optimize transportation systems, reduce traffic congestion, and improve emergency response times.

There are many examples of smart city initiatives around the world including Seoul (Lim, 2021), Paris, Amsterdam, London, and others (Noori et al., 2020). In the city of Barcelona, for example, the smart aspect has been affected by installing a string of smart lighting system that uses sensors to adjust the brightness of streetlights based on pedestrian and vehicle traffic (Mora & Bolici, 2016). As a result of that system, the city has managed to reduce energy consumption by approximately 30% and a corresponding reduction in carbon emissions. Another example is the city of Singapore, which has implemented a smart transportation system that uses real-time data to optimize traffic flow.

On its part, the smart features have resulted in a 10% reduction in travel time for commuters, as well as a reduction in traffic congestion and air pollution.

The examples cited in this section only showcase the potential the smart city concept holds in addressing numerous urban challenges, and with the emergence of the metaverse, it is anticipated that the situation can only continue to become better.

Understanding the metaverse

VR and AR technologies are the key technologies upon which the foundation for the metaverse is laid (Dwivedi et al., 2022). The VR technology immerses the user into a completely different dimension (Anderson et al., 2017), while AR overlays digital content and products onto the physical world (Arena et al., 2022). These technologies are relied upon in the process of creating the virtual spaces and experiences that make up the metaverse. The deployment of these technologies results in a new and unique experience where users are not bound by the limitations of the physical world (Lee et al., 2021). For instance, obstacles such as geographical location, race, gender, religions, and others have no room in the digital realm. The freedom of those limitations is warranted by factors like the ability of users to access and operate in the virtual realm in the form of avatars of their liking. Also, the ability is to create digital twins of the physical objects, hence making it possible for users to be in total control of their new environment in a way beyond what they can achieve in the real world. These two components of the metaverse are very critical in promoting unhindered communication, collaboration, and interaction of users despite the demographical differences that have always been a barrier in the physical realm.

Another significant features of the metaverse is its ability to create new and unique platforms for innovators and the creative industry. That it, it offers infinite possibilities for creativity and innovation including make it possible for simulations and test before actual products are mass produced (Koohang et al., 2023). It then means that improvements and changes can be made during the design phase thus helping saving on time and costs. The emergence of new industries, such as virtual fashion and virtual real estate, that are unique to the metaverse is one of the results of this feature. The metaverse also has the potential to improve accessibility and inclusivity by providing access to diverse resources and experiences that are not always available in the physical realm. A classic example on how the metaverse can help create new and unique experiences is by considering the virtual museums and galleries which are slow gaining traction across the globe. These offer art and history to people who may not be able to visit in person.

On the other front, it is possible to integrate the metaverse with emerging secure technologies such as the distributed blockchain technology which allows for the creation and subsequent ownership of digital assets. This feature is critical as it will make it possible to have some form of control and order in this new

44 The metaverse and smart cities

virtual realm (Aks et al., 2022). Without control, it would be difficult to determine who is in charge of the digital platforms and the assets, and this might result into different challenges. Coupling the blockchain technology with the artificial intelligence (AI) is expected to enhance the virtual experience, providing even more opportunities for innovation and creativity. With these two technologies and others, the metaverse has the potential to revolutionize various industries, including entertainment, education, and health care.

In the entertainment industry, developers are upbeat that the metaverse will provide new opportunities for immersive storytelling and interactive experiences. For instance, the metaverse by Meta (formerly Facebook) is anticipated to enable and enhance virtual concerts and festivals (e.g., as shown in Fig. 3.3). Already, such virtual events are gradually becoming popular in the metaverse, allowing users to attend and interact in events organized from different parts of the world.

In the education industry, the metaverse can provide new opportunities for immersive and interactive learning experiences, hence making e-learning even more intuitive (Alfaisal et al., 2022). With metaverse, it will be possible to create virtual classrooms and educational simulations aimed at enhancing the learning experience for students and providing trainers more control of the learning environment. The metaverse is further expected to allow for customization of the modules for each student according to their academic needs. In addition, it will make it possible for learners and teachers/trainers to access a wide range of resources and experiences that may not be available in traditional classroom settings. In the healthcare industry, the metaverse can provide new opportunities for advanced services such as telemedicine and remote healthcare services, providing access to healthcare services for people who may not have access to traditional healthcare services. This would also help reduce costs and reduce overcrowding of health facilities among other benefits.

Like all the other emerging digital products and platforms, the metaverse also is subject to a variety of challenges and risks. One of these is the issue

FIG. 3.3 A girl enjoying virtual concert (Getty Images, 2022).

of privacy and security, especially since modalities and frameworks to guide operations, transactions, ownership of assets, and other such issues are not yet in place (Pooyandeh et al., 2022). On other fronts, the metaverse becomes more interconnected, the risk of cyberattacks and data breaches may increasingly expose users to unimaginable challenges and vulnerabilities.

Another challenge is the potential for social isolation and addiction as people immerse themselves into exploring the unlimited potentials and adventures in the virtual realm. As the virtual world becomes more immersive, there is a risk that users may become disconnected from the real world; hence neglect the reality (Bojic, 2022). This has led to calls for responsible development and use of the metaverse, with a focus on promoting social interaction and healthy use of technology.

Intersecting the metaverse and smart cities

The metaverse and smart cities are two emerging technological phenomena that share a common goal: to create a seamless, efficient, and sustainable living environment for the inhabitants. While they are different in that the smart city represent the physical realm and the metaverse depicts the virtual world, they share a wide variety of similarities. In particular, the two are intertwined in that the metaverse has the potential to revolutionize urban planning and development, while the smart technologies installed in cities plays a critical role in the actualization of metaverse. The metaverse influences the smart city concept by enabling immersive experiences, facilitating data collection and analysis, and supporting social and cultural activities.

The metaverse further is becoming and instrumental tool of promoting public engagement and participation in decision-making (Dwivedi et al., 2022). This feat is achieved as the metaverse allows for immersive interaction where users could interact, discourse, and exchange views on how different aspects of the city can be achieved. For example, VR technologies can be used in urban planning to enable citizens to experience and provide feedback on proposed designs. This can improve the accuracy of decision-making and foster a sense of community ownership in the development process. Additionally, via the metaverse, it is possible for different stakeholders to facilitate public education and awareness campaigns on diverse issues related to smart city development, such as energy conservation, waste management, and sustainable transportation.

Another probable benefit of the metaverse in smart city development is its ability to support and consolidate the data collection strategies and analysis of real-time data. This could be achieved by deploying virtual sensors in the metaverse, which would in turn help transmit real-time information and data on various urban sectors like transport, energy, health, environment, and others (Allam, Sharifi, et al., 2022). The data collected could then be fed into the smart city's control system to optimize the use of resources and improve public services. With the help of other technologies such as the digital twins, the metaverse can also be used to simulate different scenarios and test the impact of various policy interventions before they are implemented in the real world, hence helping in cost reduction and optimizing designs. On the social sphere within smart cities, the metaverse has the potential to support social and cultural activities. For instance, it provides a platform for creating virtual spaces that reflect the city's diversity, history, and heritage, which would not only help promote social cohesion and cultural exchange, but could also play a critical role in the preservation and conservation of endangered heritage. Such would be important especially in view of the changing tourism in metaverse where it is now possible for users to make virtual tours of historical landmarks or attend and even participate in virtual cultural festivals (Hemmati, 2022).

In order for the smart cities to benefit from the potential benefits that the metaverse makes possible, several key considerations must be made and a variety of challenges be addressed. First, it will be important to upgrade the wireless connectivity to allow for seamless transfer of data in the two realms. On this, the 5G network or the anticipated 6G will play a leading role in ensuring high-speed internet connectivity, data storage, and cybersecurity measures (Allam & Jones, 2021). Further, investing on other infrastructure that would promote the security of smart cities security is paramount. Additionally, the metaverse's integration into smart cities may require significant changes to the existing legal and regulatory frameworks, especially in areas such as intellectual property rights, liability, transaction, governance, and others (Gupta et al., 2023; Lubin, 2022). This is important to ensure order, and sanity is observed even in the virtual world, hence void challenges such as inequality, discrimination, sexual or racial abuse, etc.

The ethical and moral concerns also need to be addressed especially with regard to the social implications of using the metaverse in smart cities (Bibri & Allam, 2022). For instance, the metaverse should not be made to exacerbate the already existing socioeconomic inequality in cities. For instance, the tools and gadgets such as VR and AR headgears should not be priced in a manner that would promote exclusion of citizens who lack access or financial capacity to purchase such technologies or who are not comfortable with them. Additionally, the diverse technologies should not be used to collect real-time data from the users, and subsequently use the data in ways that raise concerns about privacy and surveillance. On this, public participation and clear information on how the data is to be used need to be encouraged.

Case studies and examples

One successful example of the metaverse and smart city intersection is the city of Seoul, South Korea, where it is being used to enhance service delivery. Seoul has been on the forefront in adopting and implementing diverse new technologies to enhance transportation, energy efficiency, and public safety. With regard to metaverse, Seoul has created a virtual version of itself on the online gaming platform Second Life and allows its citizens to experience new and immersive social interaction approaches (Gaubert, 2021; Squires, 2021). Besides enhancing service delivery, the metaverse in Seoul has provided the residents with a platform for engagement and collaboration with the urban management and other stakeholders. The city management is also exploring the ways it could exploit the metaverse in other frontiers such as virtual real estate, in the education sector and in the commerce and industry.

Singapore is another classic case where the metaverse initiative may taking shape through the Smart Nation initiative in Singapore. This initiative was launched in 2014 with the aim of using technology to create a more efficient and sustainable city that has the potential to offer improved livability status to residents (Christiansen & Koc, 2017). While focus during the launch was to leverage on technology, the government of Singapore has recognized the potential of the metaverse in achieving these goals and has invested in the development of virtual environments that can be used for education, training, and entertainment. For example, the National Heritage Board has created a virtual museum that allows visitors to experience Singapore's new and immersive cultural heritage. In addition, there is increased attention on blockchain technology, which is seen as a foundation for many metaverse projects that may be initiate in the country in the future (Aks et al., 2022).

Another outstanding example worth mentioning is the Shanghai city which is on course in implementing its own version of the metaverse. Already, the local government is reported to propose a $52 billion metaverse industry expected to be complete by 2025 (Knight, 2022). As of 2023, approximately 20 locations with the city had been identified as potential pilot for the initiative, with the objective being to give the residents an immersive digital experience in different urban dimensions (Yuche & Lanlan, 2023). The main target urban dimension includes public service, business, entertainment, industrial manufacturing, and production safety.

These classical examples highlight the potential of the metaverse in smart city development. However, there are some perennial challenges that need to be addressed. First one is in related to accessibility, which in this case focus on ubiquitousness of the technologies and the associated costs of purchasing relevant tools and gears. Another challenge is in regard to the need for collaboration and coordination, to ensure that technologies are not in silos, or they access is not barred by proprietary claims. This is important because smart cities require the integration of multiple technologies and stakeholders, and the metaverse is no exception. As virtual environments become increasingly complex, it will be important to ensure that all stakeholders are involved in their development and use. This will require new forms of governance and collaboration that go beyond traditional models of city planning and management (Lubin, 2022).

Ethical, legal, and social implications

The metaverse allows for the creation of immersive virtual environments that collect vast amounts of personal data. This data can be used to manipulate users' behavior and preferences, raising genuine privacy and security concerns. Besides privacy, the metaverse is deemed to blur the line between public and private spaces, thus attracting questions on whether individual privacy of users could be guaranteed, especially at a time when there is no clear legal or ethical framework in place to guide operations. To address these concerns, it is obvious that the policymakers have no option but to establish clear guidelines and regulations for data collection, use, storage, and sharing in the metaverse.

The privacy concerns in the metaverse do not only focus on individuals, but also stretch to the needs of both the communities and society as a whole (Ceyhan, 2022). For instance, with the realization that the collection of data in the metaverse can be used to create digital profiles of an entire communities, which could then be exploited for discriminatory practices, such as redlining or targeted advertising, it is inevitable to seal the loopholes. Such could be sealed by ensuring proactive legislations, laws, and regulations are fast tracked. In particular, those frameworks should make it explicit the need ethical and transparent approaches in data collection. They should further spell out who have control of the data of both individuals and communities collected for the sake of the metaverse.

The legal challenges related to intellectual property rights also need to be addressed amicably. On this, there are already live concerns, especially in view that users create and share virtual assets, such as avatars and buildings, and it would be critical to define their ownership and copyright. In the absence of clear regulations, virtual assets can be easily copied or stolen, leading to legal disputes. Like is the case in the physical realm, the legal framework on ownership would also need to protect the rights of the creators in owning and transferring those rights (Filipova, 2023). For instance, virtual asset registries can be created to track ownership and transfers, similar to the way physical assets are tracked in the real world. Similarly, the legal framework will need to protect the rights of the metaverse creator, in events where digital assets such as apps are created within their platform.

Another social issue related to the metaverse is the potential for exacerbating existing inequalities on different fronts such as education, economic (purchasing power), physical conditions (more so in regard to those with disabilities such as blindness and deafness), etc. (Henz, 2022). On this, it has rightly been stated that access to the metaverse requires technological infrastructure and digital literacy. This then puts off a wide range of constituents who are either constrained financially, or have not acquired prerequisite digital literacy. The physically challenged (blind and deaf in particular) are at high risks of being left out in sharing the benefits brought about by the metaverse, and in cases where governments may decide to shift their service provision to such platform, these minority groups would then be alienated. This can lead to a digital divide, where access to the metaverse is limited to those with the means to access it. To ensure equitable access, policymakers must prioritize digital inclusion efforts and invest in infrastructure development. The stakeholders in the creation of the metaverse should also consider collaboration to avoid "silolization" which leads to unstandardized protocols and frameworks (Dwivedi et al., 2022). As a result, compatibility becomes a challenge, hence leading to expensive devices and technologies. However, it is possible to reduce the discrimination by adopting strategies such as providing access to affordable broadband, digital literacy training, and support for underrepresented groups, such as people with disabilities.

The environmental footprint of the metaverse also needs to be accounted for, especially in regard to energy demand and consumption. It has been appreciated that the metaverse requires significant computational power; hence, its development metaverse could contribute to an increase in carbon emissions, especially if conventional energy production approaches are adopted. However, it is possible to reduce its carbon footprint by prioritizing sustainable and energy-efficient metaverse development. This could include investing in renewable energy sources, energy-efficient hardware, and optimizing software to reduce energy consumption (Verdict, 2021). The metaverse also has the potential to impact the physical urban environments by blurring the boundary between virtual and physical spaces, raising questions about how the two will interact seamlessly. Such challenges could be addressed by having clear guidelines in place for the interaction between the metaverse and physical urban spaces. This would include guarantees that virtual assets would not interfere with physical infrastructure, and that virtual spaces are designed after thoughtful consideration of their physical impact.

The ethical, moral, legal, and environmental considerations are critical in the course of creating the metaverse in smart city development, to avoid rolling-over the already existing challenges. It then becomes imperative for the policymakers to establish effective policy and governance frameworks. These frameworks will need to prioritize the protection of individual privacy and data security, the promotion of equitable access, and the development of sustainable and energy-efficient infrastructure. This way, it will become possible to harness the metaverse as a tool for enhancing the quality of life of citizens and promoting urban development. Furthermore, effective policy and governance frameworks must also consider the potential impact of the metaverse on social and cultural dimensions and values of the urban residents. It will need to be streamlined such that its presence will not disillusion the citizenly between reality and simulation, thus influencing the way they perceive reality and interact with each other.

Policymakers must make it a priority to engage and encourage dialogue with stakeholders, including citizens, businesses, and community groups, on the best way forward. This would include soliciting feedback on proposed regulations and frameworks and providing opportunities for public participation in decision-making processes. Such engagement could help build trust in the metaverse and promote a sense of ownership among citizens, which is essential for ensuring responsible and equitable use.

Future directions

The integration of the metaverse and smart city technologies presents a wide range of possibilities for the future, especially for the urban areas that are experiencing a myriad of challenges. The increased attention, advancement, and activities on these technologies paint a promising future with numerous benefits to urban environments and their inhabitants.

One anticipated implication of the metaverse on the smart cities is the potential for increased efficiency and sustainability, which forms the basis of modern urban planning pursuits. The maturation of the metaverse is expected to help smart cities to optimally leverage data and analytics, thus positively impacting on frontiers such as the energy production and consumption, waste management, environmental conservation, and shifting to alternative mobility. This has been demonstrated in various studies, such as the research conducted by Zhao et al. (2022), which found that smart city technologies can significantly reduce energy consumption and greenhouse gas emissions. Moreover, the integration of the metaverse and smart city technologies could also result in more equitable and accessible cities, especially if current trends such as remote working, e-learning, e-commerce, and telemedicine among others are to continue. For instance, VR and AR applications could facilitate remote access to city services and cultural experiences for individuals who face physical or financial barriers. They are also expected to help increase and improve tourism experience especially for people with diverse limitation such as geographical distance, advanced in years, or those with no time or opportunities to physically visit attraction sites. All those possible will in turn help improve social inclusion and diversity in urban areas. In addition, incorporation of the metaverse into the smart city technologies could lead to enhanced mobility, especially through reduced traffic as people shift their operations and schedules such as entertainment, shopping, working, and learning into the virtual realm. Further, it will prove even more beneficial to individuals with disabilities or limited access to transportation.

Furthermore, the metaverse and smart city technologies are anticipated to revamp and enhance public safety and security. For example, the use of sensors and artificial intelligence algorithms could enable early detection of potential security threats and allow for rapid response times. This is supported in a report by Woetzel et al. (2018), who found that smart city technologies can significantly improve public safety and emergency response.

In order for the urban residents to maximize the benefits of both the metaverse and smart city technologies, there will be need to be addressed some assorted challenges that they attract. First, it will be critical to overcome the fears and concerned on data privacy and security. These are more pronounced by the risks of cyberattacks and breaches, which exposes private data and sensitive infrastructures. As such, robust cybersecurity protocols and privacy policies need to be implemented to safeguard the sensitive data collected by these technologies. It will also be critical to ensure that both the virtual and physical realms presented by these two technologies are not exploited by ill-minded groups such as terrorists, sexual offenders, and others.

Another challenge is ensuring that the implementation of smart city technologies is inclusive and equitable. As noted by Ahmadi Marzaleh et al. (2022), there is a risk of exacerbating existing social and economic disparities if the benefits of these technologies are not distributed equitably. Therefore, policy-makers and urban planners need to consider the needs of all residents and ensure that the implementation matrix of these technologies is designed to benefit the entire community, not just specific groups.

In conclusion, it is worth reminding that the integration of the metaverse and smart city technologies presents a wealth of opportunities for the future of urban development pursuits. It will then be important to increase the attention on ensuring that the two technologies succeed at their own right and in a complementary manner. This will include ensuring that potential challenges are addressed at the earliest opportunity to avoid rolling-over challenges that already exist in the current urban planning setups. It will also be critical to ensure that the implementation is inclusive and target to positive change the situation of everyone despite their demographic limitations.

References

Ahmadi Marzaleh, M., Peyravi, M., & Shaygani, F. (2022). A revolution in health: Opportunities and challenges of the metaverse. *EXCLI Journal, 21*, 791–792. https://doi.org/10.17179/excli2022-5017.

Aks, S. M. Y., Karmila, M., Givan, B., Hendratna, G., Setiawan, H. S., Putra, A. S., Winarno, S. H., Kurniawan, T. A., Simorangkir, Y. N., Taufiq, R., Herawaty, M. T., & Asep. (2022). A review of blockchain for security data privacy with metaverse. In *2022 international conference on ICT for smart society (ICISS), (10-11 August 2022)*.

Alfaisal, R., Hashim, H., & Azizan, U. H. (2022). Metaverse system adoption in education: A systematic literature review. *Journal of Computers in Education, 1*. https://doi.org/10.1007/s40692-022-00256-6.

Allam, Z. (2020a). Biometrics, privacy, safety, and resilience in future cities. In *Biotechnology and future cities* (pp. 69–87). Cham: Palgrave Macmillan.

Allam, Z. (2020b). *Urban governance and smart city planning: Lessons from Singapore*. Emerald Group Publishing.

Allam, Z., Bibri, S. E., Chabaud, D., & Moreno, C. (2022). The theoretical, practical, and technological foundations of the 15-Minute City model: Proximity and its environmental, social and economic benefits for sustainability. *Energies, 15*(16), 6042. https://doi.org/10.3390/en15166042.

Allam, Z., & Dhunny, Z. A. (2019). On big data, artificial intelligence and smart cities. *Cities, 89*, 80–91. https://doi.org/10.1016/j.cities.2019.01.032.

Allam, Z., & Jones, D. S. (2021). Future (post-COVID) digital, smart and sustainable cities in the wake of 6G: Digital twins, immersive realities and new urban economies. *Land Use Policy, 101*, 105201. https://doi.org/10.1016/j.landusepol.2020.105201.

Allam, Z., & Newman, P. (2018). Redefining the smart city: Culture, metabolism and governance. *Smart Cities, 1*(1), 4–25. https://doi.org/10.3390/smartcities1010002.

Allam, Z., Nieuwenhuijsen, M., Chabaud, D., & Moreno, C. (2022). The 15-minute city offers a new framework for sustainability, liveability, and health. *The Lancet Planetary Health, 6*(3), e181–e183.

Allam, Z., Sharifi, A., Bibri, S. E., Jones, D. S., & Krogstie, J. (2022). The metaverse as a virtual form of smart cities: Opportunities and challenges for environmental, economic, and social sustainability in urban futures. *Smart Cities, 5*, 771–801. https://doi.org/10.3390/smartcities5030040.

Anderson, A. P., Mayer, M. D., Fellows, A. M., Cowan, D. R., Hegel, M. T., & Buckey, J. C. (2017). Relaxation with immersive natural scenes presented using virtual reality. *Aerospace Medicine and Human Performance, 88*(6), 520–526. https://doi.org/10.3357/amhp.4747.2017.

Arena, F., Collatta, M., Pau, G., & Termine, F. (2022). An overview of augmented reality. *Computers, 11*(2), 28. https://doi.org/10.3390/computers11020028.

Ball, M. (13 January 2020). *The metaverse: What it is, where to find it, and who will build it*. Matthew Ball. Retrieved 2nd December 2021 from https://www.matthewball.vc/all/themetaverse.

Banse, L. (7 April 2017). *Timelapse photo of city with vehicles*. Unsplash. Retrieved 8th June 2023 from https://unsplash.com/photos/mjXf6po0TWs.

Batty, M. (2018). Artificial intelligence and smart cities. *Environment and Planning B: Urban Analytics and City Science, 45*(1), 3–6. https://doi.org/10.1177/2399808317751169.

Bibri, S. E. (2021). A novel model for data-driven smart sustainable cities of the future: The institutional transformations required for balancing and advancing the three goals of sustainability. *Energy Informatics, 4*(1), 4. https://doi.org/10.1186/s42162-021-00138-8.

Bibri, S., & Krogstie, J. (2020). Data-driven smart sustainable cities of the future: A novel model of urbanism and its core dimensions, strategies, and solutions. *Journal of Futures Studies, 25*(2), 77–94. https://doi.org/10.6531/JFS.202012_25(2).0009.

Bibri, S. E., & Allam, Z. (2022). The metaverse as a virtual form of data-driven smart cities: The ethics of the hyper-connectivity, datafication, algorithmization, and platformization of urban society. *Computational Urban Science, 2*, 22. https://doi.org/10.1007/s43762-022-00050-1.

Bibri, S. E., Allam, Z., & Krogstie, J. (2022). The metaverse as a virtual form of data-driven smart urbanism: Platformization and its underlying processes, institutional dimensions, and disruptive impacts. *Computational Urban Science, 2*, 24. https://doi.org/10.1007/s43762-022-00051-0.

Bojic, L. (2022). Metaverse through the prism of power and addiction: What will happen when the virtual world becomes more attractive than reality? *European Journal of Futures Research, 10*(1), 22. https://doi.org/10.1186/s40309-022-00208-4.

Ceyhan, C. (20 April 2022). *Data privacy concerns in the metaverse. May the privacy be with us!*. Lexology. Retrieved 30th May 2022 from https://www.lexology.com/library/detail.aspx?g=319620e2-09b4-46e3-bf20-0d4afd537a7b.

Cheng, X., Zhang, S., Fu, S., Liu, W., Guan, C., Mou, J., Ye, Q., & Huang, C. (2022). Exploring the metaverse in the digital economy: An overview and research framework. *Journal of Electronic Business & Digital Economics, 1*(1/2), 206–224. https://doi.org/10.1108/JEBDE-09-2022-0036.

Christiansen, B., & Koc, G. (2017). *Transcontinental strategies for industrial development and economic growth*. IGI Global.

Dasgupta, S., Lall, S., & Wheeler, D. (5 January 2022). *Cutting global carbon emissions: Where do cities stand?*. The World Bank. Retrieved 2nd February 2022 from https://blogs.worldbank.org/sustainablecities/cutting-global-carbon-emissions-where-do-cities-stand.

Dwivedi, Y. K., Hughes, L., Baabdullah, A. M., Ribeiro-Navarrete, S., Giannakis, M., Al-Debei, M. M., Dennehy, D., Metri, B., Buhalis, D., Cheung, C. M. K., Conboy, K., Doyle, R., Dubey, R., Dutot, V., Felix, R., Goyal, D. P., Gustafsson, A., Hinsch, C., Jebabli, I., … Wamba, S. F. (2022). Metaverse beyond the hype: Multidisciplinary perspectives on emerging challenges, opportunities, and agenda for research, practice and policy. *International Journal of Information Management*, *66*, 102542. https://doi.org/10.1016/j.ijinfomgt.2022.102542.

Faraboschi, P., Frachtenberg, E., Laplante, P., Milojicic, D., & Saracco, R. (2022). Virtual worlds (metaverse): From skepticism, to fear, to immersive opportunities. *Computer*, *55*(10), 100–106. https://doi.org/10.1109/MC.2022.3192702.

Filipova, I. (2023). Creating the metaverse: Consequences for economy, society, and law (2023). *Journal of Digital Technologies and Law*, *1*(1), 1.

Gaubert, J. (11 November 2021). Seoul to become the first city to enter the metaverse. What will it look like? *Euro News*. Retrieved 4th December 2021 from https://www.euronews.com/next/2021/11/10/seoul-to-become-the-first-city-to-enter-the-metaverse-what-will-it-look-like.

Getty Images. (13 September 2022). *Metaverse digital cyber world technology, girl with virtual reality VR goggles playing augmented reality game, futuristic lifestyle*. Unsplash. Retrieved 8th June 2023 from https://unsplash.com/photos/m625SHCmYm0.

Ghobakhloo, M. (2020). Industry 4.0, digitization, and opportunities for sustainability. *Journal of Cleaner Production*, *252*, 119869. https://doi.org/10.1016/j.jclepro.2019.119869.

Glazebrook, G., & Newman, P. (2018). The city of the future. *Urban Planning*, *3*(3), 1–20. https://doi.org/10.17645/up.v3i2.1247.

Gupta, A., Khan, H. U., Nazir, S., Shafiq, M., & Shabaz, M. (2023). Metaverse security: Issues, challenges and a viable ZTA model. *Electronics*, *12*(2), 391. https://doi.org/10.3390/electronics12020391.

Hemmati, M. (2022). The metaverse: An urban revolution effect of the metaverse on the perceptions of urban audience. *Tourism and Culture*, *2*(7), 53–60.

Henz, P. (2022). The societal impact of the metaverse. *Discover Artificial Intelligence*, *2*(1), 19. https://doi.org/10.1007/s44163-022-00032-6.

Heo, K., Lee, D., Seo, Y., & Choi, H. (2020). Searching for digital technologies in containment and mitigation strategies: Experience from South Korea COVID-19. *Annals of Global Health*, *86*(1), 109. https://doi.org/10.5334/aogh.2993.

Knight, O. (12 July 2022). *Shanghai plans to cultivate $52B metaverse industry by 2025*. CoinDesk. Retrieved 10th March from https://www.coindesk.com/business/2022/07/12/shanghai-plans-to-cultivate-52b-metaverse-industry-by-2025/.

Koohang, A., Nord, J. H., Ooi, K.-B., Tan, G. W.-H., Al-Emran, M., Aw, E. C.-X., Baabdullah, A. M., Buhalis, D., Cham, T.-H., Dennis, C., Dutot, V., Dwivedi, Y. K., Hughes, L., Mogaji, E., Pandey, N., Phau, I., Raman, R., Sharma, A., Sigala, M., … Wong, L.-W. (2023). Shaping the metaverse into reality: A holistic multidisciplinary understanding of opportunities, challenges, and avenues for future investigation. *Journal of Computer Information Systems*, *1-31*. https://doi.org/10.1080/08874417.2023.2165197.

Lee, L.-H., Braud, T., Zhou, P., Wang, L., Xu, D., Lin, Z., Kumar, A., Bermejo, C., & Hui, P. (2021). All one needs to know about metaverse: A complete survey on technological singularity, virtual ecosystem, and research agenda. *arXiv*, *3*. https://doi.org/10.48550/arXiv:2110.05352.

LeFebvre, D. (20 December 2018). *Gray nest thermostat displaying at 63*. Unsplash. Retrieved 8th June 2023 from https://unsplash.com/photos/RFAHj4tI37Y.

Lim, J. (16 July 2021). Seoul will have a city-wide public IoT network by 2023. *Tech Wire Asia*. Retrieved 12th September 2021 from https://techwireasia.com/2021/07/seoul-will-have-a-city-wide-public-iot-network-by-2023/.

Lubin, A. (26 April 2022). Governance in the metaverse. *DataSphere*. Retrieved 12th February 2023 from https://www.thedatasphere.org/news/governance-in-the-metaverse/.

Menon, G., & Guttikunda, S. (2010). *Electronic road pricing: Experience & lessons from Singapore*. https://doi.org/10.13140/RG.2.2.27671.83363.

Mora, L., & Bolici, R. (2016). The development process of smart city strategies: The case of Barcelona. In J. Rajaniemi (Ed.), *Re-city: Future city—Combining discipline* (pp. 155–181). Juvenes Print.

Noori, N., Hoppe, T., & de Jong, M. (2020). Classifying pathways for smart city development: Comparing design, governance and implementation in Amsterdam, Barcelona, Dubai, and Abu Dhabi. *Sustainability*, *12*(10), 4030. https://doi.org/10.3390/su12104030.

Paiva, S., Ahad, M. A., Tripathi, G., Feroz, N., & Casalino, G. (2021). Enabling technologies for urban smart mobility: Recent trends, opportunities and challenges. *Sensors*, *21*(6). https://doi.org/10.3390/s21062143.

Park, S. M., & Kim, Y. G. (2022). A metaverse: Taxonomy, components, applications, and open challenges. *IEEE Access*, *10*, 4209–4251. https://doi.org/10.1109/ACCESS.2021.3140175.

Parry, R. L. (15 February 2023). Conspiracy theories on '15-minute cities' flourish. *Phy Org*. Retrieved 5th March 2023 from https://phys.org/news/2023-02-conspiracy-theories-minute-cities-flourish.html.

Pasca, L., Carrus, G., Loureiro, A., Navarro, Ó., Panno, A., Tapia Follen, C., & Aragonés, J. I. (2021). Connectedness and well-being in simulated nature. *Applied Psychology. Health and Well-Being*. https://doi.org/10.1111/aphw.12309.

Pooyandeh, M., Han, K.-J., & Sohn, I. (2022). Cybersecurity in the AI-based metaverse: A survey. *Applied Science*, *12*(24), 12993. https://www.mdpi.com/2076-3417/12/24/12993.

Squires, C. (21 November 2021). Seoul will be the first city government to join the metaverse. *Quartz*. Retrieved 4h November 2021 from https://qz.com/2086353/seoul-is-developing-a-metaverse-government-platform/.

Stephenson, N. (2003). *Snow crash: A novel*. Random House Publishing Group. https://books.google.co.ke/books?id=RMd3GpIFxcUC.

Toppeta, D. (2010). The smart city vision: How Innovation and ICT can build smart, "livable", sustainable cities. *The innovation knowledge foundation*, *5*, 1–9.

Verdict. (18 November 2021). Calculating the future of environmental impacts of the metaverse. *Verdict*. Retrieved 4th December 2021 from https://www.verdict.co.uk/metaverse-environmental-impact/.

Woetzel, J., Remes, J., Boland, B., Katrina, L., Sinha, S., Strube, G., Means, J., Law, J., Cadena, A., & Tann, v. d. V. (2018). *Smart cities: Digital solutions for a more livable future*. McKinsey Global Institute. https://www.mckinsey.com/business-functions/operations/our-insights/smart-cities-digital-solutions-for-a-more-livable-future.

Yuche, L., & Lanlan, H. (17 January 2023). Shanghai starts metaverse services at 20 urban spots as part of pilot program. *Global Times*. Retrieved 10th March from https://www.globaltimes.cn/page/202301/1283918.shtml.

Zhang, X., Shen, J., Saini, P. K., Lovati, M., Han, M., Huang, P., & Huang, Z. (2021). Digital twin for accelerating sustainability in positive energy district: A review of simulation tools and applications [mini review]. *Frontiers in Sustainable Cities*, *3*(35). https://doi.org/10.3389/frsc.2021.663269.

Zhao, Y., Jiang, J., Chen, Y., Liu, R., Yang, Y., Xue, X., & Chen, S. (2022). Metaverse: Perspectives from graphics, interactions and visualization. *Visual Informatics*, *6*(1), 56–67. https://doi.org/10.1016/j.visinf.2022.03.002.

Chapter 4

The metaverse and sustainable cities

Introduction

The concept of sustainable cities hinges on the economic, environmental, and social sustainability pillars (Mensah, 2019). On the other hand, smart cities are current emerging concepts in urban areas that leverage technology to enhance the livability status of the residents, promote economic growth, and foster environmental sustainability (Allam, 2018a, 2021). However, in recent years, the emergence of the metaverse (a virtual reality space comprising interconnected digital environments) has continued to garner significant attention especially for its promising prospect in the ability to contribute in the development of sustainable cities.

The metaverse can facilitate sustainable urban development by enhancing seamless interlinkages between the digital and physical realms, which allows for among other things efficient allocation and consumption of scarce natural resources and subsequent reduction of environmental impact (Allam, Sharifi, et al., 2022). For instance, the metaverse is enabling the virtualization of physical activities, such as remote work environment and virtual meetings, thus reducing the need for transportation. This translates into significant reduction of greenhouse gas emissions as well as minimization of the economic associated with the transport sector. The ability for metaverse users to acquire virtual goods such as real estates and other properties, plus the ability to enhance their experiences increases the sustainability aspect, particularly when such benefits are compared to what they have in the physical world. As such, the metaverse can be argued to be key in reducing waste and resource depletion (Cheng et al., 2022; Dwivedi et al., 2022).

The metaverse also plays a pivotal role in advancing economic sustainability in cities by making it possible to create virtual marketplaces and digital platforms. In the business world, the metaverse has been enabling businesses to reach an infinite global audience without the need for a physical presence, thereby reducing infrastructure costs and promoting economic growth. Furthermore, the metaverse is becoming paramount in fostering innovation and entrepreneurship by providing a virtual space where individuals can collaborate, develop, and market new products and services in a more immersive way than in the physical realm (Lv et al., 2022).

In regard to the social aspect, the metaverse is slowly gaining grounds through its ability to promote social cohesion and inclusivity by offering unmatched virtual social environment for the users. It offers a platform for diverse communities to interact and engage in cultural exchange while also fostering a sense of belonging and mutual understanding among users (Henz, 2022). Moreover, the metaverse has the potential to facilitate civic engagement by providing a virtual space for citizens to voice their opinions and participate in the decision-making process, ultimately leading to more equitable urban development.

In addition to the above, the critical relationship between the metaverse and sustainable cities can further be elucidated by examining specific individual applications and case studies. For instance, in the realm of urban planning, the metaverse has been argued to provide an immersive environment for simulating and visualizing the impacts of proposed urban developments (Lv et al., 2022). This allows planners and stakeholders to comprehensively and keenly assess the three pillars of sustainability and how such would be impacted by diverse decisions. A case in point to demonstrate this further is the city of Helsinki which utilized a virtual model to assess the viability of a proposed urban development project, ultimately leading to a more sustainable outcome (Hämäläinen, 2021).

The metaverse is also anticipated to have significant impacts on the sustainable city development pursuits especially in the domain of transportation. One area that it will enhance is in the provision of real-time data on traffic patterns and public transportation schedules, hence, facilitate the optimization of urban mobility, leading to reduced congestion and pollution (noise and air pollution in particular). Additionally, the metaverse is expected to promote the adoption of alternative, sustainable transportation modes, such as cycling and walking, by offering immersive virtual experiences that would encourage users to explore their surroundings (Allam, Bibri, et al., 2022; Allam, Moreno, et al., 2022). This will be increasingly welcome particular in the current and near future, where sustainable options such as the adoption of the 15-minute city concept and others are being pursued.

The potential of the metaverse to contribute to sustainable city development is also evident in the energy production, distribution, and management. Through the integration of modern, advanced technologies such as the digital twins and the Internet of Things (IoT), the metaverse can facilitate the monitoring and optimization of energy consumption in buildings and urban infrastructure (Bibri et al., 2022). A classic case is the city of Amsterdam which in 2020 implemented a digital twin of itself to monitor energy consumption in real time, resulting in significant energy savings and a reduction in greenhouse gas emissions (City of Amsterdam, 2020). On another front, the metaverse has the potential to promote the adoption of renewable energy sources by enabling users to visualize and interact with virtual representations of solar panels, wind turbines, and other sustainable energy technologies, hence allowing for their widespread adoption in different cities.

In the context of waste management, the metaverse is expected to contribute to the development of sustainable cities by advancing the circular economy principles, thus enabling efficient waste tracking and disposal. In perspective, the metaverse can facilitate the identification and recycling of waste materials by providing a digital platform for tracking waste flows and connecting waste generators with recycling facilities (City of Amsterdam, 2020). Additionally, the metaverse can encourage sustainable waste management practices by offering virtual incentives, such as gamification and social recognition, to users who actively initiate or participate in already existing waste reduction and recycling initiatives.

The metaverse can also play a leading role in strengthen the resilience and adaptability aspects of cities in the face of climate change and other potential environmental challenges. By providing a virtual platform for simulating and visualizing the potential impacts of climate change, such as sea-level rise and extreme weather events, the metaverse would enable city planners and stakeholders to develop and implement adaptive strategies that minimize the risks associated with these threats. Such feat would be particularly very instrumental in saving coastal cities, and most significant number of Small Island Developing States (SIDS), which are already very vulnerable to the impacts of climate change (Climate Change Secretariate (United Nations Framework Convention On Climate Change), 2005). Furthermore, the metaverse can facilitate the sharing of knowledge and best practices among cities, fostering a collaborative approach to sustainable urban development (Pasca et al., 2022).

The metaverse holds substantial potential to contribute to the development of sustainable cities by fostering both the economic, environmental, and social sustainability. Through the integration of virtual and physical dimensions, the metaverse enables the efficient allocation of resources, the reduction of environmental impact, and the promotion of social cohesion and inclusivity. Specific applications of the metaverse in areas such as urban planning, transportation, energy management, waste management, and climate resilience further underscore the symbiotic relationship between the metaverse and sustainable cities. By harnessing the power of the metaverse, cities can embark on a transformative journey toward sustainability, ultimately improving the quality of life for current and future generations as is further elucidated in this chapter.

Sustainable cities: Challenges and opportunities

Sustainable cities are urban areas designed and managed to promote environmental sustainability, social well-being, and economic prosperity.

Sustainable cities, frequently referred to as ecocities, are urban environments designed to incorporate the tenets of social, economic, and environmental sustainability (Allam & Newman, 2018). These cities strive to minimize their ecological footprint while concurrently enhancing the well-being of residents and fostering economic growth. Achieving this equilibrium presents a plethora of challenges, as urban planners must harmonize conflicting interests, limited resources, and intricate interactions between diverse urban systems.

One primary challenge in establishing sustainable cities is the rapid urbanization occurring on a global scale. The United Nation (2019) reports that over half of the world's population now resides in urban areas, with projections suggesting this figure will reach 68% by 2050. This swift urbanization places tremendous pressure on existing urban infrastructure, public services, and natural resources, intensifying the challenge of ensuring sustainability.

A further challenge lies in the effective coordination of numerous stakeholders, including governments, the private sector, and civil society organizations. Efficient collaboration among these actors is crucial for the successful implementation of sustainable urban policies (Allam, 2012; Bibri & Krogstie, 2020). However, differing objectives, priorities, and timeframes can impede this coordination, leading to disjointed efforts and suboptimal outcomes. The United Nation (2019) reports that over half of the world's population now resides in urban areas, with projections suggesting this figure will reach 68% by 2050. This swift urbanization places tremendous pressure on existing urban infrastructure (Fig. 4.1), public services, and natural resources, intensifying the challenge of ensuring sustainability.

Financing the transition to sustainable cities also presents a significant challenge. The Global Commission on the Economy and Climate approximates an annual investment of $4.5–5.4 trillion is required for sustainable

FIG. 4.1 Sustainable transportation option in Brisbane, Australia (Staines, 2016).

infrastructure by 2030. Traditional financing mechanisms often fail to provide the necessary funds, necessitating innovative financial models and public-private partnerships to bridge the funding gap (International Labour Organization, 2018). In addition, sustainable cities must confront the issues of social inequality and spatial segregation. A just and equitable distribution of resources and opportunities is essential for true sustainability (Agyeman et al., 2003). However, social and economic disparities can lead to uneven access to public services, housing, and employment opportunities, thereby exacerbating existing inequalities (Nijman & Wei, 2020).

Despite these challenges, there are several opportunities and benefits associated with sustainable cities. A significant opportunity is the potential for an improved quality of life. Sustainable urban environments prioritize the well-being of their inhabitants by providing green spaces, promoting public transportation, and reducing air and noise pollution (Allam & Dhunny, 2019). These measures have been linked to numerous health benefits, including reduced respiratory ailments, lower levels of stress, and increased physical activity (Frumkin et al., 2017). Additionally, sustainable cities offer substantial environmental benefits. By reducing greenhouse gas emissions, implementing waste management strategies, and conserving natural resources, sustainable cities can mitigate climate change and protect ecosystems (Seto et al., 2016). For example, adopting energy-efficient building standards can reduce energy consumption by 50%–90%, significantly decreasing carbon emissions (Gef, 2022).

Sustainable cities are also associated with substantial economic benefits especially in view of the fact that investments in green infrastructure can create jobs, stimulate local economies, and reduce long-term costs associated with resource depletion and environmental degradation (Gramkow, 2020). A study by the International Renewable Energy Agency (2021) found that doubling the share of renewables in the global energy mix by 2030 could generate over 24 million jobs while saving up to $4.2 trillion per year in externalities related to health and environmental impacts.

Furthermore, sustainable cities provide a platform for technological innovation and experimentation. Advances in information and communication technologies (ICTs), such as the Internet of Things (IoT) and Big Data analytics, enable cities to monitor and optimize urban systems more effectively (Allam, 2018b; Batty, 2018). These technologies can facilitate the integration of renewable energy sources, optimize transportation networks, and improve waste management systems, contributing to the overall sustainability of urban environments (Kramers et al., 2014). Moreover, sustainable cities promote social cohesion and community engagement by designing public spaces that encourage interaction and participation (Gehl, 2010). These spaces can foster a sense of belonging and social capital, which are essential for building resilient communities capable of addressing and adapting to various challenges.

Case studies of the metaverse in sustainable cities

This section highlights the case four cities that are in advanced stage of transforming to become truly sustainable. There diverse stories are interesting because they have also embraced the concept of metaverse, despite the fact that it is an emerging technology that requires substantial concerted effort to streamline it and make work. However, these shortcomings have not been a deterrent to these cities, but instead, have helped them to reap forward in providing livable environments for the residents, as well as help the city to overcome some perennial urban challenges. Despite the divergent approaches taken by each of the individual cities, the convergent reality is that the metaverse has an indisputable potential to bring the best of the cities, as well as help them speed up the processes of achieving sustainable status.

Copenhagen: Virtual collaboration for climate adaptation

Copenhagen, Denmark, is recognized for its commitment to sustainable urban development and climate resilience (ICLEI, 2021). The city has embraced the metaverse through the use of 3D visualization and virtual collaboration platforms in its climate adaptation planning. By creating a digital twin of the city, stakeholders can virtually explore different scenarios, assess the potential impacts of climate change, and design effective adaptation measures. This approach has facilitated the development of innovative solutions, such as the cloudburst management plan, which combines green and grey infrastructure to mitigate flood risks and enhance urban livability (e.g., as depicted in Fig. 4.2 below).

FIG. 4.2 Grey infrastructure in Copenhagen (Juggins, 2018).

Singapore: Smart nation initiative and virtual Singapore

Singapore's Smart Nation Initiative aims to harness digital technologies and the metaverse to create a more sustainable and inclusive urban environment. A notable example is the Virtual Singapore project, a dynamic 3D model of the city that integrates real-time data from IoT devices, sensors, and geospatial databases (Riaz et al., 2023). This digital twin enables urban planners, policymakers, and citizens to simulate various urban interventions, optimize resource allocation, and monitor the performance of urban systems (City2City, 2022). Virtual Singapore has contributed to the city's sustainable development goals, such as the reduction of energy consumption, the improvement of public transportation, and the enhancement of green spaces (White et al., 2021).

Barcelona: Superblocks and the metaverse

Barcelona has implemented the Superblocks concept to promote urban sustainability and improve the quality of life for its residents (Eggimann, 2022). Superblocks are defined as pedestrian-centric zones in which traffic is restricted, allowing for the expansion of green spaces, the enhancement of public transportation, and the promotion of cycling and walking (as depicted in Fig. 4.3 below) (López et al., 2020). The city has utilized the metaverse to facilitate public participation in the planning and implementation of the Superblocks project. Through the use of virtual reality (VR) and 3D modeling, citizens can engage in the cocreation of urban spaces, offering feedback and suggestions to ensure that the Superblocks cater to diverse needs and preferences (Calavita & Ferrer, 2000).

FIG. 4.3 Image of Superblocks in the city of Barcelona (Hesry, 2017).

Amsterdam: Circular economy and the metaverse

Amsterdam is committed to becoming a fully circular city by 2050, with an intermediary goal of reducing material consumption by 50% by 2030 (City of Amsterdam, 2020). This objective can be made possible by the integration of the metaverse concept which has played a crucial role in fostering collaboration among stakeholders and enabling data-driven decision-making in the pursuit of a circular economy. For instance, the Amsterdam Circular Innovation Program (ACIP) employs digital twins and data visualization tools to monitor resource flows, identify circular opportunities, and design interventions that optimize material use and reduce waste generation. This approach has facilitated the development of innovative circular projects, such as the Buiksloterham district, which incorporates principles of circular urban planning, construction, and resource management (Metabolic, 2014).

Lessons learned and implications for future applications

The case studies presented above demonstrate the potential of the metaverse in promoting sustainability in urban environments. Key lessons that can be drawn from these examples include:

1. The importance of multistakeholder collaboration: The successful integration of the metaverse in sustainable cities requires the involvement of diverse stakeholders, including governments, private sector entities, and citizens as envisioned by Bibri and Krogstie (2020). This collaboration fosters innovation, ensures the relevance and effectiveness of urban interventions, and promotes social inclusion and equity.
2. The value of data-driven decision-making: The metaverse enables the collection, integration, and analysis of vast amounts of data, facilitating evidence-based decision-making in urban planning and management. This approach contributes to the optimization of resource allocation, the enhancement of urban systems' performance, and the monitoring of progress towards sustainability goals (Allam, Sharifi, et al., 2022).
3. The potential for public engagement and cocreation: The metaverse provides accessible platforms for spirited and concerted public consultation and participation, empowering citizens to contribute to the development of sustainable urban policies and projects (Dwivedi et al., 2022). This participatory approach fosters social cohesion, enhances the sense of community, and ensures that urban interventions reflect the diverse needs and aspirations of city residents.
4. The role of innovative technologies: The metaverse, coupled with other digital technologies, such as IoT devices, sensors, 5G advanced analytics, and others, can contribute to the development of more sustainable, efficient, and inclusive urban environments (Theo, 2021). By harnessing the power of these technologies, urban planners and policymakers can address the

complex challenges associated with sustainable cities and capitalize on the opportunities they present.

The case studies discussed above demonstrate the significant potential of the metaverse in facilitating sustainable urban development. By drawing on the lessons learned from these examples, cities around the world can leverage the metaverse, in conjunction with other advanced technologies to create more sustainable, efficient, and inclusive urban environments that contribute to global sustainability efforts and enhance the livability status of the urban citizens and the visitors.

Benefits and challenges of using the metaverse in sustainable cities

As a tool for promoting sustainability

The metaverse offers numerous benefits in promoting sustainability, particularly in urban environments, and would be very instrumental in the fast-urbanizing global sphere. One such benefit is reduced environmental impact through the optimization of resource consumption and waste generation (Bibri et al., 2022). By leveraging digital twins and real-time data from IoT devices, urban planners can design more efficient systems for energy, water, and waste management (Dwivedi et al., 2022). Additionally, the metaverse facilitates remote collaboration, reducing the need for physical meetings and the associated carbon emissions from transportation.

Improved quality of life for urban residents is another significant benefit of using the metaverse in sustainable cities. By enabling the cocreation of urban spaces, the metaverse fosters social cohesion and ensures that urban interventions cater to the diverse needs and preferences of city residents (Chapman, 2021). Furthermore, the metaverse allows for the seamless integration of public services, enhancing the accessibility, efficiency, and responsiveness of urban systems (Duan et al., 2021).

Challenges and limitations of using the metaverse

Despite its potential benefits, the metaverse faces several challenges and limitations in promoting sustainable cities. Equity and inclusivity are critical concerns, as the digital divide may exacerbate existing social inequalities and limit access to the benefits of the metaverse for marginalized communities (Filipova, 2023). Policymakers must address this digital divide by investing in digital infrastructure, promoting digital literacy, and ensuring that digital services cater to the needs of all residents.

Cultural sensitivity is another challenge associated with the metaverse, as different cultures have unique perspectives on urban spaces and public engagement. The metaverse must be designed with respect for local cultures, customs, and values, ensuring that urban interventions are contextually appropriate and culturally sensitive including to the plight of small and vulnerable societies (Henz, 2022).

Potential risks and unintended consequences

The use of the metaverse in sustainable cities may also result in potential risks and unintended consequences, affecting both the human and the installed infrastructure. For instance, the metaverse's reliance on vast amounts of data raises concerns about privacy and surveillance (Ahmad & Corovic, 2022; Bosworth & Gregg, 2021). Moreover, the metaverse may contribute to increased energy consumption and e-waste generation, undermining its sustainability objectives (Allam, Sharifi, et al., 2022). Lastly, the rapid pace of technological change may result in obsolescence and stranded assets, as urban systems become outdated or incompatible with new technologies (Pardo-Vicente et al., 2022).

Ethical considerations

Ethical considerations play a crucial role in the use of the metaverse in sustainable cities. The collection, storage, and use of data must be guided by principles of transparency, accountability, privacy, and goodwill (Bibri & Allam, 2022). Furthermore, the metaverse should prioritize social and environmental objectives over profit maximization, ensuring that its benefits are distributed equitably among city residents. There should also be concerted efforts to curb and derail the negative social impacts such as addiction, misuse by outlawed groups among other issues (Bojic, 2022; Todorovic & Trifunovic, 2020).

Recommendations for addressing challenges and maximizing benefits

To address the challenges and maximize the benefits of using the metaverse in sustainable cities, several recommendations can be proposed:

(a) Develop context-specific and culturally sensitive solutions that cater to the unique needs and values of different communities.
(b) Foster multistakeholder collaboration, ensuring that diverse perspectives are considered in the development of urban interventions (Adinarayan, 2021).
(c) Address the digital divide through investment in digital infrastructure, digital literacy programs, and inclusive digital services.
(d) Implement robust data governance frameworks that ensure transparency, accountability, and privacy in the collection and use of data (Lubin, 2022).
(e) Prioritize energy-efficient and environmentally friendly technologies, minimizing the environmental impact of the metaverse and urban digital systems

(f) Encourage continuous innovation and adaptation to emerging technologies, fostering resilience and flexibility in urban systems
(g) Develop ethical guidelines and best practices for the metaverse, ensuring that its use in sustainable cities aligns with social and environmental objectives.

By addressing these challenges and leveraging the benefits of the metaverse, sustainable cities can harness the full potential of this transformative technology in fostering more resilient, inclusive, and environmentally friendly urban environments. It would also help address even emerging challenges that have largely been prompted by the serious impacts of the COVID-19 pandemic, especially on the future of work, education system, and urban neighborhoods

Future directions and implications for research

The metaverse is rapidly evolving, offering new opportunities for sustainable urban development to be pursued earnestly. One noteworthy trend is the increasing decentralization, facilitated by the blockchain technology. This development allows for more democratic and inclusive decision-making processes in urban planning (Gadekallu et al., 2022). Decentralization in the metaverse can lead to a more equitable distribution of resources and empower marginalized communities by giving them greater control over their local environment (Aks et al., 2022; Gadekallu et al., 2022).

Additionally, the integration of VR in the metaverse is enhancing user experiences and allowing for more realistic simulations of urban environments, which can aid in designing sustainable cities (Rosenberg, 2022). By offering immersive and interactive experiences, VR can help planners visualize the potential impacts of their decisions on the urban environment, leading to better-informed choices that promote sustainability (Faraboschi et al., 2022).

The proliferation of Internet of Things (IoT) devices and sensor networks is expected to facilitate real-time data collection and analysis in the metaverse, providing valuable insights for sustainable urban development (Bibri et al., 2022). The integration of IoT in the metaverse can create a more comprehensive understanding of the urban environment, enabling planners to identify trends and patterns in resource consumption and develop targeted strategies for reducing waste and improving efficiency (Theo, 2021). Furthermore, advanced AI algorithms and machine learning techniques will proof very critical in helping to analyze and process vast amounts of urban data in the metaverse, facilitating more efficient and sustainable urban planning and management (Huynh-The et al., 2023). AI can help identify optimal solutions for complex urban challenges, such as transportation planning and energy management, leading to smarter and more sustainable cities (Henz, 2022).

As the metaverse continues to evolve, several key areas for future research and inquiry have and continue to emerge. One important area is the examination of the implications of the metaverse on urban governance and policy, particularly in terms of how it influences decision-making, citizen engagement, and collaboration among stakeholders (Lubin, 2022; Rodríguez Bolívar & Alcaide Muñoz, 2019). The metaverse has the potential to reshape urban governance by facilitating more transparent, participatory, and accountable decision-making processes, leading to more equitable and sustainable outcomes.

The role of community engagement in metaverse-based sustainable development projects should also be explored, with a focus on understanding how to maximize the benefits of citizen participation in the planning and implementation of such projects. Engaging local communities in the metaverse can help planners better understand their needs and preferences, resulting in more effective and context-specific solutions for sustainable development (Benrimoh et al., 2022).

Interdisciplinary collaboration is another crucial aspect of metaverse research in the context of sustainable cities. Researchers from diverse fields, including urban planning, computer science, and social sciences, need to collaborate to understand the complex interactions between the metaverse, urban systems, and social dynamics (Dwivedi et al., 2022). Such collaboration will help develop innovative solutions that address the challenges of using the metaverse for sustainable urban development and promote knowledge exchange between different disciplines, leading to more holistic and integrated approaches to urban planning.

The metaverse has the potential to revolutionize the field of sustainable urban planning and design. By leveraging the immersive capabilities of the metaverse, urban planners have the opportunity to engage in more effective participatory processes, gather valuable data and insights, and create more informed and sustainable urban designs in a quicker and universally agreed approach (Koohang et al., 2023). For example, by fostering collaboration between urban planners, architects, engineers, and environmental specialists, the metaverse can facilitate the development of innovative solutions that address multiple dimensions of sustainability, such as energy efficiency, green infrastructure, and social cohesion (Dwivedi et al., 2022). Moreover, the metaverse can be adopted as an active platform for public-private partnerships (PPPs) in urban development, encouraging collaboration between governments, businesses, and civil society organizations. By providing a shared virtual space for stakeholders to exchange ideas, knowledge, and resources, the metaverse can help drive sustainable urban development initiatives and foster a sense of collective responsibility for the well-being of cities (Ascott, 2021; Dwivedi et al., 2022).

The metaverse presents both numerous opportunities for sustainable cities, but also some real challenges that would require to be addressed amicably. As such, it would be important for the stakeholders to understand the implications of the metaverse on urban governance and policy, the role of community engagement in metaverse-based sustainable development projects, and the need for interdisciplinary collaboration. This will help them come up with robust frameworks of addressing the possible challenges that may slow down its fully implementation in cities. Addressing the challenges will in turn help cities leveraging the benefits of the metaverse to harness the full potential of this transformative technology in fostering more resilient, inclusive, and environmentally friendly urban environments.

Conclusions

As the metaverse continues to develop and expand, urban planners and policymakers must remain adaptable and responsive to the shifting landscape of technological advancements, increasing rates of urbanization and population growth and societal needs. Embracing the potential of the metaverse for sustainable urban development will, however, require continuous learning, experimentation, and adjustment, as well as a willingness to reevaluate and refine strategies and approaches as new insights and challenges keep on emerging as the metaverse become even more complex.

Moreover, the ethical implications of the metaverse must never be overlooked as they may be escalated to become counterproductive in the pursuit of sustainability, resilience, and livable urban environments. The potential for surveillance, data misuse, and privacy breaches within the metaverse raises concerns that must be addressed to ensure equitable and responsible implementation, as well as enhanced security from both internal and external threats. Urban planners and policymakers must collaborate with technology developers, legal experts, and the general public to establish ethical guidelines and best practices for the use of the metaverse in sustainable urban development.

Finally, in addressing the challenges of sustainable urban development, the metaverse should be considered not as a standalone solution, but rather as one component of a broader "whole." While the metaverse offers exciting possibilities for advancing sustainability, urban planners and policymakers must remain committed to a diverse array of strategies and approaches to achieve truly resilient, inclusive, and environmentally friendly cities. It should not be seen or deemed as another modern urban planning fad that would only lead to alienating the public and help expand the already existing inequality gulf that has been exacerbated by modernist approach of planning the urban environments.

References

Adinarayan, T. (2021). Metaverse only gets real when Apple joins, Morgan Stanley says [Online]. *Bloomberg*. Available: https://www.Bloomberg.Com/News/Articles/2021-11-12/Metaverse-Only-Gets-Real-When-Apple-Joins-Morgan-Stanley-Says. (Accessed 1 December 2021).

Agyeman, J., Bullard, R. D., & Evans, B. (2003). *Just sustainabilities: Development in an unequal world*. MIT Press.

Ahmad, I., & Corovic, T. (2022). *Privacy in a parallel digital universe: The metaverse [Online]*. Norton Rose Fulbright. Available: https://www.Dataprotectionreport.Com/2022/01/Privacy-In-A-Parallel-Digital-Universe-The-Metaverse/. (Accessed 30 May 2022).

Aks, S. M. Y., Karmila, M., Givan, B., Hendratna, G., Setiawan, H. S., Putra, A. S., Winarno, S. H., Kurniawan, T. A., Simorangkir, Y. N., Taufiq, R., Herawaty, M. T., & Asep. (2022). A review of blockchain for security data privacy with metaverse. In *2022 International conference on ICT for smart society (ICISS), 10-11 August* (pp. 1–5).

Allam, Z. (2012). Sustainable architecture: Utopia or feasible reality? *Journal of Biourbanism, 2*, 47–61.

Allam, M. Z. (2018a). *Redefining the smart city: Culture, metabolism and governance. Case study Of Port Louis, Mauritius*. Curtin University.

Allam, Z. (2018b). Contextualising the smart city for sustainability and inclusivity. *New Design Ideas, 2*, 124–127.

Allam, Z. (2021). On complexity, connectivity and autonomy in future cities. In *The rise of autonomous smart cities*. Cham: Palgrave Macmillan.

Allam, Z., Bibri, S. E., Jones, D. S., Chabaud, D., & Moreno, C. (2022). Unpacking the 15-Minute City via 6g, Iot, and digital twins: Towards a new narrative for increasing urban efficiency, resilience, and sustainability. *Sensors, 22*, 1369.

Allam, Z., & Dhunny, Z. A. (2019). On big data, artificial intelligence and smart cities. *Cities, 89*, 80–91.

Allam, Z., Moreno, C., Chabaud, D., & Pratlong, F. (2022). Proximity-based planning and the "15-Minute City": A sustainable model for the city of the future. In *The Palgrave handbook of global sustainability*.

Allam, Z., & Newman, P. (2018). Redefining the smart city: Culture, metabolism and governance. *Smart Cities, 1*.

Allam, Z., Sharifi, A., Bibri, S. E., Jones, D. S., & Krogstie, J. (2022). The metaverse as a virtual form of smart cities: Opportunities and challenges for environmental, economic, and social sustainability in urban futures. *Smart Cities, 5*, 771–801. https://doi.org/10.3390/smartcities5030040.

Ascott, E. (2021). *How the metaverse will change the future of work [Online]*. All Work. Available: https://Allwork.Space/2021/09/How-The-Metaverse-Will-Change-The-Future-Of-Work/. (Accessed 3 December 2021).

Batty, M. (2018). Artificial intelligence and smart cities. *Environment and Planning B: Urban Analytics and City Science, 45*, 3–6.

Benrimoh, D., Chheda, F. D., & Margolese, H. C. (2022). The best predictor of the future-the metaverse, mental health, and lessons learned from current technologies. *JMIR Mental Health, 9*, E40410.

Bibri, S., & Krogstie, J. (2020). Data-driven smart sustainable cities of the future: A novel model of urbanism and its core dimensions, strategies, and solutions. *Journal of Futures Studies, 25*, 77–94.

Bibri, S. E., & Allam, Z. (2022). The metaverse as a virtual form of data-driven smart cities: The ethics of the hyper-connectivity, datafication, algorithmization, and platformization of urban society. *Computational Urban Science, 2*, 22. https://doi.org/10.1007/s43762-022-00050-1.

Bibri, S. E., Allam, Z., & Krogstie, J. (2022). The metaverse as a virtual form of data-driven smart urbanism: Platformization and its underlying processes, institutional dimensions, and disruptive impacts. *Computational Urban Science, 2*, 24. https://doi.org/10.1007/s43762-022-00051-0.

Bojic, L. (2022). Metaverse through the prism of power and addiction: What will happen when the virtual world becomes more attractive than reality? *European Journal of Futures Research, 10*, 22.

Bosworth, A., & Gregg, N. (2021). Building the metaverse responsibly [Online]. *Meta*. Available: https://About.Fb.Com/News/2021/09/Building-The-Metaverse-Responsibly/. (Accessed 22 April 2022).

Calavita, N., & Ferrer, A. (2000). Behind Barcelona's success story: Citizen movements and planners' power. *Journal of Urban History*, *26*, 793–807.

Chapman, M. (2021). Is the metaverse a friend or foe to travel? [Online]. *Phocus Wire*. Available: https://www.Phocuswire.Com/Metaverse-Friend-Foe-Travel. (Accessed 4 December 2021).

Cheng, X., Zhang, S., Fu, S., Liu, W., Guan, C., Mou, J., Ye, Q., & Huang, C. (2022). Exploring the metaverse in the digital economy: An overview and research framework. *Journal of Electronic Business & Digital Economics*, *1*, 206–224.

City of Amsterdam. (2020). Amsterdam circular strategy 2020-2025 [Online]. *City of Amsterdam*. Available: https://www.Amsterdam.Nl/En/Policy/Sustainability/Circular-Economy/. (Accessed 15 March 2023).

City2City. (2022). *Virtual Singapore: A digital 'twin' for planning [Online]*. Available: Undp https://City2city.Network/Virtual-Singapore-Digital-Twin-Planning-Innovation-Type-Institutional-Pioneer. (Accessed 15 March 2023).

Climate Change Secretariate (United Nations Framework Convention On Climate Change). (2005). *Climate change, small island developing states*. Bonn, Germany: UNFCCC.

Duan, H., Li, J., Fan, S., Lin, Z., Wu, X., & Cai, W. (2021). *Metaverse for social good: A university campus prototype*. New York, NY: Association For Computing Machinery.

Dwivedi, Y. K., Hughes, L., Baabdullah, A. M., Ribeiro-Navarrete, S., Giannakis, M., Al-Debei, M. M., Dennehy, D., Metri, B., Buhalis, D., Cheung, C. M. K., Conboy, K., Doyle, R., Dubey, R., Dutot, V., Felix, R., Goyal, D. P., Gustafsson, A., Hinsch, C., Jebabli, I., ... Wamba, S. F. (2022). Metaverse beyond the hype: Multidisciplinary perspectives on emerging challenges, opportunities, and agenda for research, practice and policy. *International Journal of Information Management*, *66*, 102542.

Eggimann, S. (2022). The potential of implementing superblocks for multifunctional street use in cities. *Nature Sustainability*, *5*, 406–414.

Faraboschi, P., Frachtenberg, E., Laplante, P., Milojicic, D., & Saracco, R. (2022). Virtual worlds (metaverse): From skepticism, to fear, to immersive opportunities. *Computer*, *55*, 100–106.

Filipova, I. (2023). Creating the metaverse: Consequences for economy, society, and law (2023). *Journal of Digital Technologies and Law*, *1*(1), 1.

Frumkin, H., Bratman, G. N., Breslow, S. J., Cochran, B., Kahn, P. H., Jr., Lawler, J. J., Levin, P. S., Tandon, P. S., Varanasi, U., Wolf, K. L., & Wood, S. A. (2017). Nature contact and human health: A research agenda. *Environmental Health Perspectives*, *125*, 075001.

Gadekallu, T., Huynh-The, T., Wang, W., Yenduri, G., Ranaweera, P., Pham, V., Costa, D. B., & Liyanage, M. (2022). *Blockchain for the metaverse: A review*.

Gef. (2022). *Energy efficiency: Main issue [Online]*. Gef. Available: https://www.Thegef.Org/What-We-Do/Topics/Energy-Efficiency. (Accessed 10 March 2023).

Gehl, J. (2010). *Cities for people*. Washington, DC: Island Press.

Gramkow, C. (2020). *Green fiscal policies: An armoury of instruments to recover growth sustainably*. Santiago: United Nations.

Hämäläinen, M. (2021). Urban development with dynamic digital twins in Helsinki city. *IET Smart Cities*, *3*, 201–210.

Henz, P. (2022). The societal impact of the metaverse. *Discover Artificial Intelligence*, *2*, 19.

Hesry, E. (2017). *Barcelona superblock [Online]*. La Sagrada Familia: Unsplash. Available: https://Unsplash.Com/Photos/Pm3o5kxwktw. (Accessed 10 June 2023).

Huynh-The, T., Pham, Q.-V., Pham, X.-Q., Nguyen, T. T., Han, Z., & Kim, D.-S. (2023). Artificial intelligence for the metaverse: A survey. *Engineering Applications of Artificial Intelligence, 117*, 105581.

ICLEI. (2021). *Copenhagen: A green and sustainable city [Online]*. Available: https://Iclei.Org/En/Member/Copenhagen. (Accessed 15 March 2023).

International Labour Organization, & Richter, P. (2018). In P. Elmer, E. Zhang, & M. Marino (Eds.), *Innovative finance: Putting your money to (decent) work*. Geneva: ILO.

International Renewable Energy Agency. (2021). *Renewable energy and jobs—Annual review 202*. Irena: Renewable Energy.

Juggins, T. (2018). *Low angle view photography of street and parked bikes [Online]*. Copenhagen, Denmark: Unsplash. Available: https://Unsplash.Com/Photos/Awguzekl5dg. (Accessed 10 June 2023).

Koohang, A., Nord, J. H., Ooi, K.-B., Tan, G. W.-H., Al-Emran, M., Aw, E. C.-X., Baabdullah, A. M., Buhalis, D., Cham, T.-H., Dennis, C., Dutot, V., Dwivedi, Y. K., Hughes, L., Mogaji, E., Pandey, N., Phau, I., Raman, R., Sharma, A., Sigala, M., ... Wong, L.-W. (2023). Shaping the metaverse into reality: A holistic multidisciplinary understanding of opportunities, challenges, and avenues for future investigation. *Journal of Computer Information Systems*, 1–31.

Kramers, A., Höjer, M., Lövehagen, N., & Wangel, J. (2014). Smart sustainable cities—Exploring ICT solutions for reduced energy use in cities. *Environmental Modelling & Software, 56*, 52–62.

López, I., Ortega, J., & Pardo, M. (2020). Mobility infrastructures in cities and climate change: An analysis through the superblocks in Barcelona. *Atmosphere [Online], 11*.

Lubin, A. (2022). Governance in the metaverse [Online]. *DataSphere*. Available: https://www.Thedatasphere.Org/News/Governance-In-The-Metaverse/. (Accessed 12 February 2023).

Lv, Z., Shang, W.-L., & Guizani, M. (2022). Impact of digital twins and metaverse on cities: history, current situation, and application perspectives. *Applied Sciences [Online], 12*.

Mensah, J. (2019). Sustainable development: Meaning, history, principles, pillars, and implications for human action: LITERATURE review. *Cogent Social Science, 5*, 1653531.

Metabolic. (2014). *Circular Buiksloterham: Vision and ambition for a new urban development in Amsterdam [Online]*. Metabolic. Available: https://www.Metabolic.Nl/Projects/Circular-Buiksloterham/. (Accessed 16 March 2023).

Nijman, J., & Wei, Y. D. (2020). Urban inequalities in the 21st century economy. *Applied Geography (Sevenoaks, England), 117*, 102188.

Pardo-Vicente, M.-A., Camacho-Magriñan, P., & Pavon-Dominguez, P. (2022). Influence of technology on perceived obsolescence though product design properties. *Sustainability [Online], 14*.

Pasca, L., Carrus, G., Loureiro, A., Navarro, Ó., Panno, A., Tapia Follen, C., & Aragonés, J. I. (2022). Connectedness and well-being in simulated nature. *Applied Psychology. Health And Well-Being, 14*(2), 397–412.

Riaz, K., Mcafee, M., & Gharbia, S. S. (2023). Management of climate resilience: Exploring the potential of digital twin technology, 3d city modelling, and early warning systems. *Sensors, 23*, 2659.

Rodríguez Bolívar, M. P., & Alcaide Muñoz, L. (2019). *E-participation in smart cities: Technologies And models of governance For citizen engagement*. Cham: Springer International Publishing.

Rosenberg, L. (2022). Regulation of the metaverse: A roadmap. In *6th International conference on virtual and augmented reality simulations (ICVARS 2022), Brisbane, Australia*.

Seto, K. C., Davis, S. J., Mitchell, R. B., Stokes, E. C., Unruh, G., & Ürge-Vorsatz, D. (2016). Carbon lock-in: Types, causes, and policy implications. *Annual Review of Environment and Resources*, *41*, 425–452.

Staines, Z. (2016). *Assorted commuter bicycle park ahead [Online]*. Brisbane, Australia: Unsplash. Available: https://Unsplash.Com/Photos/Kehncocldbk. (Accessed 10 June 2023).

Theo. (2021). Digital twins, IoT and the metaverse [Online]. *Medium*. Available: https://Medium.Com/@Theo/Digital-Twins-Iot-And-The-Metaverse-B4efbfc01112. (Accessed 3 December 2021).

Todorovic, B., & Trifunovic, D. (2020). Prevention of (AB-) use of the internet for terrorist plotting and related purposes. In A. P. Schmid (Ed.), *Handbook of terrorism prevention and preparedness*. The Hague: ICCT Press.

United Nation. (2019). *World population prospects 2019*. Washington, DC: United Nations.

White, G., Zink, A., Codecá, L., & Clarke, S. (2021). A digital twin smart city for citizen feedback. *Cities*, *110*, 103064.

Chapter 5

The metaverse and future cities

Introduction

As cities continue to grapple with issues like climate change, inequality, and rapid urbanization, increased urban population, and others, the metaverse serves as among the most potent tools for reimagining urban spaces and fostering more sustainable, equitable, and resilient cities.

> The Metaverse is a virtual universe that blends digital and physical realities seamless and has shown immense potentials in its ability to revolutionize the field of urban planning and design.

One of the most profound ways the metaverse can transform future city planning is through the emerging concept of virtual urban planning. This innovative approach leverages the immersive and interactive nature of the metaverse made possible by the availability of technologies such as VR, AR, AI, 5G, and others, enabling urban planners to experiment with city designs in a cost-effective and risk-free environment. Adopting virtual simulations can help planners test various scenarios and interventions, allowing them to assess and gauge the potential impacts of their decisions before implementing them in the physical world (Allam, Bibri, et al., 2022; Dimov & Dimov, 2022). This data-driven approach can facilitate evidence-based decision-making and foster more effective, innovative urban solutions.

Moreover, the Metaverse has been argued to provide significant potential to enhance stakeholder engagement and collaboration in the urban planning process. Traditionally, public participation in city planning has been limited by factors such as time, resources, bureaucracy, costs, and access to information (Rodríguez Bolívar & Alcaide Muñoz, 2019). However, with the Metaverse's immersive experiences, stakeholders can better actively participate in discourse and decision-making platforms, visualize and understand proposed developments, ensuring that their voices are heard and their concerns are addressed. This enhanced engagement can lead to more inclusive and democratic urban planning processes, ultimately resulting in cities that better serve the needs and aspirations of their residents.

> The metaverse holds immense potential to revolutionize urban infrastructure, offering a plethora of opportunities for cities to optimize resource utilization and enhance connectivity.

At the global scale, several pioneering examples showcase how the metaverse and virtual simulations are being leveraged for urban planning and stakeholder engagement. In Singapore, for instance, there is the Virtual Singapore project which has created a detailed 3D digital model of the city, incorporating real-time data on demographics, transportation, and environmental factors (City2City, 2022). This model enables urban planners and policymakers to analyze the potential impacts of various planning interventions, allowing for more informed and effective decision-making.

Another notable example is the use of VR in the planning and design of the Los Angeles River Revitalization project which was initiated by Major of LA Eric Garcetti (Miranda, 2020). By creating an immersive VR experience, stakeholders could virtually explore the proposed changes to the river and its surrounding areas, fostering a deeper understanding of the project from when its history, its present and future prospects, and its potential impacts on the city and the residents. This innovative approach to public engagement facilitates impactful discourses and collaboration between the project team, stakeholders and sponsors, and the local community, ultimately leading to a more inclusive and successful revitalization effort (Miranda, 2020).

In addition to the aforementioned case studies, recent advancements in AI and machine learning (ML) offer further opportunities for innovations within the metaverse's urban planning applications. For example, generative design algorithms can be adopted to generate numerous potential design solutions based on specific criteria and constraints, such as environmental sustainability, social equity, or economic viability (Huynh-The et al., 2023). These AI-driven design processes can foster more innovative and contextually sensitive urban interventions, ultimately leading to better-designed cities that can effectively respond to the complex challenges of the 21st century.

Furthermore, as the metaverse continues to evolve and gain traction, it is likely that new technologies and applications will emerge that can further enhance the urban planning process. For example, the integration of the IoT and smart city technologies within the metaverse will facilitate real-time monitoring and management of urban systems, such as transportation, energy, and water (Theo, 2021). Also, the emergence of the 6G that is anticipated to be actualized between 2028 and 2030 will increase the potential of metaverse, especially by reducing the latency further, while also increasing the connectivity speed by almost 1000% from what the 5G is offering today. This convergence of digital and physical realms can enable more adaptive and resilient urban environments that can better respond to changing conditions and unforeseen challenges.

Metaverse-enabled smart infrastructure for future cities

By harnessing the power of virtual and augmented reality, the metaverse can enable the development of cutting-edge solutions for transportation, energy, and water management (Dwivedi et al., 2022). Several cities across the globe such as Singapore, Seoul, and others have already taken the pioneer status by being the first cities that are using the metaverse technologies to create more sustainable and efficient infrastructure, to enhance the service delivery as well as enhance the livability status and experiences of the residents.

One of the most significant applications of the metaverse in smart infrastructure is its ability to transform and improve transportation systems. One way it has managed to achieve this is by enabling city planners to visualize traffic flow, assess public transportation networks, and predict future transportation needs more effectively (Fig. 5.1). For instance, as expressed in the previous section, Singapore's Land Transport Authority utilizes virtual reality simulations to optimize its public transportation system, reducing congestion and improving mobility for its citizens (City2City, 2022). Additionally, the metaverse can facilitate the

FIG. 5.1 One of the transport systems in Singapore.

development of intelligent traffic management systems, utilizing real-time data analysis to optimize traffic signal timings and reduce congestion (Lim, 2021).

In the realm of energy management, the metaverse can significantly contribute to the optimization of smart grids. Through virtual and augmented reality, utility companies have an added advantage in their pursuit to monitor energy consumption patterns and predict energy demand more accurately; hence, help resolve the connection problems, as well as help cities to gradually shift their energy production and consumption to renewable alternatives. This enhanced visibility allows for the efficient allocation of resources, reducing energy waste and promoting the use of renewable energy sources. The city of Amsterdam, for example, has implemented a metaverse-based smart grid system that enables citizens to monitor their energy consumption in real-time, fostering more sustainable energy usage practices (City of Amsterdam, 2020).

Water management is another critical area in which the metaverse can support smart infrastructure development. By utilizing virtual and augmented reality, water utilities can model and simulate complex water distribution networks, optimizing water usage and reducing waste (Lv et al., 2022). The metaverse also enables the development of advanced leak detection systems that can identify and locate leaks in real-time, mitigating the risk of water loss and minimizing the need for costly infrastructure repairs. In Israel, for instance, the national water company Mekorot has successfully implemented a metaverse-based system for monitoring and controlling water distribution, resulting in improved efficiency and resource management (Jerusalem Post, 2021).

While the aforementioned examples demonstrate the metaverse's potential in enhancing smart infrastructure, it is crucial to note the importance of robust governance frameworks and public-private partnerships in realizing these benefits. The deployment of metaverse technologies in infrastructure development requires concerted and collaborative efforts from various stakeholders, including governments, private sector organizations, and citizens themselves (Allam, Sharifi, et al., 2022). By fostering collaboration and creating a conducive environment for innovation, cities can harness the power of the metaverse to build resilient, sustainable, and efficient urban systems.

Through the use of advanced simulations, planners can explore various development scenarios and evaluate their implications on environmental, social, and economic factors. For instance, Swinburne University of Technology is employing the metaverse technologies to create a 3D digital twins of Swinburne's factory, allowing planners to assess the impact of proposed production system and policy interventions before their implementation (Swinburne University of Technology, 2023).

Moreover, the metaverse can play a vital role in fostering community engagement and participation in the decision-making process. By providing immersive and interactive platforms, citizens can actively participate in urban planning and contribute to shaping their cities' futures (Bingöl, 2022). This heightened level of civic engagement has the potential to create more equitable and inclusive urban environments, reflecting the diverse needs and aspirations of city dwellers (Allam, Sharifi, et al., 2022; Lv et al., 2022).

The metaverse also has significant implications for the deployment of IoT technologies in smart cities. Through integrating virtual and physical environments, the metaverse can serve as a platform for the seamless exchange of data between various IoT devices and systems. This enhanced connectivity can lead to the development of innovative solutions that improve the efficiency and resilience of urban infrastructure. For example, Barcelona has implemented a metaverse-based IoT platform to optimize waste management by utilizing sensor data to monitor waste levels in containers and optimize collection routes (Bibri, 2022).

Furthermore, the metaverse is taunted to have the potential to contribute to the development of more sustainable urban environments. By offering real-time insights into resource consumption and emissions, metaverse technologies can inform targeted interventions aimed at reducing cities' ecological footprints. For instance, Seoul, South Korea, has utilized metaverse technologies under its virtual city model dubbed *Metaverse Seoul* to monitor air quality in real time and implement data-driven policies aimed at reducing air pollution. Though this project is anticipated to be complete by 2026, already, substantial benefits have been experienced by the residents and the urban management too (Gaubert, 2021).

In addition to the benefits discussed above, the metaverse can also facilitate the evolution of the sharing economy in urban settings. By providing platforms for the exchange of resources and services, the metaverse can enhance the accessibility and affordability of essential amenities such as housing, transportation, and workspace by reducing demand, as people will have the latitude in the virtual realm. That is, the virtual world also allows people to own virtual assets such as real-estate properties. It also allows people to work and interact virtually, thus reducing the need for travel, renting of office places and so on. This can lead to more equitable distribution of resources, reduced environmental impact, and increased economic opportunities for city residents (Youde, 2022).

However, the successful integration of metaverse technologies into urban infrastructure also presents several challenges that require urgent and amicable solutions. Ensuring data privacy and security is of paramount importance, as the vast amount of data generated and shared within the metaverse can potentially expose individuals to significant privacy risks (Ahmad & Corovic, 2022; Aks et al., 2022; Allam, Sharifi, et al., 2022; Ceyhan, 2022). Additionally, bridging the digital divide is crucial to ensuring that the benefits of metaverse-enabled smart infrastructure are accessible to all citizens, irrespective of their socio-economic backgrounds (Dwivedi et al., 2022).

Metaverse-enabled urban experience and engagement

The metaverse has the potential to significantly enhance the urban experience and engagement of city dwellers, especially on the social spheres, through the use of diverse advanced technologies. By creating a seamless bridging between the digital and physical spaces, the metaverse offers new opportunities for cultural and social engagement, creating immersive urban experiences that can make cities more livable and enjoyable (Allam, Sharifi, et al., 2022).

One key aspect of metaverse-enabled urban experiences is the blending of virtual and physical dimensions, often referred to as mixed reality (MR) or AR. This fusion allows for the creation of interactive, immersive environments that allow uses to seamlessly operate in the two distinctive dimensions, with little or no hitches. The proliferation of AR and MR technologies has led to the development of novel applications in various domains, including entertainment, education, health, culture and art, and urban planning among others (Allam, Sharifi, et al., 2022; Marr, 2022; Qi, 2022; Zhang et al., 2022).

In the context of urban spaces, metaverse technologies are expected to enable city dwellers to access and engage with digital layers of information and services that are superimposed onto the physical environment. For instance, residents and visitors can use AR-enabled devices to explore historical sites or artworks, access real-time information about public transportation, and participate in interactive events and performances, just like it has been done in the city of Seoul, where residents are able to access government services virtually. These immersive experiences not only provide novel ways of interacting with the urban environment but also foster social connections and a sense of community among users (Benrimoh et al., 2022; Facebook, 2021).

Furthermore, the metaverse can facilitate new forms of cultural and social engagement by allowing users to create, recreate, share, and consume content within virtual spaces (Anderson et al., 2017; Huynh-The et al., 2023). Such abilities have immeasurable benefits to the artists, performers, and other cultural producers especially in facilitating their ability to showcase their work and engage with audiences in novel ways (Hwang & Koo, 2023). Additionally, the metaverse can foster crosscultural exchange and collaboration, as users from diverse backgrounds can interact and cocreate within shared virtual environments. On the same vein, the metaverse would also help in the conservation and regeneration pursuits for culture and heritage especially those that at the risk of disappearing, or those that have not yet been officially recognized.

Several cities around the world have already begun to harness the potential of metaverse technologies to create more engaging and interactive public spaces. In Tokyo, the Mori Building Digital Art Museum, created in collaboration with the art collective teamLab, offers an immersive, interactive experience that blends art, technology, and design (Quito, 2018). Following such initiatives, visitors can explore a vast, interconnected digital world that responds to their movements and actions, allowing for a unique and dynamic engagement with the artworks on display.

Another example is the Smart City Sandbox initiative in Toronto, which aims to transform a waterfront district into a living lab for urban innovation (Flynn & Valverde, 2019). While the project was not initially fashioned with the metaverse in mind, the technologies such as AR and MR already deployed make it metaverse ready as such have the capacity to create an interactive public realm that fosters citizen engagement and fosters a sense of community. Through partnerships with local artists, cultural organizations, and technology companies, the Smart City Sandbox aims to create a vibrant, inclusive urban environment that encourages creativity, collaboration, and social interaction.

The city of Melbourne has also embraced metaverse technologies to enhance urban experiences and engagement. In 2017, the Australian Centre for the Moving Image (ACMI) launched an innovative exhibition called "Wonderland," which combined physical and digital elements to create an immersive, interactive journey through the history of Alice in Wonderland adaptations (Thomson et al., 2019). Visitors could explore the exhibition using AR-enabled devices, engaging with the content in new and exciting ways. This project demonstrated the potential of metaverse technologies to transform traditional cultural institutions and create more engaging, participatory experiences for audiences (Acmi, 2018).

Moreover, metaverse technologies can also play a crucial role in facilitating civic engagement and participation in the urban planning process. For example, the city of Helsinki has developed a virtual platform called Virtual Helsinki, which enables residents and stakeholders to explore and interact with 3D models of the city (Hämäläinen, 2021). This platform allows users to visualize proposed urban development projects, provide feedback, and participate in virtual workshops, fostering a more inclusive and participatory approach to urban planning.

Similarly, in Barcelona, the Superilla (Superblock) project has utilized metaverse technologies to engage citizens in the process of reimagining public spaces. This is being achieved by creating a virtual environment that replicates the physical layout of the city where residents can contribute ideas and suggestions for improving their neighborhoods, fostering a sense of ownership and agency in the urban transformation process (López et al., 2020). According to Salvador Rueda, the project would only require 300 million euros to implement, but its benefits, especially with the prospect of metaverse, would be immense and far reaching (The Overview, 2022).

Despite the numerous benefits of metaverse-enabled urban experiences, it is essential to recognize and address potential challenges and limitations. The digital divide, which refers to disparities in access to information and communication technologies, can exacerbate existing social inequalities and limit the potential of metaverse technologies to create inclusive urban experiences (Timmermans & Kaufman, 2020). Therefore, it is crucial for policymakers, urban planners, and technology developers to collaborate and ensure that metaverse-enabled initiatives are accessible and equitable for all city dwellers.

The metaverse offers a promising avenue for enhancing urban experiences and engagement by fostering immersive, interactive environments that blend digital and physical spaces. Cities around the world have already begun to harness the potential of these technologies, creating innovative public spaces, cultural experiences, and participatory urban planning initiatives. As metaverse technologies continue to evolve and mature, they hold the potential to transform urban life, making cities more livable, enjoyable, and inclusive for all.

Metaverse-enabled work and education in future cities

The advent of the metaverse has the potential to transform work and education paradigms in the cities of the future, particularly by enabling virtual workspaces and classrooms that offer flexibility and remote collaboration opportunities. In respect to this, the metaverse can be described as a collective virtual shared space created by the convergence of virtually augmented physical reality and physically persistent virtual spaces that allows users to engage in immersive experiences and interact in novel ways.

One of the key drivers of metaverse-enabled workspaces is the growing demand for remote work opportunities. According to a study conducted by Gartner (2020), 82% of company leaders plan to continue offering remote work options even after the pandemic (Gartner, 2020). Another study done by Intuition found out that even postpandemic, approximately 48% of employees have continued to work remotely, while 62% of the employees would be very pleased if their employers allowed them to work remotely (O'donnellan, 2022). The metaverse can facilitate this shift by providing virtual workspaces that replicate the collaborative aspects of physical offices while enabling employees to work from anywhere. For instance, Spatial, a start-up company, offers a platform that allows users to collaborate in shared virtual spaces using avatars, which can be accessed through various devices such as VR headsets, smartphones, and computers (Winn, 2020). By bridging the gap between physical and virtual work environments, the metaverse has and could continue to help organizations adapt to the changing nature of work and maintain productivity. It could help by ensuring users have total, immersive experiences, which most of the existing technologies that have been adopted for remote activities such as work have not managed to avail to individual users.

Another area where the metaverse is poised to revolutionize work is in the realm of skill development and training. To begin with, virtual reality simulations have already demonstrated their efficacy and unmatched capacities in providing immersive, realistic training environments for various professions, including healthcare, aviation, and construction, and these could serve as the stepping stone for things to come in the future. The metaverse can take this a step further by enabling workers to acquire new skills and knowledge through social interactions and collaborations with experts and peers in virtual environments. For example, it would be easy to learn from Strivr, a company specializing in immersive learning which has developed a platform that leverages the metaverse for workplace training, enabling employees to practice skills and receive feedback in real time (Accenture, 2022). This approach to skill development can lead to greater retention and faster learning, as well as increased access to specialized expertise.

In the realm of education, there is anticipation that the metaverse could facilitate the creation of virtual classrooms that offer personalized learning experiences and foster global collaboration among students and educators. To put this in perspective, it is worth considering a study conducted by Villena-Taranilla et al. (2022) who found out that VR can increase student engagement and improve learning outcomes by providing immersive, hands-on learning experiences. In the future, the metaverse could expand on this by offering virtual classrooms that allow students to interact with instructors and peers in real time, regardless of geographical location (Alfaisal et al., 2022). This can democratize access to quality education, as students from all corners of the globe can participate in courses offered by prestigious institutions, which could be a toll order in the case of the traditional educational setup (Fig. 5.2).

Moreover, the metaverse is also being fashioned in a way that it could contribute in promoting a more inclusive and diverse learning environment. Virtual classrooms for instance would be expected to accommodate various learning styles and needs, providing personalized learning experiences for students with disabilities or those who face barriers to traditional classroom learning (Sghaier et al., 2022). Additionally, the metaverse can create opportunities for crosscultural exchanges and collaborations that would be difficult to achieve in physical classrooms. For instance, the Global Nomads Group, a nonprofit organization, has utilized virtual reality to connect students from different countries, fostering empathy and understanding through shared experiences (Fabris, 2018).

Several educational institutions have already started to explore the potential of the metaverse for teaching and learning. In 2021, the University of California, Berkeley, launched a pilot program that utilized virtual reality headsets to provide students with immersive learning experiences, including virtual field trips and interactive simulations (Mao, 2020). Similarly, the Massachusetts Institute of Technology (MIT) has established the MIT nano Immersion Lab,

FIG. 5.2 Students engaging in virtual classroom.

which offers a space for researchers and students to experiment with metaverse technologies and develop innovative educational experiences (MIT, 2021). These early adopters serve as examples of how educational institutions can harness the metaverse to create more engaging and effective learning environments for students, hence reduce challenges prompted by geographical distances, limited housing facilities for patients, and some overheads that could be avoided in the case of virtual environment.

The metaverse also has the potential to transform the way research is conducted and disseminated. Virtual conferences and symposiums can democratize access to cutting-edge knowledge, as attendees from around the world can participate without incurring travel costs or visa restrictions (Alfaisal et al., 2022). Furthermore, the metaverse can facilitate novel forms of collaboration among researchers, enabling interdisciplinary teams to work together in shared virtual spaces and explore complex problems from multiple perspectives. For instance, the Networked Minds Lab at Stanford University has developed a virtual reality platform that allows researchers to collaborate on complex scientific visualizations, fostering a deeper understanding of data and promoting innovative problem-solving.

While the metaverse holds immense potential of transforming work and education systems in future cities, it is paramount to address potential challenges and ethical considerations. One concern is the digital divide, as access to the necessary technology and infrastructure required to engage in metaverse-enabled work and education may be limited for economically disadvantaged individuals and communities. Moreover, issues related to privacy, data security, and the potential for surveillance in virtual spaces must be addressed to ensure that metaverse technologies are used responsibly and ethically (Ceyhan, 2022).

Overall, the metaverse is poised to revolutionize how people work and learn, especially in cities and urban areas in the days to come. Its potential to enable virtual workspaces and classrooms that offer greater flexibility and remote collaboration opportunities will help organizations adapt to changing work demands and democratize access to quality education. Early adopters, such as innovative companies and educational institutions, are already utilizing metaverse technologies to create more engaging and effective work and learning environments. However, to fully realize the potential of the metaverse in transforming work and education, it is essential to address the challenges and ethical considerations that accompany this paradigm shift.

Challenges and limitations of metaverse-enabled future cities

In the ambit of urban development, the metaverse has emerged as a transformative force, promising to reshape the very fabric of cities. However, the integration of metaverse technologies in the urban landscape is not without its challenges and limitations as has been pointed out in the sections above.

This section delves deeper into the complex issues that have already been identified concerning access, inclusivity, and privacy, examining their implications on the development and adoption of metaverse technologies in cities. It also highlights the strategies adopted in different cities to address these challenges and surmount potential barriers.

From a wide scope of literature, it has been elucidated that the metaverse relies heavily on advanced technology and infrastructure, and as is the case with other modern technologies, it inadvertently creates a digital divide (Allam & Newman, 2018; Sghaier et al., 2022). This gap manifests itself in different forms, such as disparities in the quality and affordability of internet connections, and the availability of compatible devices. Consequently, individuals and communities with limited resources may be unable to access the metaverse, further exacerbating existing socioeconomic inequalities (Allam, Sharifi, et al., 2022). Thus, it is crucial for city planners and policymakers to ensure equitable access to metaverse technologies, enabling all citizens to partake in the digital urban experience. This could be achieved by streamlining and standardizing some protocols, especially in regard to compatibility of devices across different platforms. By doing so, it would be possible for people from different socioeconomic background to access the metaverse using devices that they can comfortably afford.

Another challenge that emerges in the context of metaverse-enabled cities is the question of inclusivity. The design of the metaverse, its content, and its interfaces have the potential to either promote or hinder social inclusion (Bosworth & Gregg, 2021). Currently, there is sufficient evidence that most metaverse platforms are not inclusive, and only favors those in the higher economic cadre, those that are technologically savvy, and those living in areas covered by diverse infrastructural developments that smoothly supports the application of metaverse. In this regard, the metaverse's architecture must be cognizant of the diverse needs and preferences of its users, such as linguistic, cultural, and physical barriers. For instance, the design of virtual public spaces should accommodate users with disabilities, providing them with the necessary tools and resources to navigate the metaverse (Sghaier et al., 2022). Moreover, city planners and metaverse developers must collaborate to create inclusive virtual spaces that foster social cohesion and crosscultural understanding, rather than perpetuating stereotypes or reinforcing biases (Winn, 2020). Collaboration would further help in bringing down the cost of accessing the metaverse, hence promoting inclusivity (Fig. 5.3).

Privacy concerns represent another significant challenge in the adoption of metaverse technologies within cities, and if not addressed early, it might become the bane of metaverse. The convergence of the physical and digital realms in metaverse-enabled cities generates vast amounts of data, necessitating robust privacy frameworks to protect users' personal information. The absence of relevant safeguards aimed at protecting the data and the privacy of those whose data is being used may deter or demoralize citizens from engaging with

84 The metaverse and smart cities

FIG. 5.3 An elderly woman enjoying the virtual environment.

the metaverse, impeding its widespread adoption. In this regard, it is crucial for city administrators, in collaboration with technology companies, to establish stringent data protection regulations and promote transparency in data handling practices. Such measures will engender trust among users and foster the responsible development and use of metaverse technologies in urban settings (Lubin, 2022; Lv et al., 2022).

In response to these challenges, several cities have adopted innovative strategies to ensure the equitable development and adoption of metaverse technologies. For example, some municipalities have implemented PPPs to improve digital infrastructure and provide affordable internet access to underserved communities. These PPPs have the potential to bridge the digital divide and facilitate broader participation in the metaverse, promoting digital equity within cities (Squires, 2021).

Furthermore, the concept of "participatory design" has gained traction in addressing the issue of inclusivity in metaverse-enabled cities. This approach entails the active involvement of diverse stakeholders, including citizens, in the design and development of metaverse applications and environments (Dwivedi et al., 2022). By soliciting input from a wide range of users, participatory design fosters the creation of inclusive virtual spaces that cater to the needs and preferences of all citizens, regardless of their background or abilities.

In the quest to address privacy concerns, some cities have adopted data protection frameworks and guidelines, which emphasize transparency, accountability, and user control (Dwivedi et al., 2022). For instance, the European Union's General Data Protection Regulation (GDPR) serves as a benchmark for data privacy standards, imposing strict requirements on data collection, storage, and usage practices (Hoofnagle et al., 2019). By adhering to such regulations, cities can ensure the responsible and ethical use of metaverse technologies, fostering trust among citizens and facilitating their integration into urban life.

Conclusions and future directions for metaverse-enabled future cities

In synthesizing the insights garnered from the discussions above, it is evident that the metaverse holds immense potential in shaping cities today and in the future. But it is in the future that the full strength and benefits of it will be realized, especially after the teething challenges in the normative phase of this technologies are addressed. The potential of metaverse in cities extends across a broad spectrum of urban planning, smart infrastructure, urban experience, work and education, as well as addressing potential challenges and limitations. The vision for metaverse-enabled future cities is one that encompasses sustainable, inclusive, and livable urban environments, which have been the pursuit of urban planners, in the recent decades.

The metaverse has demonstrated the capacity to revolutionize urban planning through virtual simulations and immersive experiences, allowing for more experimentation and innovation in city design (Allam, Sharifi, et al., 2022). This capability will have immense advantage, as it helps overcome the "trial-and-error" approach which could be attributed to the "nonstart" of a wide range of modern planning models that have emerged in the recent years, but failed to gain traction. Virtual urban planning offers stakeholders the opportunity to test different scenarios, receive immediate feedback, and refine designs iteratively. For instance, the city of Helsinki utilized a virtual model of the city to engage stakeholders in the planning process, enabling more informed decision-making and fostering a sense of ownership among citizens (Hämäläinen, 2021).

Metaverse technologies, such as VR and AR have emerged as powerful tools in supporting the development of smart infrastructure in future cities. These technologies can optimize transportation, energy, and water systems, making more efficient use of resources and enhancing connectivity (Dwivedi et al., 2022). For example, the technology could become invaluable in helping actualize innovative approaches like the Singapore's Virtual Singapore project which target to serves as a comprehensive 3D model of the city-state, facilitating urban planning, disaster management, and infrastructure maintenance (City2City, 2022 #2234). This exemplifies the potential of metaverse technologies in contributing to more sustainable and efficient infrastructure not only in the current dispensation, but also in future cities.

The metaverse also has the potential to enhance urban experiences and engagement for city dwellers, making cities more livable and enjoyable. Immersive urban experiences can create new forms of cultural and social engagement, transforming public spaces into interactive environments (Cronenwett, 2002; Faraboschi et al., 2022). For instance, the installation of augmented reality art in public spaces, as seen in Melbourne, Australia, fosters a sense of community and enriches the urban experience. This potential of the metaverse could even be amplified if the cities across the world embrace emerging urban planning model like the 15-Minute City concept, which emphasize on human-centric approaches on planning, especially in regard to proximity, density, technology, and diversity. However, regardless of the planning model that the cities across the world will settle for, the concept of metaverse will remain priceless and invaluable.

In the discussion above, it has been comprehensively demonstrated how the metaverse technologies have begun to reshape the way people across different cities work, learn, interact and spend their recreation time. From virtual workspaces and classrooms that offer flexibility and remote collaboration, to borderless entertainment and cultural enjoyments that breaking down geographical barriers and promoting innovation (Allam, Sharifi, et al., 2022; Benrimoh et al., 2022; Bibri, Allam, & Krogstie, 2022; Zhang et al., 2022). At the heart of these transformations are companies such as Spatial, Teamlab, and educational institutions like Stanford University that have already embraced metaverse technologies to create more engaging and immersive work and learning environments. It is anticipated that in the future, as the vision of metaverse become even more clearer, more and more companies, both existing and startups, plus a wide range of both public and private institutions will shift their operations to this virtual world, which, in reality does not take away the operations in the physical realm, but only affirm and strengthen them by giving them and extra edge to become even better.

While the potential of metaverse-enabled future cities is undeniable, challenges and limitations must be acknowledged and addressed at the earliest opportunity to void them from recurring when the concept become common, and most activities shifts to the virtual realm. It then means that resolving challenges such as access, inclusivity, and privacy concerns cannot wait for the concept to be fully embraced as they are paramount in ensuring that the metaverse contributes to a more equitable urban future (Rosenberg, 2022 #160; Shou, 2021 #124). Cities must develop strategies to overcome obvious and anticipated issues such as the digital divide, inequality, infrastructure underdevelopment, and others. More importantly, the focus should be to ensure that all citizens regardless of the demographic profiles and backgrounds benefit from metaverse technologies. Inclusivity initiatives, such as New York City's LinkNYC program, which provides free public Wi-Fi and digital services, serve as examples of how cities can address these challenges.

As we look toward the future of metaverse-enabled cities, several developments and challenges merit further exploration. Firstly, the integration of metaverse technologies with emerging fields such as the IoT, 6G, AI, and others can further enhance the potential of smart cities (Güven & Balli, 2022). By leveraging these synergies, cities can harness vast amounts of data to make informed decisions, optimize resource usage, and improve quality of life.

Secondly, the governance of metaverse-enabled cities will require the development of new frameworks that balance innovation with privacy, security, and ethical considerations (Kitchin, 2016). City governments and technology providers must collaborate in establishing standards and protocols to ensure that metaverse technologies are deployed responsibly, equitably and in ethical manner (Koohang et al., 2023). A leaf on the these can be borrowed from the approach adopted in the city of Barcelona, where Barcelona's Data Commons model which emphasizes citizen participation and the ethical use of data is strictly emphasized (Noori et al., 2020).

Thirdly, fostering PPPs will be crucial in advancing metaverse technologies and ensuring their successful integration into urban systems. Collaborative efforts between city governments, technology providers, and local stakeholders can enable the pooling of resources, knowledge, and expertise, accelerating the development and adoption of innovative solutions (Radoff, 2021).

Moreover, addressing the environmental impact of metaverse technologies is critical in ensuring that future cities are sustainable (Allam, Sharifi, et al., 2022). Energy-efficient infrastructure, such as data centers and servers, as well as efforts to reduce the carbon footprint of metaverse platforms, will be vital in mitigating any adverse environmental consequences.

Lastly, a focus on human-centric design and ensuring that metaverse technologies serve the needs of citizens will be essential in creating inclusive and livable future cities. This approach involves considering the diverse needs of various demographic groups, such as the elderly, people with disabilities, and culturally diverse populations, and integrating these considerations into the design and deployment of metaverse technologies.

References

Accenture. (2022). Accenture invests in strivr to help advance immersive learning in the metaverse continuum era [Online]. *Accenture*. Available: https://Newsroom.Accenture.Com/News/Accenture-Invests-In-Strivr-To-Help-Advance-Immersive-Learning-In-The-Metaverse-Continuum-Era.Htm. (Accessed 2 April 2023).

Acmi. (2018). *Wonderland: Imagine a world where nothing is impossible*. [Online]. Available: https://www.Acmi.Net.Au/About/Touring-Exhibitions/Wonderland-Touring/. (Accessed 31 March 2023).

Ahmad, I., & Corovic, T. (2022). *Privacy in a parallel digital universe: The metaverse [Online]*. Norton Rose Fulbright. Available: https://www.Dataprotectionreport.Com/2022/01/Privacy-In-A-Parallel-Digital-Universe-The-Metaverse/. (Accessed 30 May 2022).

Aks, S. M. Y., Karmila, M., Givan, B., Hendratna, G., Setiawan, H. S., Putra, A. S., Winarno, S. H., Kurniawan, T. A., Simorangkir, Y. N., Taufiq, R., Herawaty, M. T., & Asep. (2022). A review of blockchain for security data privacy with metaverse. In *2022 International conference on ICT for smart society (ICISS), 10-11 August* (pp. 1–5).

Alfaisal, R., Hashim, H., & Azizan, U. H. (2022). Metaverse system adoption in education: A systematic literature review. *Journal of Computers in Education, 1*.

Allam, Z., Bibri, S. E., Jones, D. S., Chabaud, D., & Moreno, C. (2022). Unpacking the 15-Minute City via 6g, Iot, and digital twins: Towards a new narrative for increasing urban efficiency, resilience, and sustainability. *Sensors, 22*, 1369.

Allam, Z., & Newman, P. (2018). Redefining the smart city: culture, metabolism and governance. *Smart Cities, 1*.

Allam, Z., Sharifi, A., Bibri, S. E., Jones, D. S., & Krogstie, J. (2022). The metaverse as a virtual form of smart cities: Opportunities and challenges for environmental, economic, and social sustainability in urban futures. *Smart Cities*, *5*(3), 771–801. https://doi.org/10.3390/smartcities5030040.

Anderson, A. P., Mayer, M. D., Fellows, A. M., Cowan, D. R., Hegel, M. T., & Buckey, J. C. (2017). Relaxation with immersive natural scenes presented using virtual reality. *Aerospace Medicine and Human Performance*, *88*, 520–526.

Benrimoh, D., Chheda, F. D., & Margolese, H. C. (2022). The best predictor of the future-the metaverse, mental health, and lessons learned from current technologies. *JMIR Mental Health*, *9*, E40410.

Bibri, S. E. (2022). Eco-districts and data-driven smart eco-cities: Emerging approaches to strategic planning by design and spatial scaling and evaluation by technology. *Land Use Policy*, *113*, 105830.

Bibri, S. E., Allam, Z., & Krogstie, J. (2022). The metaverse as a virtual form of data-driven smart urbanism: Platformization and its underlying processes, institutional dimensions, and disruptive impacts. *Computational Urban Science*, *2*, 24. https://doi.org/10.1007/s43762-022-00051-0.

Bingöl, E. S. (2022). Citizen participation in smart sustainable cities. In E. A. Babaoğlu, & O. Kulaç (Eds.), *Research anthology on citizen engagement and activism for social change* IGI Global.

Bosworth, A., & Gregg, N. (2021). *Building the metaverse responsibly* [Online]. Meta. Available: https://About.Fb.Com/News/2021/09/Building-The-Metaverse-Responsibly/. (Accessed 22 April 2022).

Ceyhan, C. (2022). *Data privacy concerns in the metaverse. May the privacy be with us! [Online]*. Lexology. Available: https://www.Lexology.Com/Library/Detail.Aspx?G=319620e2-09b4-46e3-Bf20-0d4afd537a7b. (Accessed 30 May 2022).

City of Amsterdam. (2020). Amsterdam circular strategy 2020-2025 [Online]. *City of Amsterdam*. Available: https://www.Amsterdam.Nl/En/Policy/Sustainability/Circular-Economy/. (Accessed 15 March 2023).

City2City. (2022). *Virtual Singapore: A digital 'twin' for planning [Online]*. Undp. Available: https://City2city.Network/Virtual-Singapore-Digital-Twin-Planning-Innovation-Type-Institutional-Pioneer. (Accessed 15 March 2023).

Cronenwett, W. (2002). The metaverse: A fully-realized virtual world. *Journal of Interactive Technology and Smart Education*, *1*, 95–104.

Dimov, R., & Dimov, D. (2022). *Metaverse implementation In real life. Augmented and virtual reality*.

Dwivedi, Y. K., Hughes, L., Baabdullah, A. M., Ribeiro-Navarrete, S., Giannakis, M., Al-Debei, M. M., Dennehy, D., Metri, B., Buhalis, D., Cheung, C. M. K., Conboy, K., Doyle, R., Dubey, R., Dutot, V., Felix, R., Goyal, D. P., Gustafsson, A., Hinsch, C., Jebabli, I., … Wamba, S. F. (2022). Metaverse beyond the hype: Multidisciplinary perspectives on emerging challenges, opportunities, and agenda for research, practice and policy. *International Journal of Information Management*, *66*, 102542.

Fabris, B. (2018). Bridging the divide: A critical analysis of intercultural dialogue through videoconference as a peace education practice [Online]. *Academia*. Available: https://www.Academia.Edu/89459874/Bridging_The_Divide_A_Critical_Analysis_Of_Intercultural_Dialogue_Through_Videoconference_As_A_Peace_Education_Practice?F_Ri=9491. (Accessed 2 April 2023).

Facebook. (2021). *Connect 2021: Our vision for the metaverse [Online]*. Meta. Available: https://Tech.Fb.Com/Connect-2021-Our-Vision-For-The-Metaverse/. (Accessed 1 December 2021).

Faraboschi, P., Frachtenberg, E., Laplante, P., Milojicic, D., & Saracco, R. (2022). Virtual worlds (metaverse): From skepticism, to fear, to immersive opportunities. *Computer*, *55*, 100–106.

Flynn, A., & Valverde, M. (2019). Planning on the waterfront: Setting the agenda for Toronto's 'smart city' project. *Planning Theory & Practice, 20*, 769–775.

Gartner. (2020). *Gartner survey reveals 82% of company leaders plan to allow employees to work remotely some of the time [Online]*. Available: Gartner https://www.Gartner.Com/En/Newsroom/Press-Releases/2020-07-14-Gartner-Survey-Reveals-82-Percent-Of-Company-Leaders-Plan-To-Allow-Employees-To-Work-Remotely-Some-Of-The-Time. (Accessed 2 April 2023).

Gaubert, J. (2021). Seoul to become the first city to enter the metaverse. What will it look like? [Online]. *Euro News*. Available: https://www.Euronews.Com/Next/2021/11/10/Seoul-To-Become-The-First-City-To-Enter-The-Metaverse-What-Will-It-Look-Like. (Accessed 4 December 2021).

Güven, İ., & Balli, O. (2022). *Empowering metaverse through artificial intelligence*.

Hämäläinen, M. (2021). Urban development with dynamic digital twins in Helsinki city. *IET Smart Cities, 3*, 201–210.

Hoofnagle, C. J., Van Der Sloot, B., & Borgesius, F. Z. (2019). The European Union general data protection regulation: What it is and what it means. *Information & Communications Technology Law, 28*, 65–98.

Huynh-The, T., Pham, Q.-V., Pham, X.-Q., Nguyen, T. T., Han, Z., & Kim, D.-S. (2023). Artificial intelligence for the metaverse: A survey. *Engineering Applications of Artificial Intelligence, 117*, 105581.

Hwang, S., & Koo, G. (2023). Art marketing in the metaverse world: Evidence from South Korea. *Cogent Social Science, 9*, 2175429.

Jerusalem Post. (2021). Mekorot launches startup for remote monitoring of water data [Online]. *Jerusalem Post*. Available: https://www.Jpost.Com/Jpost-Tech/Mekorot-Launches-Startup-For-Remote-Monitoring-Of-Water-Data-671722. (Accessed 29 March 2023).

Kitchin, R. (2016). The ethics of smart cities and urban science. *Philosophical Transactions of the Royal Society A: Mathematical, Physical and Engineering Sciences, 374*, 1–15.

Koohang, A., Nord, J. H., Ooi, K.-B., Tan, G. W.-H., Al-Emran, M., Aw, E. C.-X., Baabdullah, A. M., Buhalis, D., Cham, T.-H., Dennis, C., Dutot, V., Dwivedi, Y. K., Hughes, L., Mogaji, E., Pandey, N., Phau, I., Raman, R., Sharma, A., Sigala, M., ... Wong, L.-W. (2023). Shaping the metaverse into reality: A holistic multidisciplinary understanding of opportunities, challenges, and avenues for future investigation. *Journal of Computer Information Systems*, 1–31.

Lim, J. (2021). Seoul will have a city-wide public Iot network By 2023 [Online]. *Tech Wire Asia*. Available: https://Techwireasia.Com/2021/07/Seoul-Will-Have-A-City-Wide-Public-Iot-Network-By-2023/. (Accessed 12 September 2021).

López, I., Ortega, J., & Pardo, M. (2020). Mobility infrastructures in cities and climate change: An analysis through the superblocks in Barcelona. *Atmosphere [Online], 11*.

Lubin, A. (2022). Governance in the metaverse [Online]. *Datasphere*. Available: https://www.Thedatasphere.Org/News/Governance-In-The-Metaverse/. (Accessed 12 February 2023).

Lv, Z., Shang, W.-L., & Guizani, M. (2022). Impact of digital twins and metaverse on cities: History, current situation, and application perspectives. *Applied Sciences [Online], 12*.

Mao, M. (2020). Op-Ed: Virtual reality has powerful potential in education and experiential learning [Online]. *Berkeley*. Available: https://Funginstitute.Berkeley.Edu/News/Op-Ed-Virtual-Reality-Has-Powerful-Potential-In-Education-And-Experiential-Learning/. (Accessed 2 April 2023).

Marr, B. (2022). The metaverse, digital dressing rooms and the future of the fashion retail [Online]. *Forbes*. Available: https://www.Forbes.Com/Sites/Bernardmarr/2022/07/01/The-Metaverse-Digital-Dressing-Rooms-And-The-Future-Of-Fashion-Retail/?Sh=4cfd06816b90. (Accessed 10 February 2023).

Miranda, C. A. (2020). *The Los Angeles river as you've never seen it—In augmented reality* [Online]. *Los Angeles Times*. Available: https://Www.Latimes.Com/Entertainment-Arts/Story/2020-07-30/Los-Angeles-River-Augumented-Reality-History-App. (Accessed 30 March 2023).

MIT. (2021). *Mit. nano's immersion lab opens for researchers and students [Online]*. Mit (Accessed).

Noori, N., Hoppe, T., & De Jong, M. (2020). Classifying pathways for smart city development: Comparing design, governance and implementation in Amsterdam, Barcelona, Dubai, and Abu Dhabi. *Sustainability, 12*, 4030.

O'donnellan, R. (2022). *Remote working statistics you need to know in 2023 [Online]*. Intuition. Available: https://www.Intuition.Com/Remote-Working-Statistics-You-Need-To-Know-In-2023/. (Accessed 30 March 2023).

Qi, W. (2022). The investment value of metaverse in the media and entertainment industry. *BCP Business & Management, 34*, 279–283.

Quito, A. (2018). Digital art sensation teamlab will open its own immersive museum in Tokyo [Online]. *Quartz*. Available: https://Qz.Com/Quartzy/1199864/Digital-Art-Sensation-Teamlab-Will-Open-Its-Own-Immersive-Museum-In-Tokyo. (Accessed 30 March 2023).

Radoff, J. (2021). Clash of the metaverse Titans: Microsoft, Meta and Apple [Online]. *Medium*. Available: https://Medium.Com/Building-The-Metaverse/Clash-Of-The-Metaverse-Titans-Microsoft-Meta-And-Apple-Ce505b010376. (Accessed 1 December 2021).

Rodríguez Bolívar, M. P., & Alcaide Muñoz, L. (2019). *E-participation in smart cities: Technologies and models of governance for citizen engagement*. Cham: Springer International Publishing.

Rosenberg, L. (2022). Regulation of the metaverse: A roadmap. In *6th International conference on virtual and augmented reality simulations (ICVARS 2022), Brisbane, Australia*.

Sghaier, S., Elfakki, A. O., & Alotaibi, A. A. (2022). Development of an intelligent system based on metaverse learning for students with disabilities. *Frontiers in Robotics and AI, 9*, 1006921.

Shou, D. (2021). I want my daughter to live in a better metaverse [Online]. *Wired*. Available: https://www.Wired.Com/Story/I-Want-My-Daughter-To-Live-In-A-Better-Metaverse/. (Accessed 25 February 2022).

Squires, C. (2021). Seoul will be the first city government to join the metaverse [Online]. *Quartz*. Available: https://Qz.Com/2086353/Seoul-Is-Developing-A-Metaverse-Government-Platform/. (Accessed 4 November 2021).

Swinburne University of Technology. (2023). Swinburne enters the metaverse with factory of the future digital twin [Online]. *Swinburne University Of Technology*. Available: https://www.Swinburne.Edu.Au/News/2023/03/Swinburne-Enters-The-Metaverse-With-Factory-Of-Future-Digital-Twin/. (Accessed 30 March 2023).

The Overview. (2022). Barcelona superblock project: Blueprint for the green city of the future? [Online]. *The Overview*. Available: https://Theoverview.Art/Superblocks-Barcelona-Blueprint-For-The-Livable-City-Of-The-Future/. (Accessed 30 March 2023).

Theo. (2021). Digital twins, Iot and the metaverse [Online]. *Medium*. Available: https://Medium.Com/@Theo/Digital-Twins-Iot-And-The-Metaverse-B4efbfc01112. (Accessed 3 December 2021).

Thomson, G., Newton, P., & Newman, P. (2019). Sustainable precincts: Transforming Australian cities one neighbourhood at a time. In P. Newton, D. Prasad, A. Sproul, & S. White (Eds.), *Decarbonising the built environment: Charting the transition*. Singapore: Palgrave Macmillan.

Timmermans, S., & Kaufman, R. (2020). Technologies and health inequities. *Annual Review of Sociology, 46*, 583–602.

Villena-Taranilla, R., Tirado-Olivares, S., Cózar-Gutiérrez, R., & González-Calero, J. A. (2022). Effects of virtual reality on learning outcomes In K-6 education: A meta-analysis. *Educational Research Review*, *35*, 100434.

Winn, Z. (2020). Bringing the benefits of in-person collaboration to the virtual world [Online]. *Massachusetts Institute of Technology*. Available: https://News.Mit.Edu/2020/Spatial-Vr-Collaboration-0710. (Accessed 2 April 2023).

Youde, K. (2022). Social housing and the metaverse: A future vision [Online]. *Inside Housing*. Available: https://www.Insidehousing.Co.Uk/Insight/Social-Housing-And-The-Metaverse-A-Future-Vision-78407. (Accessed 30 March 2023).

Zhang, X., Chen, Y., Hu, L., & Wang, Y. (2022). The metaverse in education: definition, framework, features, potential applications, challenges, and future research topics. *Frontiers in Psychology*, *13*.

Chapter 6

The impact of the metaverse on urban life

Introduction

> The metaverse is an immersive and interconnected virtual environment that represents a new frontier in the realm of urban life and urban planning.

In particular, the metaverse opens new opportunities and potentials for cities, more so in the current dispensation where the urban areas are experiencing immense growth and evolution. With it, there is unlimited potential for cities to overcome traditional urban challenges through the numerous innovative urban solutions that are emerging. It therefore becomes important to adopt an interdisciplinary approach that combines insights from technology, social sciences, and urban planning to fully appreciate the potential impact of the metaverse when it is incorporated into the urban sphere (Theo, 2021).

In the recent past, the metaverse has gained substantial popularity for its capacity to enhance areas such as immersive communication capabilities, increased collaboration, and creativity. It has helped transcend physical boundaries that have been a hindrance in many cases and has also been instrumental in fostering new forms of interaction (Bailenson, 2021). For this reason, urban planners, designers, and other stakeholders have begun to explore the different potential applications of the metaverse to address perennial, pressing issues such as environmental sustainability, transportation, social cohesion, livability status, and others.

In the modern days, one of the pressing challenges in urban planning is the pursuit of sustainable investment and development. Attention has been on identifying a potent technology that would warrant subtle development, while at the same time, promoting sustainability agendas (Allam, 2012; Allam et al., 2020). As such, the emergence and subsequent adoption of the metaverse into urban planning processes is taunted to have the potential to become instrumental in addressing this challenge. On this, a case can be drawn on how the metaverse can facilitate data-driven decision-making by enabling planners to visualize and manipulate spatial data in real-time, allowing for the identification of environmentally sound solutions (Bibri, Allam, & Krogstie, 2022). Furthermore, it has been argued that the virtual environments within the metaverse have the potential to serve as platforms for social interactions and community engagement, thus, fostering collaboration, dialogues, and discourses between various stakeholders in the urban planning process (Rosenberg, 2022).

The metaverse also has immeasurable potential in the transportation sector which is another vital domain in the urban realm. Since the early 1980, as the number of cars on the roads continued to increase, issues such as congestion, pollution, and accessibility have become pervasive issues in contemporary urban environments, and it is anticipated that the metaverse will open new opportunities that would help to mitigate these challenges (Pamucar et al., 2023). For instance, through the implementation of intelligent transportation systems made possible by the adoption of modern technologies such as artificial intelligence (AI), Internet of Things (IoT), and others, plus the metaverse could enable the development of dynamic, real-time traffic management strategies that optimize efficiency and minimize environmental impact (Zamponi & Barbierato, 2022). Further, the metaverse is being created in such a way that it can facilitate the creation of virtual workspaces that would play a critical role in reducing the need for daily commutes to and from work, hence, alleviating pressure on urban transportation networks (Allam, Sharifi, et al., 2022).

The metaverse's potential to positively influence social cohesion in urban spheres is particularly an important, and crucial aspect to consider. As cities continue to become increasingly diverse and complex, the need to build strong social networks and communities can never be overlooked. This makes the metaverse an attractive option as it has been proven to have the potential to serve as a platform for social interaction, providing immersive virtual spaces where people from different backgrounds can come together, share ideas, and collaborate on projects (Dwivedi et al., 2022) (Fig. 6.1).

FIG. 6.1 People exploring the virtual environment (Sorkin, 2019).

By providing new platforms for civic engagement, the metaverse can contribute to the development of inclusive and vibrant urban communities, which conventional urban planning models have failed to achieve. Despite the potential benefits of the metaverse, it is important to be cognizant of the possible negative impacts that may arise when it becomes part of urban life. One major concern about the metaverse is its potential to exaggerate the already existing debacle on the digital divide. For example, the overdependency on digital technologies may exacerbate the existing gap between have and have-nots, further marginalizing disadvantaged populations who lack access to the necessary infrastructure (Sadowski, 2020). Additionally, the widespread adoption of virtual realms within the metaverse is expected to exacerbate concerns on pertinent and sensitive issues such as privacy, surveillance, and control over personal data (Falchuk et al., 2018; Gupta et al., 2023).

To fully harness the potential of the metaverse in urban planning and designing, it would be important to adopt a holistic approach that considers the complex interplay between technological innovation, and social and spatial dynamics. This calls for a concerted effort from multiple disciplines to ensure all aspects are conclusively addressed. Further, it would be important for the development of collaborative partnerships between researchers, policymakers, and urban stakeholders (Allam, Sharifi, et al., 2022). By embracing this interdisciplinary perspective, urban planners and designers can effectively navigate the myriad opportunities and challenges presented by the metaverse, ultimately contributing to the creation of smarter, more sustainable, and inclusive cities for the future.

Challenges of urban life

In the modern days, urban life presents a myriad of challenges to both residents and visitors including issues of accessibility, traffic gridlock, and socioeconomic issues. On the bare minimum, these challenges impact the well-being of urban dwellers and derail the potential of cities to be livable, equitable, and sustainable. It then becomes paramount to understand these challenges as the knowledge helps to leverage the potential of the metaverse and emerging technologies to come up with innovative and cost-effective solutions for the urban challenges as described in the following.

Accessibility

Accessibility is a fundamental aspect of urban life in all spheres, encompassing the ease and efficiency with which urban dwellers can access diverse services, amenities, and opportunities. This is however not the case in most cases, as despite the immense investments and concentration of resources in most urban areas, obvious disparities in accessibility remain a pervasive issue (Nijman & Wei, 2020). A case can be made here by considering the lifestyle of the

FIG. 6.2 A crowded neighborhood in the city of Jerusalem, Israel (Brandon, 2020).

low-income demographic that often resides in areas with limited access to essential services, such as healthcare, education, and employment opportunities. Despite this population living in urban areas, they are all marginalized when compared to their counterparts in the middle- and upper-income cadres (Kawachi & Berkman, 2014) (Fig. 6.2).

These disparities in accessibility play significant roles in exacerbating the persistence of social and economic inequalities within cities. As a result, urban residents experience diverse challenges including mobility, health, education, and recreation. For instance, inaccessibility in the transport sector, exacerbated by limited transportation options has been argued to compound challenges such as marginalization of the vulnerable populations, restricting their ability to participate in the social and economic life of the city (Hidayati et al., 2021).

Congestion

In the recent past, the world has experienced significant population growth (over 55% of the current global population lives in cities) and immeasurable urbanization. As the population increased, so did the number of vehicles, and the demand for housing too. As a result, cities have experienced notable congestion especially on the roads and in the residential areas. It has been widely documented that the increasing number of vehicles on the road contributes to a myriad of negative consequences, such as traffic delays, reduced air quality, and heightened noise pollution (Mackett, 2014). In the United States, for example, urban dwellers spend an average of 54 h/year in traffic congestion, resulting in an annual cost of $166 billion (McCarthy, 2020). Urban residents, on average, spend the equivalent of up to 8 days per year in traffic, when daily commute times are accumulated over the year (Fleming, 2019) (Fig. 6.3).

FIG. 6.3 Queen's Road Central, Hong Kong (Yin, 2022).

The environmental impacts of congestion are particularly concerning, with transportation accounting for nearly a quarter of global greenhouse gas emissions, noting that over 95% of energy worldwide consumed in the transport sector is sourced from fossil fuels. The pollutants from vehicles have been linked to adverse health outcomes, including respiratory and cardiovascular diseases (Mackett, 2014). Thus, congestion not only affects the daily experiences of urban dwellers but also poses long-term challenges to public health and environmental sustainability.

Social isolation

Whereas cities are known for high density and notable diversity, cases of social isolation remain a prevalent issue for many urban dwellers. This has been prompted by factors such as the fragmentation of traditional social networks, the prevalence of single-person households, and the proliferation of digital technologies that have contributed to the erosion of social connections in cities (Holt-Lunstad et al., 2015).

From a psychological point of view, social isolation has significant implications on the well-being of both humans and animals; hence, it should be of pertinent concern for urban residents who are mostly affected due to the factors cited earlier. It has been documented that social isolation is associated with health-related issues such as increased rates of depression, anxiety, and cognitive decline (Cornwell & Waite, 2009). Lack of social connections has more challenges including hindering the development of social capital and reducing the ability of urban dwellers to respond effectively to challenges and pursue collective goals.

The magnitude and complexity of the earlier challenges underscore the need for innovative, and proactive approaches to urban planning and design that promote equity, high livability status, and sustainability (Allam, Bibri, et al., 2022b). One such approach could be the adoption of metaverse and smart city technologies that have been argued to have the potential to address these issues. In particular, the metaverse would be instrumental in fostering new forms of communication, collaboration, and resource allocation, while being complemented by the diverse smart technologies. However, to effectively harness this potential, it is essential to adopt a holistic and interdisciplinary approach that recognizes the multifaceted nature of urban life.

It is possible to come up with novel and far-reaching solutions for urban challenges by leveraging the affordance of the metaverse and smart city technologies coming up in the modern days. However, this will require integrating insights from diverse backgrounds such as technology, social sciences, and urban planning. To put this into perspective, a case could be made of how the metaverse can be exploited to facilitate the creation of virtual workspaces that reduce the need for daily commutes, thereby alleviating congestion and its associated environmental impacts (Bailenson, 2021). Similarly, the metaverse can serve as a platform for social interaction and civic engagement, helping to reduce the cases of social isolation and foster the development of social capital within urban communities (Dwivedi et al., 2022).

Emerging technologies such as the Smart city models and associated concepts such as the 15-minute planning model can also play a critical role in addressing accessibility challenges in urban environments (Allam, 2019, 2021; Allam, Bibri, et al., 2022a, 2022b). Such would be particularly beneficial by leveraging data-driven decision-making to effect digital solutions such as the intelligent transportation systems (Bibri, Allam, & Krogstie, 2022), which have been found to have the capacity to optimize the allocation of resources and improve the overall quality of life for urban residents (Zhang, 2021). Furthermore, these technologies can help to pursue more inclusive urban planning processes, which in turn would help in empowering communities to allow them to participate in the design and development of their urban environments (Fig. 6.4).

Despite the promising outcomes that would be realized when the two technologies (the metaverse and the smart city concept) are integrated into urban life, there is a need for a critical understanding of the potential risks and ethical

FIG. 6.4 La Rochele, France (Torgonskaya, 2023). Bicycles will be very important in the 15-minute city structure.

considerations. Furthermore, it's crucial to address concerns related to privacy, surveillance, and digital inequality to ensure the use of these technologies fosters social and environmental well-being (Sadowski, 2020).

Potential applications of the metaverse in urban life

There are numerous frontiers within the urban setups that the metaverse can be applied. In the earlier discussion, it has been demonstrated how it holds significant potential to address the challenges of urban life, such as enhancing accessibility, reducing congestion, and improving social interactions. In the planning and designing phases of urban areas, the metaverse would come in handy, especially in allowing for simulation before actual work starts. The numerous fetes are achieved through the deployment of immersive technologies, such as virtual realities, and augmented reality (VR/AR), which make it possible for urban experiences and services to be transformed, leading to more inclusive, sustainable, and resilient cities. In view of this brief, this section discusses various applications of the metaverse in urban life and provides a few examples of how these technologies are already being utilized to address urban challenges in different cities across the world.

A. *Enhancing accessibility*

In most cities, the issue of accessibility to different services remains critical. However, the emergence of the metaverse is a welcome relief as this concept can play a pivotal role in enhancing accessibility in urban environments by creating virtual platforms that connect residents with essential services and opportunities. For instance, in the medical realm, it could be used to enhance telemedicine platforms by providing remote access to healthcare services, reducing the need for physical travel, and ensuring that residents in underserved areas can receive the care they need (Hollander & Carr, 2020). On other fronts, the metaverse can be deployed in the education sector, for instance, in creating virtual classrooms to allow for continuity in learning. Metaverse also holds immense potential in transforming the work environment by enabling the creation of remote workspaces; thus promoting equitable access to employment opportunities regardless of geographical location (Bailenson, 2021). These benefits in the education, health, employment, and other sectors also help in reducing the need for regular travel, and building more physical buildings, thus, in the long run promoting the sustainability agendas.

In addition to those direct applications, the metaverse is also very instrumental in indirect ways such as in facilitating inclusive urban planning processes by providing accessible tools and platforms for community engagement. It also provides diverse platforms such as virtual workshops and public consultation arenas for urban designers to obtain valuable input from residents and stakeholders, ensuring that urban development reflects the needs and aspirations of diverse communities (Rosenfeld, 2021).

B. *Reducing congestion*

Regarding urban congestion detailed in the previous section, the metaverse could help in the mitigation process by offering alternatives to physical travel and promoting more efficient transportation systems. For example, virtual workspaces and meeting platforms can minimize the need for daily commutes, thereby alleviating traffic congestion and its associated environmental impacts (Bailenson, 2021).

Coupled with other technologies such as AI, IoT, and Blockchain, et cetera, the metaverse can robustly enhance the development of intelligent transportation systems that optimize traffic flows and improve the efficiency of public transit. This could be achieved by integrating real-time data and advanced analytics approaches, which dynamically adjust traffic signals, route planning, and transportation schedules to minimize congestion and reduce travel times (Zhang et al., 2023).

C. *Improving social interactions*

Another indisputable benefit about the metaverse is its ability to foster social interactions in and within the urban environments. It does this by fostering new forms of communication in the virtual realm, collaboration, and community-building. The virtual public spaces within the metaverse are increasingly observed to provide opportunities for social interaction and civic engagement. For instance, the metaverse by Meta is fashioned in a way that users can interact in an immersive way while donning avatars of their liking. This way, they can freely interact without limitations of color, race, gender, age, or geographical location. With the metaverse, it is therefore very possible to connect residents with shared interests and facilitate the development of social capital.

In addition, it has been proven that the metaverse has the potential to significantly influence the creation of inclusive and accessible environments that cater to the needs of the diverse urban demographic. By employing VR/AR technologies, urban designers can develop adaptable public spaces that appeal to a wide range of users, including individuals with disabilities, older adults, and families with young children (Winn, 2020).

D. *Enhancing urban experiences and services*

One of the most profound benefits that the metaverse avails to urban residents is enhancing their experiences and services through immersive technologies such as VR/AR. It does this by providing rich, interactive platforms for information, entertainment, interactions, and engagement. To put this in perspective, it is becoming common in diverse cities for cultural activities and services to be performed in the virtual realm. A practical demonstration of this is the use of the metaverse as a platform for immersive cultural experiences, such as virtual museum tours, art exhibitions, and live performances. The main objective of such is to enable residents to access and enjoy cultural amenities without the need for physical travel or physical presence (Adato, 2020).

In addition, the VR and AR technologies which are very pertinent for the metaverse can be employed to improve the delivery of urban services by providing intuitive, user-friendly interfaces for accessing information and resources. Such has been tried and tested in Seoul City, where a sizable number of public services are now accessible in the virtual realm after the city fashioned its own form of metaverse. Another case is how AR applications are being used to overlay contextual information on the physical environment, such as directions, public transit schedules, or points of interest, making it easier for residents to navigate and engage with their urban surroundings.

Examples of metaverse applications in urban life

Several examples highlighted in the following demonstrate how the metaverse is already being used to address urban challenges.

1. *Virtual Singapore*

The Virtual Singapore project is an astounding example of how the metaverse's can be exploited for urban planning and development. The

Singaporean's initiative is fashioned to create a digital twin of the city, which would enable different stakeholders such as the urban planners, architects, local governments, and residents to visualize and interact with the urban environment in a virtual setting (City2City, 2022). This platform allows for data-driven decision-making, improved communication among stakeholders, and more inclusive planning processes, ultimately enhancing the city's livability and sustainability status.

2. *Sidewalk Toronto*

   The Sidewalk Toronto project is a collaboration between Alphabet's Sidewalk Labs and Waterfront Toronto aimed at creating a smart city district that leveraged digital technologies, including the metaverse, to address urban challenges such as housing affordability, sustainability, and mobility (Flynn & Valverde, 2019). Although the project was ultimately discontinued due to concerns about data privacy and governance (Jacobs, 2022), it highlights the potential of the metaverse and smart city technologies to transform urban life.

3. *CityVR in Helsinki*

   In Helsinki, Finland, a unique project dubbed the CityVR project was proposed in 2018, and it aimed to use the VR technology to provide an immersive, interactive platform for urban planning and community engagement. With this project, it was anticipated that urban residents would manage to actively visualize any proposed development initiative in the city, and provide feedback in a virtual setting. Such an approach does not only foster a more inclusive and transparent planning process but it also ensures that urban development reflects the needs and aspirations of diverse communities living within the city.

4. *Neom, Saudi Arabia*

   In Saudi Arabia, the deployment of the metaverse is showcased by Neom City located in Tabuk Province. Among the anticipated highlights of the planned city include the integration of the metaverse in urban design and services. Further, this project aims to create a futuristic, sustainable, and technologically advanced urban environment that seamlessly blends digital and physical spaces, hence providing the residents with an immersive experience. By incorporating the metaverse into its development plans, Neom intends to foster innovation, enhance the quality of life, and create new economic opportunities for its residents.

5. *Virtual reality art exhibitions*

   The availability of numerous, advanced technologies has prompted many cities around the world to leverage the metaverse to create virtual art exhibitions and immersive cultural experiences. A case in point is the Louvre Museum in Paris which launched a VR experience in 2019 that allows users to explore the museum and interact with its famous artworks in a virtual setting (Katz, 2019). Another example is the *Museum of Other Realities* in the metaverse offers a platform for artists to showcase their work and engage with audiences in novel ways, transcending the limitations of physical galleries (Realities, 2023).

6. *AR-enhanced public spaces*
    The application of AR technologies is gradually gaining traction in the urban realm, with several cities already experimenting with it to enhance public spaces and urban service delivery. A practical example is the New York City which has created and deployed a mobile app dubbed Time-Looper which provides users with AR-guided walking tours of the city (Timelooper, 2015). The app overlays historical scenes and information onto the physical environment, giving the users an immersive and unforgettable experience. Another citable example is in Barcelona, where another AR-based mobile app titled "Past View" has been created that allows users to explore the city's historical sites through an immersive, interactive experience that combines the digital and physical realms.

    The earlier examples showcase the capability of the metaverse to offer amicable solutions to the challenges of urban life and serve as a foundation for future applications in urban environments. By leveraging the power of immersive technologies such as VR and AR, coupled with other emerging technologies such as Blockchain, AI, Cloud Computing, Digital Twins, and others, cities can transform urban experiences and services, leading to more inclusive, sustainable, and resilient urban spaces.

Benefits and challenges of using the metaverse in urban life

The potential of the metaverse in revolutionizing urban life by addressing diverse challenges while unlocking new opportunities can never be overstated. However, there it also possesses some challenges that require amicable and urgent solutions if it is to become successful. In view of that knowledge, this section explores the potential benefits and challenges associated with the use of the metaverse in urban life, offering examples of how these challenges have been addressed and lessons learned for future implementations.

Potential benefits of the metaverse in urban life

1. *Improving urban services*
    The metaverse can improve the efficiency and effectiveness of different urban services, including healthcare, education, transportation, and utilities to public safety, et cetera. A practical example of this is the use of digital twins of urban infrastructure by city managers to help them monitor and regulate energy consumption, water distribution, and waste management systems in real-time (Batty, 2018). Additionally, the metaverse can enable remote access to diverse essential services, such as land registry, telemedicine, and virtual education, thus, minimizing the strain on physical infrastructure and improving the quality of life for urban dwellers.
2. *Increasing social connectivity*
    In the era where a sense of community and interpersonal relationships has been greatly affected by the emergence of technologies, capitalist

ideologies, and the nature of occupations, the metaverse is anticipated to bring some paradigm shift, especially regarding interactions. In particular, it is expected to continue fostering a sense of community and social connectivity, as people can interact in an immersive way in the virtual realm (Allam, Sharifi, et al., 2022). By providing virtual spaces and platforms for social interaction, cultural exchange, gaming and adventure, and civic engagement, the metaverse can enable more meaningful connections among urban residents, transcending physical barriers and fostering a sense of belonging.

3. *Reducing environmental impact*

The metaverse offers numerous platforms and virtual spaces that have the potential to positively contribute to more sustainable urban development. For example, it offers a potent platform for immersive virtual meetings and remote working, which would translate into a significant reduction in the need for private cars and travel; hence, a reduction in greenhouse gas. On the issue of wanton consumption of natural resources, the metaverse can help reduce the need for travel, physical office spaces, and physical entertainment joints among other such developments, hence, fostering a reduction in resource use. Similarly, by enabling immersive tourism experiences, it can alleviate the environmental pressures of mass tourism on urban destinations, hence, promoting conservation and regeneration efforts. Additionally, the metaverse can facilitate the sharing of resources, such as energy and water, through smart city applications that optimize the use and distribution of these resources.

Challenges and limitations of the metaverse in urban life

1. *Equity and inclusivity*

The widespread adoption of the metaverse in urban life is nevertheless all positive, as it has been observed to raise pertinent concerns about its potential to exacerbate social exclusion (Bosworth & Gregg, 2022). This is particularly due to the eminent digital divide that already exists and would be worsened by the cost of securing necessary tools and devices such as headsets that would allow people to access the metaverse. Ensuring equitable access to the metaverse and its benefits requires addressing disparities in digital infrastructure, affordability, and digital literacy among urban populations. Strategies for promoting digital equity could include initiatives such as conscious public investment in broadband infrastructure, digital skills training, and targeted subsidies for low-income households (Maceviciute & Wilson, 2018).

2. *Privacy and security*

The metaverse's reliance on third parties for data collection, storage, and analysis has been argued to raise concerns about privacy and security, particularly regarding private data (Kitchin, 2016). It then becomes important to ensure that the data used in the metaverse does not compromise individual privacy. To achieve this, robust data governance frameworks encompassing factors such as transparent data policies, secured data storage, and anonymization techniques are necessary. It would also be important to address cybersecurity risks associated with the metaverse, thus, promoting trust and transparency. Addressing the privacy concerns would further encourage urban residents to share data and participate in making the metaverse even more robust and better.

Addressing challenges in the metaverse

Several initiatives could be deployed to help address the challenges associated with using the metaverse in urban environments. Among those include the Digital Equity Initiative in Portland, Oregon which aims to bridge the digital divide by providing affordable broadband access, digital literacy training, and access to devices for low-income residents (Portland Government, 2023). Another initiative worth noting is the EU General Data Protection Regulation (GDPR) which provides a comprehensive framework for ensuring data privacy and security in the digital realm, including the metaverse (Hoofnagle et al., 2019).

Informing the design and implementation of the metaverse in urban settings

Addressing the challenges associated with the metaverse in urban life necessitates a collaborative approach that involves various stakeholders, including governments, technology corporations, urban planners, community organizations, and other players. By drawing on lessons learned from previous initiatives and considering the unique context of each urban setting, these stakeholders can develop tailored solutions that maximize the benefits of the metaverse while minimizing potential drawbacks.

Participatory design

Involving urban residents in the decision-making concerning the design and implementation of the metaverse is essential for ensuring encompasses and aligns with their needs and expectations (Bingöl, 2022). Participatory design approaches, such as workshops, focus groups, and cocreation sessions, can help gather valuable insights into user preferences and concerns, leading to more inclusive and user-friendly metaverse solutions. For example, the Smart Dubai initiative actively engages citizens in the development of smart city applications through regular public consultations and feedback mechanisms, hence, drawing the city closer to achieving the four pillars (seamless, efficient, safe, and personalized) of its strategic plan (Smart City Dubai, 2021).

Policy and regulatory frameworks

Developing comprehensive policy and regulatory frameworks can help address challenges related to concerns such as equity, inclusivity, privacy, security, and affordability in the metaverse. In this regard, the frameworks need to be formatted in a way that promotes digital inclusion by ensuring affordable access to digital tools and infrastructure and promoting digital literacy among diverse urban demographics. Moreover, they should identify and establish clear guidelines for data privacy, security, and governance, including the use of anonymization techniques and the implementation of cybersecurity measures to foster the security and privacy of the users.

Interdisciplinary collaboration

The metaverse's potential to transform urban environments requires interdisciplinary collaboration between technology providers, urban planners and designers, policymakers, community organizations, and other potential stakeholders. The aspect of working together between these stakeholders can ensure that the metaverse is designed and implemented in a way that complements existing urban systems and enhances the overall quality of life for urban residents. For instance, the collaboration observed between the city of Helsinki, Finland, and the technology company ZOAN has resulted in the creation of a virtual Helsinki, which has been used for urban planning, cultural events, and tourism (Hämäläinen, 2021).

Case studies of metaverse in urban life

Virtual Helsinki: Urban planning and cultural events

Virtual Helsinki, which is borne from a cordial collaboration between the City of Helsinki and technology company ZOAN, is a classical illustration of how the metaverse can be utilized for urban planning and designing, as well as for cultural events (Zoan, 2023). The initiative provides a 3D digital twin of this Finnish capital, which allows planners to visualize proposed developments and assess their impact on the urban environment before implementation. Additionally, Virtual Helsinki has hosted various cultural events, such as virtual concerts (for instance, the Helsinki Biennial Facebook Open Arts VR experience) and art exhibitions (e.g., at Amos Rex), enhancing social connectivity and access to cultural experiences for residents and visitors alike (Zoan, 2023). However, the implementation of this initiative has encountered several challenges including ensuring that the platform remains up-to-date and accurately reflects the city's evolving landscape.

The New York City virtual hub: Accessibility and inclusivity

The New York City Virtual Hub (NYCVH) is a metaverse initiative aimed at enhancing accessibility and inclusivity in urban life in New York City. The platform provides a virtual environment where users can actively access essential city services, attend virtual public meetings, and participate in community events, devoid of both physical or financial barriers. The NYCVH has been successful in increasing civic engagement and fostering a sense of belonging among residents. Those benefits notwithstanding, the initiative is crowded by issues such as digital literacy concerns and unequal access to relevant technologies.

Virtual Singapore: Data-driven urban decision-making

Virtual Singapore is a government-led initiative that leverages the metaverse to facilitate data-driven urban decision-making (City2City, 2022). The platform benefits from the 3D models of the city coupled with real-time data on various urban systems, such as transportation, energy, and public services, enabling planners and policymakers to make informed decisions based on comprehensive data insights. While this initiative has been largely successful and has demonstrated immeasurable potential in streamlining urban processes and improving service delivery, concerns regarding data privacy and security remain as challenges that need to be addressed.

Seoul's metaverse city project: Enhancing public spaces and fostering innovation

Seoul's Metaverse City Project which was launched in 2021 aims to create a digital twin of the city, focusing on fostering public spaces and enhancing unmetered innovation (Squires, 2021). The project combines both virtual and augmented reality technologies to transform urban spaces, providing immersive experiences and interactive services for residents and visitors alike. Beyond that, the initiative targets to support start-ups and small business enterprises (SMEs) by creating a virtual incubation platform where they can collaborate, develop, and showcase their products and services. Amid those positives, a few issues like the need for equitable access to the platform and addressing potential social isolation resulting from excessive reliance on virtual interactions need to be proactively and urgently addressed.

Virtual Barcelona: Collaborative urban planning and citizen engagement

Virtual Barcelona is an initiative that utilizes the metaverse for collaborative urban planning and citizen engagement (Eggimann, 2022). The platform features a 3D model of the city, allowing urban planners, architects, and citizens to participate in the planning process by visualizing proposed developments and providing feedback on their potential impact on diverse issues such as the urban environment. This collaborative approach has led to increased community involvement and participation, leading to the development of more informed, sustainable urban plans. However, the implementation of this initiative has faced challenges ranging from unequal representation of locals in decision-making, and the notably skewed accessibility of citizens with varying levels of digital literacy.

Virtual Melbourne: Emergency management and climate adaptation

In the City of Melbourne, a unique smart-oriented initiative dubbed Virtual Melbourne that benefits from the emergence of the metaverse was borne back in 2020. The project aims to facilitate emergency management and climate adaptation efforts within the city. The platform integrates real-time data on weather, traffic, and infrastructure with a 3D model of the city, enabling emergency teams to assess potential risks, develop response strategies, and coordinate efforts during disaster events without endangering their own lives (City of Melbourne, 2023). Additionally, the platform supports climate adaptation initiatives by allowing planners to model and assess the impacts of climate change scenarios on the urban environment, informing the development of adaptive strategies. Challenges associated with this application include maintaining data accuracy and ensuring that the platform is scalable and adaptable to a rapidly changing urban landscape.

Virtual London: Heritage preservation and cultural tourism

Virtual London is a metaverse-based project that aims to foster diverse heritage preservation and cultural tourism (University College London, 2023). The platform comprises a digital twin of the city, complete with historical landmarks and cultural sites, allowing users to explore and learn about London's rich cultural heritage. From the assessment done by different stakeholders, the Virtual London initiative has been successful in providing accessible and immersive experiences for tourists and residents, fostering greater appreciation for the city's history and cultural assets. However, the initiative faces challenges related to content curation and ensuring that the platform accurately represents the diverse cultural heritage of the city while respecting the rights and interests of the various stakeholders involved.

Ethical and social implications of the metaverse in urban life

After the difficult period warranted by the COVID-19 pandemic, the metaverse, as an immersive digital environment has proven to hold significant potential for transforming urban life, especially in frontiers such as work environment, transport, and social interactions. However, its integration into the urban fabric raises pertinent ethical and social concerns that warrant careful consideration. Weighty issues such as privacy, data ownership, and cultural sensitivity are particularly salient in this context, as they directly impact the well-being and agency of urban dwellers.

Regarding privacy, there are real and salient concerns that have been reported, not only in respect to the metaverse but also in relation to smart technologies. On this, it is worthwhile to note that privacy is a critical ethical concern in the metaverse, as the collection, storage, and use of personal data becomes an integral part of the digital experience. As a result, concerns about the ability of people to track users' movements, preferences, and interactions within the metaverse raise questions about surveillance, consent, and the potential misuse of data by governments, corporations, and malicious actors (Gupta et al., 2023). This concern is essentially pertinent for marginalized and vulnerable demographics, who may be disproportionately affected by privacy breaches or targeted surveillance (Koohang et al., 2023). One approach to addressing privacy concerns in the metaverse is the implementation of robust data protection frameworks that prioritize user consent, transparency, and accountability. For example, the European Union's General Data Protection Regulation (GDPR) discussed earlier offers a comprehensive model for data protection, with strict requirements for obtaining consent, providing notice, and ensuring the right to erasure (Hoofnagle et al., 2019). Adapting these principles to the metaverse context can help protect users' privacy and promote trust in the digital environment.

Data ownership is another ethical challenge that confronts the metaverse, especially in the view that the lines between creators, users, and platform providers continue to become increasingly blurred. As a result, questions of intellectual property, copyright, and fair use arise, with implications for creative expression, economic opportunity, and the equitable distribution of resources (Sadowski, 2020). Data ownership concerns are particularly pertinent to the marginalized and vulnerable groups within the urban society as these often lack the resources or legal expertise to navigate complex intellectual property frameworks. As such, they could be susceptible to exploitation or exclusion from the benefits that would accrue from the implementation of metaverse (Lubin, 2022). To address data ownership issues, initiatives such as the use of decentralized technologies such as blockchain may become inevitable. With these, it is believed that issues concerning transparent, tamper-proof records of digital assets and transactions may be enhanced (Aks et al., 2022). A practical example of this includes the Decentraland which is a virtual world built on the Ethereum blockchain that allows users to own, trade, and monetize virtual land and digital assets using nonfungible tokens (NFTs) (Decentraland, 2023). This approach could provide a more equitable distribution of resources and empower users to retain control over their creations in the metaverse.

Cultural sensitivity is another notable concern in the metaverse prompted by the convergence of diverse communities and cultural perspectives in the virtual space. Among pertinent concern includes issues of representation, appropriation with the digital realm, and also the possibilities of exclusion especially of marginalized and vulnerable population. Any compromise on those can escalate to potential negative consequences on social cohesion, identity formation, and intercultural understanding. In urban contexts, where diverse populations coexist, it is paramount to ensure that digital tools, including the metaverse foster inclusivity, respect, and positive cultural exchange. One approach that can be adopted to address cultural sensitivity in the metaverse is through promoting participatory design processes, which involve community members in the development and decision-making of digital spaces (Lv et al., 2022). For example, the Virtual Harlem project, a digital recreation of the Harlem Renaissance, sought to engage local residents, educators, and cultural institutions in the curation and interpretation of cultural assets, ensuring that the platform accurately and respectfully represented the community's history and identity (Sosnoski et al., 2006). Such approaches can promote cultural sensitivity, ignite a sense of ownership and belonging, and contribute to social cohesion in the metaverse.

Opportunities for collaboration and cocreation in metaverse and urban life

The aspect of collaboration and cocreation has been elusive due to factors like geographical distances, language barriers, and others. However, the emergence of the metaverse is argued to help overcome those challenges, by offering virtual spaces and environments to people with shared objectives and visions (Allam, Sharifi, et al., 2022). As such, it is now playing a critical role in helping to shape urban environments in more inclusive, equitable, and sustainable ways. Through the aforementioned platforms, diverse stakeholders such as residents, policymakers, businesses, and researchers get unique opportunities to contribute to the designing and implementation of the urban environment as per the aspirations of different communities and create spaces that foster innovation, social cohesion, and resilience.

One primary benefit of collaborative and cocreative processes is the ability to draw upon the collective intelligence and expertise of diverse stakeholders (Surowiecki, 2004). This can lead to more informed decision-making and the generation of innovative ideas, which can ultimately influence the quality and sustainability of urban environments. For example, crowd-sourced data and citizen science initiatives have the potential to provide valuable insights into local issues, such as air quality, mobility patterns, resource consumption, and access to services, et cetera, which can inform the design and implementation of urban interventions (Haklay, 2013).

Inclusive cocreation processes are further believed to have the potential to promote social equity and empowerment by giving voice to marginalized and underrepresented communities. By involving these groups in the design and implementation phases of the metaverse, urban planners, designers, and developers can better understand and internalize their needs and aspirations, hence, creating spaces that are more accessible, welcoming, and culturally appropriate. Moreover, participation in cocreation processes can foster a sense of ownership and belonging among urban dwellers, which can contribute to social cohesion and resilience and overall acceptance of local projects (Winn, 2020). One example of a successful cocreation process in the context of urban development is the High Line in New York City. This elevated public park, built on a disused railway line, was developed through extensive collaboration between local residents, businesses, nonprofit organizations, and government agencies (Argüelles et al., 2021). The project has been widely praised for its innovative design, environmental sustainability, and positive impact on the surrounding neighborhoods.

Another notable example to showcase the benefits of cocreation in urban settings is the transformation of Medellín, Colombia, from a city plagued by violence and social inequality to a global model of urban innovation and social inclusion (Naef, 2020). This process was made possible by the collaborative efforts of local government, community organizations, businesses, and residents, whose concerted efforts helped to develop and implement a range of innovative initiatives, such as the construction of a cable car system to improve mobility for marginalized communities, and the creation of public spaces that foster social interaction and cultural expression.

Within the metaverse, cocreation processes can involve diverse stakeholders in the designing and implementation of digital environments and applications, ensuring that they are responsive to the needs and aspirations of different user groups. For instance, the earlier discussed Virtual Harlem project, which involved the participation of local residents, educators, and cultural institutions, can serve as a model for how collaborative processes can contribute to the development of culturally sensitive and inclusive digital environments. Moreover, cocreation processes can leverage the unique ubiquitousness of the metaverse, such as real-time collaboration, virtual prototyping, and immersive simulations, to inform the quality and effectiveness of urban interventions (Dwivedi et al., 2022).

Conclusion

The metaverse presents a unique opportunity to address urban challenges and improve the livability status of urban residents by leveraging its potential for immersive experiences, real-time collaboration, and cocreation. It also presents numerous opportunities for social interaction, public participation, and mitigation of social ills such as discrimination based on color, income level, and geographical distances. However, as discussed earlier, the metaverse is not immune to some obvious challenges such as ethical and moral concerns, especially concerning privacy, data ownership, and cultural sensitivity. Those need to be urgently and comprehensively addressed if the full potential and benefits of the metaverse are to be realized. In particular, it would be critical to ensure that marginalized and vulnerable populations are protected against the aforementioned issues, as they are the most susceptible cadre.

From the earlier discussion, the plight of those groups could be addressed by focusing on the potential of the metaverse to enhance collaboration and cocreation, thus giving them an opportunity to participate in the design and implementation of digital spaces and applications. By fostering inclusive and participatory processes, the metaverse can contribute to the development of urban environments that are more equitable, sustainable, and responsive to the needs and aspirations of different communities.

As the metaverse continues to evolve, enlarge, and intersect with urban environments, it will be critical for future research to prioritize the numerous ethical and social considerations identified in this chapter and, hence, contribute to proposing further solutions to those setbacks. Such proposals could include identifying and contributing toward the development of robust data protection frameworks, the exploration of decentralized technologies for equitable resource distribution, and the incorporation of participatory design processes that foster inclusivity and respect for cultural diversity. In addition, future research could investigate the unique affordances of the metaverse in the context of urban planning and design, exploring how immersive simulations, virtual prototyping, and real-time collaboration could enhance the quality and effectiveness of urban interventions.

References

Adato, L. (13 July 2020). *Distributed computing—When everyone is working from home*. Orange Matter. Retrieved 12th September 2021 from https://orangematter.solarwinds.com/2020/07/13/distributed-computing-when-everyone-is-working-from-home/.

Aks, S. M. Y., Karmila, M., Givan, B., Hendratna, G., Setiawan, H. S., Putra, A. S., Winarno, S. H., Kurniawan, T. A., Simorangkir, Y. N., Taufiq, R., Herawaty, M. T., & Asep. (2022). A review of blockchain for security data privacy with metaverse. In *2022 international conference on ICT for smart society (ICISS), (10-11 Aug. 2022)*.

Allam, Z. (2012). Sustainable architecture: Utopia or feasible reality? *Journal of Biourbanism*, 2(1) 47–61.

Allam, Z. (2019). *Cities and the digital revolution: Aligning technology and humanity*. Springer Nature.

Allam, Z. (2021). Big data, artificial intelligence and the rise of autonomous smart cities. In *The rise of autonomous smart cities* (pp. 7–30). Cham: Palgrave Macmillan.

Allam, Z., Bibri, S. E., Chabaud, D., & Moreno, C. (2022a). The '15-minute city' concept can shape a net-zero urban future. *Humanities and Social Sciences Communications*, 9(1) 126. https://doi.org/10.1057/s41599-022-01145-0.

Allam, Z., Bibri, S. E., Chabaud, D., & Moreno, C. (2022b). The theoretical, practical, and technological foundations of the 15-minute city model: Proximity and its environmental, social and economic benefits for sustainability. *Energies*, 15(16) 6042. https://doi.org/10.3390/en15166042.

Allam, Z., Jones, D., & Thondoo, M. (2020). Decarbonization and urban sustainability. In *Cities and climate change* (pp. 33–54). Cham: Palgrave Macmillan.

Allam, Z., Sharifi, A., Bibri, S. E., Jones, D. S., & Krogstie, J. (2022). The metaverse as a virtual form of smart cities: Opportunities and challenges for environmental, economic, and social sustainability in urban futures. *Smart Cities*, 5(3) 771–801. https://doi.org/10.3390/smartcities5030040.

Argüelles, L., Cole, H. V. S., & Anguelovski, I. (2021). Rail-to-park transformations in 21st century modern cities: Green gentrification on track. *Environment and Planning E: Nature and Space*, 5(2) 810–834. https://doi.org/10.1177/25148486211010064.

Bailenson, J. N. (2021). Nonverbal overload: A theoretical argument for the causes of zoom fatigue. *Technology, Mind, and Behavior*, *2*. https://doi.org/10.1037/tmb0000030.

Batty, M. (2018). Artificial intelligence and smart cities. *Environment and Planning B: Urban Analytics and City Science*, *45*(1) 3–6. https://doi.org/10.1177/2399808317751169.

Bibri, S. E., Allam, Z., & Krogstie, J. (2022). The metaverse as a virtual form of data-driven smart urbanism: Platformization and its underlying processes, institutional dimensions, and disruptive impacts. *Computational Urban Science*, *2*, 24. https://doi.org/10.1007/s43762-022-00051-0.

Bingöl, E. S. (2022). Citizen participation in smart sustainable cities. In E. A. Babaoğlu, & O. Kulaç (Eds.), *Research anthology on citizen engagement and activism for social change* (pp. 967–987). IGI Global. https://doi.org/10.4018/978-1-7998-4978-0.ch023.

Bosworth, A., & Gregg, N. (27 September 2022). Building the metaverse responsibly. *Meta*. Retrieved 22nd April 2022 from https://about.fb.com/news/2021/09/building-the-metaverse-responsibly/.

Brandon, T. (6 September 2020). *White and brown concrete buildings*. Retrieved 11th June 2023 from https://unsplash.com/photos/Gk2wag_XpVY.

City of Melbourne. (2023). *Virtual attractions*. City of Melbourne. Retrieved 15th May 2023 from https://www.visitmelbourne.com/see-and-do/virtual-attractions.

City2City. (24 April 2022). Virtual Singapore: A digital 'twin' for planning. *UNDP*. Retrieved 15th March 2023 from https://city2city.network/virtual-singapore-digital-twin-planning-innovation-type-institutional-pioneer.

Cornwell, E. Y., & Waite, L. J. (2009). Social disconnectedness, perceived isolation, and health among older adults. *Journal of Health and Social Behavior*, *50*(1) 31–48. https://doi.org/10.1177/002214650905000103.

Decentraland. (2023). *Welcome to decentraland*. Decentraland. Retrieved 15th May 2023 from https://decentraland.org/.

Dwivedi, Y. K., Hughes, L., Baabdullah, A. M., Ribeiro-Navarrete, S., Giannakis, M., Al-Debei, M. M., Dennehy, D., Metri, B., Buhalis, D., Cheung, C. M. K., Conboy, K., Doyle, R., Dubey, R., Dutot, V., Felix, R., Goyal, D. P., Gustafsson, A., Hinsch, C., Jebabli, I., … Wamba, S. F. (2022). Metaverse beyond the hype: Multidisciplinary perspectives on emerging challenges, opportunities, and agenda for research, practice and policy. *International Journal of Information Management*, *66*, 102542. https://doi.org/10.1016/j.ijinfomgt.2022.102542.

Eggimann, S. (2022). The potential of implementing superblocks for multifunctional street use in cities. *Nature Sustainability*, *5*(5) 406–414. https://doi.org/10.1038/s41893-022-00855-2.

Falchuk, B., Loeb, S., & Neff, R. (2018). The social metaverse: Battle for privacy. *IEEE Technology and Society Magazine*, *37*(2) 52–61. https://doi.org/10.1109/MTS.2018.2826060.

Fleming, S. (19 February 2019). *Commuters in these cities spend more than 8 days a year stuck in traffic*. World Economic Forum. Retrieved 20th January 2021 from https://www.weforum.org/agenda/2019/02/commuters-in-these-cities-spend-more-than-8-days-a-year-stuck-in-traffic/.

Flynn, A., & Valverde, M. (2019). Planning on the waterfront: Setting the agenda for Toronto's 'smart city' project. *Planning Theory & Practice*, *20*(5) 769–775. https://doi.org/10.1080/14649357.2019.1676566.

Gupta, A., Khan, H. U., Nazir, S., Shafiq, M., & Shabaz, M. (2023). Metaverse security: Issues, challenges and a viable ZTA model. *Electronics*, *12*(2) 391. https://doi.org/10.3390/electronics12020391.

Haklay, M. (2013). Citizen science and volunteered geographic information: Overview and typology of participation. In D. Sui, S. Elwood, & M. Goodchild (Eds.), *Crowdsourcing geographic knowledge: Volunteered geographic information (VGI) in theory and practice* (pp. 105–122). Netherlands: Springer. https://doi.org/10.1007/978-94-007-4587-2_7.

Hämäläinen, M. (2021). Urban development with dynamic digital twins in Helsinki city. *IET Smart Cities*, *3*(4) 201–210. https://doi.org/10.1049/smc2.12015.

Hidayati, I., Tan, W., & Yamu, C. (2021). Conceptualizing mobility inequality: Mobility and accessibility for the marginalized. *Journal of Planning Literature*, *36*(4) 492–507. https://doi.org/10.1177/08854122211012898.

Hollander, J. E., & Carr, B. G. (2020). Virtually perfect? Telemedicine for Covid-19. *The New England Journal of Medicine*, *382*(18) 1679–1681. https://doi.org/10.1056/NEJMp2003539.

Holt-Lunstad, J., Smith, T. B., Baker, M., Harris, T., & Stephenson, D. (2015). Loneliness and social isolation as risk factors for mortality: A meta-analytic review. *Perspectives on Psychological Science*, *10*(2) 227–237. https://doi.org/10.1177/1745691614568352.

Hoofnagle, C. J., van der Sloot, B., & Borgesius, F. Z. (2019). The European Union general data protection regulation: What it is and what it means. *Information & Communications Technology Law*, *28*(1) 65–98. https://doi.org/10.1080/13600834.2019.1573501.

Jacobs, K. (20 June 2022). *Toronto wants to kill the smart city forever: The city wants to get right what Sidewalk Labs got so wrong*. MIT Technology Review. Retrieved 1st July 2022 from https://www.technologyreview.com/2022/06/29/1054005/toronto-kill-the-smart-city/.

Katz, B. (18 June 2019). The Louvre's first VR experience lets visitors get close to the 'Mona Lisa'. *Smithsonian Magazine*. Retrieved 15th May 2023 from https://www.smithsonianmag.com/smart-news/louvres-first-vr-experience-lets-visitors-get-close-mona-lisa-180972435/.

Kawachi, I., & Berkman, L. (2014). Social capital, social cohesion, and health. In *Social epidemiology* (pp. 290–319). https://doi.org/10.1093/med/9780195377903.003.0008.

Kitchin, R. (2016). The ethics of smart cities and urban science. *Philosophical Transactions of the Royal Society A: Mathematical, Physical and Engineering Sciences*, *374*(2083) 1–15. https://doi.org/10.1098/rsta.2016.0115.

Koohang, A., Nord, J. H., Ooi, K.-B., Tan, G. W.-H., Al-Emran, M., Aw, E. C.-X., Baabdullah, A. M., Buhalis, D., Cham, T.-H., Dennis, C., Dutot, V., Dwivedi, Y. K., Hughes, L., Mogaji, E., Pandey, N., Phau, I., Raman, R., Sharma, A., Sigala, M., … Wong, L.-W. (2023). Shaping the metaverse into reality: A holistic multidisciplinary understanding of opportunities, challenges, and avenues for future investigation. *Journal of Computer Information Systems*, 1–31. https://doi.org/10.1080/08874417.2023.2165197.

Lubin, A. (26 April 2022). Governance in the metaverse. *DataSphere*. Retrieved 12th February 2023 from https://www.thedatasphere.org/news/governance-in-the-metaverse/.

Lv, Z., Shang, W.-L., & Guizani, M. (2022). Impact of digital twins and metaverse on cities: History, current situation, and application perspectives. *Applied Sciences*, *12*(24).

Maceviciute, E., & Wilson, T. (2018). Digital means for reducing digital inequality: Literature review. *Informing Science: The International Journal of an Emerging Transdiscipline*, *21*, 269–287. https://doi.org/10.28945/4117.

Mackett, R. L. (2014). The health implications of inequalities in travel. *Journal of Transport & Health*, *1*(3) 202–209. https://doi.org/10.1016/j.jth.2014.07.002.

McCarthy, N. (10 March 2020). Traffic congestion costs U.S. cities billions of dollars every year [infographic]. *Forbes*. Retrieved 20th January 2022 from.

Naef, P. (2020). Resilience as a city brand: The cases of the Comuna 13 and Moravia in Medellin, Colombia. *Sustainability*, *12*(20) 8469. https://www.mdpi.com/2071-1050/12/20/8469.

Nijman, J., & Wei, Y. D. (2020). Urban inequalities in the 21st century economy. *Applied Geography*, *117*, 102188. https://doi.org/10.1016/j.apgeog.2020.102188.

Pamucar, D., Deveci, M., Gokasar, I., Delen, D., Köppen, M., & Pedrycz, W. (2023). Evaluation of metaverse integration alternatives of sharing economy in transportation using fuzzy Schweizer-

Sklar based ordinal priority approach. *Decision Support Systems*, 113944. https://doi.org/10.1016/j.dss.2023.113944.

Portland Government. (2023). *Digital equity strategic initiatives program*. Portland Government. https://www.portland.gov/bps/com-tech/digital-equity.

Realities, M. O. O. (2023). Museum of other realities. *Museumor*. Retrieved 15th May 2023 from https://www.museumor.com/.

Rosenberg, L. (2022). Regulation of the metaverse: A roadmap. In *6th international conference on virtual and augmented reality simulations (ICVARS 2022), Brisbane, Australia*.

Sadowski, J. (2020). Who owns the future city? Phases of technological urbanism and shifts in sovereignty. *Urban Studies*, *58*(8) 1732–1744. https://doi.org/10.1177/0042098020913427.

Smart City Dubai. (2021). *Smart Dubai 2021 strategy*. Smart Dubai. Retrieved 15th May 2023 from https://u.ae/en/about-the-uae/strategies-initiatives-and-awards/strategies-plans-and-visions/strategies-plans-and-visions-untill-2021/smart-dubai-2021-strategy.

Sorkin, S. (5 April 2019). *People wearing VR smartphone headset*. Unsplash. Retrieved 11th June 2023 from https://unsplash.com/photos/NN9HQkDgguc.

Sosnoski, J., Jones, S., Carter, B., McAllister, K., Moeller, R., & Mir, R. (2006). *Virtual Harlem as a collaborative learning environment: A project of the University of Illinois at Chicago's Electronic Visualization Lab* (pp. 1289–1320). https://doi.org/10.1007/978-1-4020-3803-7_54.

Squires, C. (21 November 2021). Seoul will be the first city government to join the metaverse. *Quartz*. Retrieved 4h November 2021 from https://qz.com/2086353/seoul-is-developing-a-metaverse-government-platform/.

Surowiecki, J. (2004). *The wisdom of crowds: Why the many are smarter than the few and how collective wisdom shapes business, economies, societies, and nations*. Doubleday & Co.

Theo. (5 August 2021). Digital twins, IoT and the metaverse. *Medium*. Retrieved 3rd December 2021 from https://medium.com/@theo/digital-twins-iot-and-the-metaverse-b4efbfc01112.

Timelooper. (2015). Timelooper travel. *Built in New York City*. Retrieved 15th May 2023 from https://www.builtinnyc.com/company/timelooper?__cf_chl_tk=9FamoKrmP7s_N.NNp1dw0wJDoZbemJHXBPH53SCHDfw-1684163425-0-gaNycGzNCyU.

Torgonskaya, A. (19 February 2023). *A row of bicycles parked next to a building*. Unsplash. Retrieved 13th June 2023 from https://unsplash.com/photos/trvwBgOol2U.

University College London. (2023). *Virtual London*. UCL. Retrieved 15th May 2023 from https://www.ucl.ac.uk/bartlett/casa/virtual-london.

Winn, Z. (10 July 2020). *Bringing the benefits of in-person collaboration to the virtual world*. Massachusetts Institute of Technology. Retrieved 2nd April 2023 from https://news.mit.edu/2020/spatial-vr-collaboration-0710.

Yin, C. (14 April 2022). *A city street filled with lots of traffic*. Unsplash. Retrieved 11th June 2023 from https://unsplash.com/photos/mdG353VBJe8.

Zamponi, M. E., & Barbierato, E. (2022). The dual role of artificial intelligence in developing smart cities. *Smart Cities*, *5*(2) 728–755. https://www.mdpi.com/2624-6511/5/2/38.

Zhang, X. (2021). *Data-driven analytics for sustainable buildings and cities: From theory to application*. Springer Singapore. https://books.google.co.ke/books?id=jZJCEAAAQBAJ.

Zhang, H., Guo, S., Long, X., & Hao, Y. (2023). Combined dynamic route guidance and signal timing optimization for urban traffic congestion caused by accidents. *Journal of Advanced Transportation*, *2023*, 5858614. https://doi.org/10.1155/2023/5858614.

Zoan. (2023). *Virtual Helsinki*. Zoan. Retrieved 15th May 2023 from https://zoan.com/en/cases/virtual-helsinki/.

Chapter 7

The metaverse and urban planning

Introduction

The potential of the metaverse in revolutionizing urban planning is becoming a reality as its acceptance continues to increase. Its capacity is hinged on the ability to transcend physical boundaries that have been the bane in the planners' and designers' efforts to collaborate and participate in multidisciplinary urban planning efforts. As a result, the metaverse stands in stark contrast to traditional urban planning approaches, which have often been criticized for being top-down, exclusionary, and unresponsive to the diverse inputs and needs of urban populations (Rossner & Tait, 2021). To the bare minimum, the metaverse enables real-time simulation, visualization, and assessment of urban environments, providing players within the urban planning realm with a more accurate understanding of the impacts of potential interventions or actions before they are actualized in the physical dimension. By leveraging the power of data-driven algorithms, the metaverse can reveal previously overlooked patterns and trends in urban areas, facilitating more targeted and effective policymaking (Allam et al., 2022).

One key tool that makes the metaverse a superior in urban planning is the virtual platform that allows stakeholders to communicate and discuss and interact with the proposed plans in a more immersive and intuitive manner (Mystakidis, 2022). This is true even with urban residents who can share their inputs; hence, increasing the sense of ownership and investment in urban development projects. Such forms of collaboration further promote more equitable and sustainable urban growth, unlike when traditional urban planning approaches are relied upon. The static and linear nature of conventional planning tools has limited their ability to respond to the dynamic and interconnected nature of urban systems (Allam, 2021; Allam et al., 2020). In addition, those models have been overcrowded by the siloed nature of planning processes leading to fragmented and uncoordinated decision-making, exacerbating existing disparities as well as negative externalities associated with rapid urbanization.

The need for the metaverse and advanced technologies to enhance the planning and designing tools that would facilitate efficiency and inclusivity cannot be overlooked as urban planning plays a critical role in shaping the livability and sustainability of cities. It also influences diverse aspects such as transportation, housing, public spaces, and environmental quality that are pertinent to the residents. Such are particularly critical as the global urban population is reported to continue to grow with projections showing that by 2050, there is the possibility of the urban population reaching approximately 70% of the world's population (Kaneda et al., 2020). It is therefore almost an urgent matter to ensure that existing and upcoming cities are both sustainable and livable, hence, reducing urban sprawl on already stretched land (Allam, 2012, 2018). As such, cities will need to be planned following innovative approaches that are adaptive, inclusive, and grounded in a thorough understanding of urban systems.

The ability of the metaverse to merge the physical and digital worlds is thus timely within the urban planning processes as it is anticipated that it will offer a more dynamic and holistic understanding of urban systems. It is opined that by helping create virtual representations of urban environments, the metaverse can facilitate more meaningful engagement with diverse stakeholders, including traditionally marginalized groups (Hudson-Smith, 2022). The increased participation, in turn, can lead to more people-oriented and equitable planning outcomes, as well as increased public trust in the planning process.

Beyond the aforementioned potential benefits, there are some challenges and limitations associated with the integration of the metaverse into urban planning processes that would require to be addressed at the earliest opportunity. One such is the digital divide which manifests in the form of skewed development and distribution of basic technological infrastructure, smart devices such as Virtual Reality (VR) headsets, and skill sets that would allow diverse demographics to easily access and enjoy the virtual spaces (Dimov & Dimov, 2022). This could exacerbate existing inequalities and further marginalize disadvantaged groups if not adequately addressed.

Another potential concern about the metaverse that is being raised is its domination by commercial interests, with implications for the democratization of urban planning processes. A classic example that showcases the risk of allowing corporations to dominate and control the metaverse is the plot in the movie, Ready Player One, where one corporation is keen to control everything within the virtual environment (Oasis as it is called in the movie) at the expense of the entire population that depends on the virtual reality to escape the hardship in the physical world. Therefore, even as the metaverse continues to become more prominent, it will be paramount to ensure careful consideration of issues related to governance, data privacy, and the ethical use of technology (Kitchin, 2016). From another perspective, there are possibilities that the metaverse would present challenges in terms of the accuracy and representativeness of the data and models used to inform planning decisions. As will be discussed in detail in the succeeding sections, it will be important to ensure that the metaverse provides a reliable and comprehensive understanding of urban systems. There will also be a need to pursue rigorous validation and verification processes, as well as ongoing collaboration between experts from diverse disciplines.

Given the earlier background, this chapter seeks to explore the positive, as well as negative consequences of integrating the metaverse as a tool in the urban planning processes.

Opportunities and benefits of using the metaverse in urban planning

In the event the metaverse is to be incorporated into the planning process, a wide range of opportunities and benefits are eminent, including, enhancing stakeholder engagement, improved collaboration, more efficient planning, increased community participation, and better decision-making. As deliberative democracy garners momentum in the urban planning discourse, the metaverse is anticipated to provide exceptional platforms for harnessing multidisciplinary intelligence and fostering real inclusivity (Hudson-Smith, 2022). It offers a radical reconfiguration of how different players can engage in urban planning by using diverse tools such as immersive 3D visualizations and interactive platforms (e.g., Fig. 7.1 showcases a 3D-rendered summer camp that can be built in a city). Such tools increase the potential for citizens to better comprehend the possible outcomes of planning decisions before actual work is done physically. Such collaborative participation can lead to increased acceptance of different local projects within the urban development setup, unlike in the case of traditional approaches, where a significant number of projects are coldly received by the intended recipient for not being involved or consulted.

The metaverse is also expected to avail some level of transparency and accessibility in urban planning decision-making. This is contrary to the traditional planning methods which have been accused of being crowded by opacity and exclusivity, making it difficult for nonexperts to comprehend and participate in any phase of planning. The metaverse is, however, changing this perception by making complex urban systems and planning scenarios more accessible and understandable, offering an interactive and immersive representation of planning proposals and their potential impacts. Allowing freedom for citizens to access and participate in decision-making is instrumental in providing opportunities for real-time feedback, public scrutiny, and improved accountability in urban planning (Goodspeed, 2014).

In addition to the earlier mentioned one, the metaverse has also been hailed for its potential to introduce cost-effective ways such as virtual simulations to test and explore different urban design scenarios, especially when coupled with technologies such as Digital Twins and Artificial Intelligence (AI). Traditional urban planning and design methods often require costly physical models and prototypes, which are time-consuming and restrictive (Allam, 2019, 2020c;

FIG. 7.1 3D render of a summer camp (Nohassi, 2023).

Pettit et al., 2018). In contrast, the metaverse enables quick and cost-effective creation and modification of digital twins and virtual prototypes, allowing planners to experiment with diverse designs and evaluate their effects under various scenarios. Such kind of potential can arguably reduce the costs and risks associated with urban development projects, while simultaneously increasing their success rate (Hudson-Smith, 2022). Importantly, the metaverse offers the urban areas the abilities and opportunities to address the diverse needs of urban communities and promote inclusive urban development. The ability and capacity to simulate and visualize diverse urban scenarios can help planners better understand and cater to the local needs of different demographic groups (Kingsley et al., 2013). Moreover, by facilitating more inclusive and participatory planning processes, the metaverse can help amplify the voices of marginalized and underrepresented groups for the plights to be heard and their needs to be addressed forthwith (Tsamados et al., 2022).

The way the metaverse is being fashioned by different groups, it will ultimately present an inherent flexibility in adapting to changing urban dynamics and trends. For instance, in the wake of rapid urbanization and global unprecedented challenges such as climate change, congestion, and scarcity of housing, et cetera, urban planners require adaptable tools that can integrate emerging trends and uncertainties into the planning process. The metaverse, with its dynamic and immersive capabilities, can incorporate real-time data, simulate future scenarios, and help planners adapt their strategies accordingly (Pettit et al., 2018). It also holds substantial potential to stimulate the creation of innovative and sustainable urban environments, that would benefit many of the urban residents. In particular, it increases the possibilities of success in the pursuit of the "smart city" concept which has been taunted as one of the best planning models in addressing modern urban challenges. The metaverse achieves this by making it possible for urban planners to easily access both the physical and digital elements of the city; hence, allowing for informed decision-making on diverse matters such as resource use, best sustainability approaches, and alternatives that could be adopted in sectors such as energy and transportation to name a few. The ability to simulate and test innovative urban solutions in a virtual environment can also inspire creative problem-solving and drive the development of sustainable urban innovations (Kitchin et al., 2015).

During urban development, one of the greatest hindrances has been the top-down decision-making approach, which has kept many residents out of the spaces where they could determine the pathway for their cities. Mostly, residents and communities in cities have been relegated to consumers of decisions made elsewhere. However, the metaverse has helped turn things around, by providing platforms and environments for immersive interactions and participation around common interests and shared goals. As such, it has helped to create stronger and more resilient communities. This sense of community and belonging is anticipated to serve as an antidote to the social isolation tag often associated with densely populated urban areas. Further, it is bound to foster social cohesion and a sense of belonging among urban dwellers, thus helping mitigate some social ills such as crime, racism, discrimination, and others. With people pulling together, other benefits such as urban innovation, and a renewed desire for conservation are natural. Through its capacity to simulate various urban scenarios and integrate diverse data sources, the metaverse can encourage the exploration of novel ideas and solutions to urban challenges (Lv et al., 2022). This can invigorate the urban planning process, prompting more creative and forward-thinking approaches to city development (Bibri et al., 2022).

The immersive and interactive profile of the metaverse is seen as a powerful educational tool not only in the realm of urban planning but also in the real education system. However, in urban planning, there are anticipations that it could help citizens and stakeholders gain a better understanding of complex planning issues and their potential impacts. As a result, it could foster a more informed and engaged citizenry, enhancing democratic decision-making, and fostering a culture of lifelong learning and curiosity about urban issues. The education potential in the metaverse could further spark renewed interest in discourses such as environmental sustainability which would ultimately help address some of the major urban concerns in the modern era.

Despite all those benefits, it is worth acknowledging the challenges and ethical concerns associated with the use of the metaverse in urban planning. Issues related to data privacy, the digital divide, and the potential for manipulation and misuse of technology by corporations and individuals must be carefully considered and addressed. These considerations emphasize the need for appropriate regulatory frameworks and ethical guidelines to ensure that the benefits of the metaverse are realized while mitigating potential risks.

Applications of the metaverse in urban planning

In the last decades, especially since the emergence of the Fourth Industrial Revolution, cities have experienced unprecedented changes and developments. However, the increased attention on the metaverse, more so after the COVID-19 pandemic has prompted a revolution in the way we conceive, create, and manage our cities (Allam & Jones, 2021). The versatility of the metaverse and its utilities that cut across several critical areas in urban planning, from stakeholder engagement to scenario visualization, real-time monitoring, mobility enhancement, community building, and professional education is the cornerstone of the revolution.

Digital simulation refers to the process of creating computer-based models or simulations that replicate and mimic real-world phenomena, systems, or processes.

In the context of stakeholder engagement and community participation, the metaverse avails unparalleled platforms and environment, that allows for virtual simulations and immersive interaction with digital twin products, et cetera. The simulations offer platforms through which stakeholders could access, experience, and interact with proposed development plans at length, thus, facilitating more informed feedback and expressions of concern (Lv et al., 2022). Consequently, this results in a more inclusive and widely acceptable decision-making process. With the diverse tools provided in the metaverse, stakeholders not only gain a clearer understanding of the propositions but also appreciate their involvement in the planning and development process. The immersive nature of the metaverse facilitates a higher degree of engagement, making urban planning more democratic and attuned to the needs of the community (Wang & Lin, 2023).

Immersive experiences brought about by the metaverse have opened up immense possibilities for creating, testing, and iterating various urban scenarios. Urban designers can experiment with different urban designs, infrastructure layouts, and sociospatial scenarios before actual implementation, thus minimizing risks of failure when actual implementation is done (Mystakidis, 2022). This virtual, level playground significantly reduces the efforts, cost, and time required for physical prototyping and enables urban planners to anticipate and find solutions to potential challenges and opportunities that could arise in the real world. The metaverse, coupled with developing technologies such as the AI, the Internet of Things (IoT), and smart city technologies, also help in real-time monitoring and analysis of urban data (Theo, 2021). This digital platform serves as a hub for collecting, analyzing, and visualizing these data (Bibri et al., 2022). Planners and urban managers can thus monitor and respond to real-time changes in the urban setups, such as traffic patterns, energy production and consumption, and environmental conditions, thereby enabling more informed and timely interventions.

The use of both virtual and augmented reality (VR and AR) to enhance urban mobility and accessibility presents another significant application of the metaverse. Among the benefits these two technologies bring into the metaverse include allowing urban planners to identify potential bottlenecks in diverse sectors. For instance, in the transport sector, using both, or either of the two technologies, planners can effectively simulate different transport scenarios, with the ultimate outcome being a well understanding of the impact of different interventions that could be deployed on urban mobility. This approach optimizes existing transportation networks and assists in designing more inclusive and accessible cities for people with diverse mobility needs.

During and after the COVID-19 pandemic, the need for social distancing became eminent. However, the pandemic only exposed a trend that was taking shape prompted by factors like remote working, increased proliferation of social media that opened opportunities for people to communicate remotely, and the ability for people to shop and trade via e-commerce platforms, et cetera. Notwithstanding, the quality of interactions and collaborations was not as robust as is the case with the metaverse. On this, the metaverse has opened opportunities for unmatched innovations where it is now possible to create virtual public spaces for community building and urban events. These spaces can host community gatherings, cultural events, and city-wide celebrations without the physical constraints of real-world urban spaces (Yang, 2023). This is and will continue to foster a strong sense of community, allowing individuals to engage in collective experiences, pursue, and explore shared interests, and contribute to the social fabric of their cities, regardless of their physical location, race, or other physical constraints (Fig. 7.2).

Another equally profound benefit that the metaverse is expected to avail is the potential for developing virtual education and training programs for urban planning professionals and stakeholders. With the metaverse, complex learning scenarios can be facilitated in virtual reality environments, equipping urban planning professionals with the necessary skills and knowledge to navigate the complexities of urban planning in the digital age (Sá & Serpa, 2023).

FIG. 7.2 A student learning how to paint (Billetto, 2017).

Challenges and limitations of using the metaverse in urban planning

The viability of the metaverse in urban planning might be compelling, but its application attracts several significant challenges and limitations, particularly in the areas of equity, technological bias, privacy, simulation fidelity, integration, and community engagement. The following Table 7.1 summarizes some of those challenges and potential solutions that could be adopted.

TABLE 7.1 Challenges and solutions of the metaverse in urban planning.

Challenge	Description	Potential solution
Equity and inclusivity	Digital divides across socioeconomic, age, and geographical lines may exclude significant segments of the population from participating in the metaverse-based urban planning	Policies and programs to increase digital literacy and access to technology across diverse demographic groups Standardization of protocols to ensure universal applicability of devices across different platforms and networks
Technological and data-driven biases	AI and machine learning algorithms, if not properly calibrated, can perpetuate existing societal biases in urban planning	Develop transparency and accountability measures for AI systems; conduct bias audits; train algorithms on diverse data sets

TABLE 7.1 Challenges and solutions of the metaverse in urban planning—cont'd

Challenge	Description	Potential solution
Privacy and security	The collection, storage, and use of personal data in the metaverse raise significant concerns about privacy and potential misuse	Implement robust data governance frameworks; ensure clear and informed consent processes; protect against data breaches
Simulation fidelity	Despite advanced simulation capabilities, the metaverse cannot fully replicate the complexities of real-world urban dynamics	Combine virtual simulations with traditional urban planning methodologies; continually refine and update models to reflect urban complexity
Integration of virtual and physical tools	Compatibility, interoperability, and learning curve issues associated with new technologies can impede the seamless integration of metaverse tools into traditional urban planning processes	Provide comprehensive training and support for urban planning professionals; develop standards and best practices for integration
Community engagement	The metaverse's virtual nature may foster a sense of detachment, reducing the sense of ownership and commitment often associated with physical community engagement processes	Create immersive and interactive experiences in the metaverse to foster a sense of community; facilitate hybrid models of engagement that combine virtual and physical meetings
Regulatory compliance	The metaverse can potentially conflict with existing laws and regulations, particularly in areas like land use and zoning	Develop new legal frameworks and regulations that account for the unique characteristics of the metaverse
Environmental impact	The energy consumption and carbon footprint associated with the servers and data centers that power the metaverse could contribute to environmental degradation	Invest in renewable energy sources and energy-efficient technologies; develop sustainable digital infrastructures
Economic impact	The introduction of the metaverse in urban planning could lead to job displacement in certain sectors, while also creating new jobs in others	Implement reskilling and upskilling programs to prepare the workforce for new job opportunities; provide social safety nets for those impacted by job displacement

The live and compelling concern lies in the question of equity and inclusivity in accessing the metaverse technologies by different segments of the population in urban areas. Despite the promise of an increased public participation during urban planning through the metaverse, the existing digital divides remain a hindrance for wholesome benefits to be realized. Socioeconomic status, age-based, and geographical disparities in technology access and cost could substantially marginalize certain population groups. This would leave them excluded from these digital participatory processes, thus suppressing their views and quests to be part of the urban planning revolution (Wang & Lin, 2023). This stark reality risks may in the long run transform the metaverse from a platform for democratizing urban planning into an exclusive domain accessible only to the technologically privileged, thereby undermining its potential for inclusive urban governance (Sadowski, 2020) (Fig. 7.3).

Alongside issues of access, the potential for technological and data-driven biases in urban planning within the metaverse is another concern that cannot be overlooked. The overreliance on advanced technologies such as the AI and Machine Learning algorithms to inform decision-making might unintentionally perpetuate existing societal biases, especially on parameters such as color, gender, and geographical location. The risk of relying on biased data inputs is that they could lead to skewed outputs, ultimately reinforcing structural inequalities in urban spaces (Tsamados et al., 2022). These concerns necessitate the need for urgent implementation of rigorous fairness, transparency, and accountability measures in all data-driven urban planning processes within the metaverse. Similar attention should be advanced to the concerns on privacy and security of metaverse uses, and their digital properties. Regarding data collection, storage, and use of personal information, there needs to be a clearly defined policy on who is responsible. This could be achieved, first by establishing a proactive

FIG. 7.3 Data privacy representation.

metaverse governance structure, which would be responsible for formulation of policies, as well as push for their implementation.

The limitations of the metaverse, surprisingly extend to its ability to accurately simulate complex urban dynamics. While this limitation will somehow self-correct in the future when the metaverse becomes robust, it is worth noting that at the current, it is not developed to the scale of matching the intricate and complex nature of the urban environment. As such, though it can provide advanced simulation capabilities, time and sufficient investment and development are required to allow it to fully replicate the nuanced complexities of real-world urban dynamics (Shi et al., 2023). This limitation underscores the importance of not abandoning the traditional urban planning methodologies yet, but instead, purpose to combine them with virtual simulations to ensure a balanced and comprehensive approach to urban planning. However, it is also worthwhile to note that even this process of integrating virtual and physical urban planning approaches and tools also presents significant challenges. This is due to factors and issues like compatibility, interoperability, and the learning curve associated with new technologies, especially due to the nonstandardization nature of protocols.

Potential developments in using the metaverse in urban planning

With the increased attention on the metaverse by diverse institutions, such as local governments (e.g., in cities like Seoul) (Gaubert, 2021) and corporations such as Meta (Newton, 2021), Apple (Radoff, 2021), Qatar Airways (Trade Arabia, 2022), and others, its application in urban planning is poised to experience significant developments. In this section, the focus will be on highlighting those potential advancements. The section will particularly emphasize on integration, accessibility, artificial intelligence, international collaboration, tailored tools, and community participation.

Greater integration and interoperability between virtual and physical urban planning tools and processes are to be crucial developments in the metaverse's application to urban planning. Those can be achieved through the help of emerging technologies such as the digital twins; virtual replicas of physical assets, which can serve as an effective bridge between the virtual and real worlds, enabling better coordination and collaboration among urban planners, architects, and engineers (Parrott et al., 2020). Achieving greater integration and interoperability would also demand untethered implementation of common standards and protocols for data sharing. With such, interoperability could contribute immensely to the seamless integration of various urban planning tools (Batty, 2018). This integration will facilitate the development of comprehensive and holistic urban planning strategies that capitalize on the strengths of both virtual and physical processes.

In addition to the earlier mentioned one, accessibility and inclusivity are another set of vital considerations that must be made possible to ensure that the metaverse is equitably applied in urban planning processes. This includes addressing the digital divide that is already very prominent by providing affordable access to technology, improving user interfaces, and offering multilingual and culturally sensitive platforms that cater to diverse populations and demographics. By prioritizing inclusivity and accessibility, the metaverse could turn out to be a truly democratized platform for urban planning.

For the benefits availed by the metaverse to continue in scale and scope, it will also be paramount to increase the use of technologies such as artificial intelligence (AI), Blockchain, and machine learning in different virtual urban planning processes. This would ensure that the planners and other involved players can conduct real-time AI-powered simulations and come up with predictive models that would eventually help in identifying patterns and trends in urban development. Machine learning algorithms on the other hand could assist in optimizing planning scenarios and identifying potential problems earlier before they become major problems in the implementation phases (Huynh-The et al., 2023). Blockchain technologies on the other hand would help in promoting and advancing the aspects of privacy and security, as well as facilitate transactions such as virtual trading, payments, et cetera. By incorporating AI and machine learning, urban planners can harness the power of these technologies to make informed decisions and develop more sustainable and resilient urban environments (Angelidou, 2015).

The potential for creating shared virtual urban environments and spaces for cross-cultural urban planning and designing collaborations is also another undeniable quality of the metaverse. By facilitating and fostering collaboration and knowledge sharing among urban planning professionals worldwide, it is anticipated that the metaverse will contribute to the development of more sustainable, resilient, and inclusive urban spaces.

As the demand for cities that are responsive to the need of the residents continue to increase, the role of metaverse and other advanced technologies will remain subtle. In particular, such will be very critical in ensuring the development of virtual urban planning tools and technologies tailored and customized to the diverse needs of urban communities. This customization will enable urban planners to address the unique and specific needs of different communities, fostering more equitable and context-sensitive urban development, as well as promoting inclusivity.

Future developments in the metaverse will need to prioritize the active engagement of local communities in the decision-making process, utilizing participatory tools such as virtual workshops, online surveys, and interactive 3D models to solicit input and feedback, that have been suppressed in the traditional urban planning approaches.

Case studies of metaverse use in urban planning

The application of the metaverse in urban planning is no longer a speculative discourse but is a reality in different parts of the world. For instance, there are concrete pioneer examples that are currently in operation, that serve as pointers to the unlimited possibilities the virtual environments can avail. Six examples of those have been cited in this section to serve as case studies that will provide a glimpse into the present and future of urban planning in the metaverse.

The first classic case is the "Virtual Singapore" project, which was initiated back in 2018 by the government of Singapore. The project presents an impressive digital twin of the city-state, in a high-resolution and a dynamic 3D model of the urban environment (City2City, 2022). This virtual platform facilitates data-driven urban planning, allowing stakeholders to visualize and simulate scenarios in real-time. The result has been a more informed, agile, and responsive planning process, benefiting citizens, planners, businesses, and even those in academia. A similar concept is being implemented in the Digital City Testbed Center in Berlin. This project allows urban scenarios and technologies to be tested and simulated in a virtual environment before physical implementation. By leveraging the metaverse, this center has managed to address issues such as traffic congestion and energy consumption, offering sustainable solutions before their real-world application.

The metaverse is proving to be a reliable tool in real estate development agendas, where it is being hailed for how developers can use virtual reality and simulations to conceptualize, design, and present projects, radically altering the design process (Georgiades, 2022). This practice not only helps in accelerating project timelines but also enhances stakeholder engagement, allowing potential buyers to experience and interact with the properties virtually.

In the architectural realm, the metaverse is increasingly influencing design and planning. Architects are now able to use virtual platforms to create, modify, and visualize structures, enabling them to experiment with innovative designs and materials (Shakeri & Ornek, 2022). This integration of the metaverse within architectural practice has transformed conventional design paradigms, fostering creativity and precision. A case in point to affirm this is the Smart City Vienna which provides a compelling evidence of how the integration of virtual and physical urban planning tools can result in tangible outcomes (Roblek, 2019). The city utilizes metaverse technologies to develop sustainable solutions, such as optimizing energy consumption and enhancing mobility. By intertwining the metaverse with urban planning processes, Vienna has emerged as a beacon of smart, sustainable urban development.

The metaverse's role during the COVID-19 pandemic, especially regarding planning and response is worth highlighting. During the height of this pandemic, in early and mid-2020, the strength of virtual simulations became evident, especially in relation to predicting disease spread, formulating response strategies, and facilitating remote collaboration among health professionals and urban planners (Allam, 2020b; Ingrassia et al., 2021). This application underscores the metaverse's potential in tackling unprecedented urban challenges, including pandemics, climate change, et cetera.

Conclusion and future outlook

The metaverse, as a concept and nascent reality, offers a tantalizing vista of transformative possibilities for urban planning. It offers the potential for the creation of cities that are not only sustainable but inclusive and responsive to the specific needs of the diverse urban population.

A key potential that the metaverse presents is the capacity for simulation and visualization of different scenarios, offering an unprecedented platform for decision-making. This is particularly very profound, when it is coupled with the digital twins of cities, like is the case with the Virtual Singapore, allowing planners to play out countless scenarios and predict outcomes before they manifest in the physical world. This predictive power, coupled with real-time data analysis, is anticipated to prompt an unprecedented revolution in the urban planning arena, leading to the creation of more sustainable, efficient, and livable cities. However, the attainment of these fetes attracts several drawbacks and challenges that have the potential to derail or even jeopardize the benefits already obtained. One such challenge is the issue to do with equity in access to these technologies which must be confronted, as widespread disparities in digital literacy and access could exacerbate existing inequalities. Likewise, the potential for data-driven biases to shape urban planning decisions is another significant concern. The reliance on data-driven processes could inadvertently perpetuate or even intensify social and spatial inequalities if not thoughtfully managed (Allam, 2020a; Yang, 2023).

Furthermore, issues of privacy and security related to the collection and use of personal data in virtual environments cannot be overstated as they pose a substantial challenge, which might even prompt the rejection of critical projects by urban residents. This issue is significant as the metaverse, by its very nature, thrives on data, and without proper checks and balances, issues touching on ethics and morals may arise. Therefore, the security and privacy of data are paramount and need to be addressed by policymakers, technologists, and urban planners alike in urgency (Kitchin, 2016). Another crucial aspect of the integration of the metaverse into the urban planning process is the participation and ownership of communities in the development and use of metaverse technologies. As we witnessed in the case of the Digital City Testbed Center in Berlin, involving communities in the planning process, even in its virtual form, can lead to more meaningful and effective outcomes. However, as already mentioned, such could be jeopardized if the privacy and security of data are not addressed.

In the future, the metaverse is poised to play an increasingly significant role in urban planning. From the integration of artificial intelligence and machine learning to the creation of shared virtual urban environments for cross-cultural collaborations, the applications of the metaverse are expected to proliferate. To avoid the problems that have already been discussed, it will be crucial to foster a balanced approach that recognizes the potential of the metaverse while addressing its limitations.

References

Allam, Z. (2012). Sustainable architecture: Utopia or feasible reality? *Journal of Biourbanism*, *2*(1), 47–61.

Allam, Z. (2018). Contextualising the smart city for sustainability and inclusivity. *New Design Ideas*, *2*(2), 124–127.

Allam, Z. (2019). *Cities and the digital revolution: Aligning technology and humanity*. Springer Nature.

Allam, Z. (2020a). Privatization and privacy in the digital city. In *Cities and the digital revolution* (pp. 85–106). Cham: Palgrave Pivot.

Allam, Z. (2020b). The rise of machine intelligence in the COVID-19 pandemic and its impact on health policy. *Surveying the Covid-19 Pandemic its Implications*, 89.

Allam, Z. (2020c). Urban chaos and the AI messiah. In *Cities and the digital revolution* (pp. 31–60). Cham: Palgrave Pivot.

Allam, Z. (2021). On complexity, connectivity and autonomy in future cities. In *The rise of autonomous smart cities* (pp. 31–47). Cham: Palgrave Macmillan.

Allam, Z., Bibri, S. E., Jones, D. S., Chabaud, D., & Moreno, C. (2022). Unpacking the 15-Minute City via 6G, IoT, and digital twins: Towards a new narrative for increasing urban efficiency, resilience, and sustainability. *Sensors*, *22*(4), 1369. https://doi.org/10.3390/s22041369.

Allam, Z., & Jones, D. S. (2021). Future (post-COVID) digital, smart and sustainable cities in the wake of 6G: Digital twins, immersive realities and new urban economies. *Land Use Policy*, *101*, 105201.

Allam, Z., Jones, D., & Thondoo, M. (2020). Economically incentivizing urban sustainability and resilience. In *Cities and climate change* (pp. 83–106). Cham: Palgrave Macmillan.

Angelidou, M. (2015). Smart cities: A conjuncture of four forces. *Cities*, *47*, 95–106. https://doi.org/10.1016/j.cities.2015.05.004.

Batty, M. (2018). Artificial intelligence and smart cities. *Environment and Planning B: Urban Analytics and City Science*, *45*(1), 3–6. https://doi.org/10.1177/2399808317751169.

Bibri, S. E., Allam, Z., & Krogstie, J. (2022). The metaverse as a virtual form of data-driven smart urbanism: Platformization and its underlying processes, institutional dimensions, and disruptive impacts. *Computational Urban Science*, *2*, 24. https://doi.org/10.1007/s43762-022-00051-0.

Billetto. (8 August 2017). *VR painting*. Unsplash. Retrieved 13th June 2023 from https://unsplash.com/photos/3eAByt3-eOw.

City2City. (24 April 2022). *Virtual Singapore: A digital 'twin' for planning*. UNDP. Retrieved 15th March 2023 from https://city2city.network/virtual-singapore-digital-twin-planning-innovation-type-institutional-pioneer.

Dimov, R., & Dimov, D. (2022). *Metaverse implementation in real life. Augmented and virtual reality*.

Gaubert, J. (11 November 2021). Seoul to become the first city to enter the metaverse. What will it look like? *Euro News*. Retrieved 4th December 2021 from https://www.euronews.com/next/2021/11/10/seoul-to-become-the-first-city-to-enter-the-metaverse-what-will-it-look-like.

Georgiades, A. (9 September 2022). 3 Aspects of the real estate industry that can benefit immensely from the metaverse. *Entrepreneur*. Retrieved 19th May from http://entrepreneur.com/science-technology/how-the-metaverse-can-enhance-the-real-estate-industry/434053.

Goodspeed, R. (2014). Smart cities: Moving beyond urban cybernetics to tackle wicked problems. *Cambridge Journal of Regions, Economy and Society, 8*. https://doi.org/10.1093/cjres/rsu013.

Hudson-Smith, A. (2022). Incoming metaverses: Digital mirrors for urban planning. *Urban Planning, 7*(2). https://doi.org/10.17645/up.v7i2.5193. Gaming, simulations, and planning: physical and digital technologies for public participation in urban planning https://www.cogitatiopress.com/urbanplanning/article/view/5193.

Huynh-The, T., Pham, Q.-V., Pham, X.-Q., Nguyen, T. T., Han, Z., & Kim, D.-S. (2023). Artificial intelligence for the metaverse: A survey. *Engineering Applications of Artificial Intelligence, 117*, 105581. https://doi.org/10.1016/j.engappai.2022.105581.

Ingrassia, P. L., Ferrari, M., Paganini, M., & Mormando, G. (2021). Role of health simulation centres in the COVID-19 pandemic response in Italy: A national study. *BMJ Simulation & Technology Enhanced Learning, 7*(5), 379–384. https://doi.org/10.1136/bmjstel-2020-000813.

Kaneda, T., Greenbaum, C., & Kline, K. (2020). *2020 World population data sheet [report]*. PRB https://www.prb.org/wp-content/uploads/2020/07/letter-booklet-2020-world-population.pdf.

Kingsley, G. T., Pettit, K. L. S., & Hendey, L. (2013). *Strengthening local capacity for data-driven decision making*. Urban Org. https://www.urban.org/sites/default/files/publication/23901/412883-Strengthening-Local-Capacity-For-Data-Driven-Decisionmaking.PDF.

Kitchin, R. (2016). The ethics of smart cities and urban science. *Philosophical Transactions of the Royal Society A: Mathematical, Physical and Engineering Sciences, 374*(2083), 1–15. https://doi.org/10.1098/rsta.2016.0115.

Kitchin, R., Lauriault, T. P., & McArdle, G. (2015). Knowing and governing cities through urban indicators, city benchmarking and real-time dashboards. *Regional Studies, Regional Science, 2*(1), 6–28. https://doi.org/10.1080/21681376.2014.983149.

Lv, Z., Shang, W.-L., & Guizani, M. (2022). Impact of digital twins and metaverse on cities: History, current situation, and application perspectives. *Applied Sciences, 12*(24).

Mystakidis, S. (2022). Metaverse. *Encyclopedia, 2*(1), 486–497.

Newton, C. (2021). Mark in the metaverse. *The Verge*. (25/10/2025). Retrieved 26th February 2022 from https://www.theverge.com/22588022/mark-zuckerberg-facebook-ceo-metaverse-interview.

Nohassi, M. (16 May 2023). *Summer camp 3D render*. Unsplash. Retrieved 14th June 2023 from https://unsplash.com/photos/eR3tnAWVYcw.

Parrott, A., Umbenhauer, B., & Warshaw, L. (15 January 2020). Digital twins: Bridging the physical and digital. *Deloitte*. Retrieved 4th January 2022 from https://www2.deloitte.com/us/en/insights/focus/tech-trends/2020/digital-twin-applications-bridging-the-physical-and-digital.html.

Pettit, C., Bakelmun, A., Lieske, S. N., Glackin, S., Hargroves, K. C., Thomson, G., Shearer, H., Dia, H., & Newman, P. (2018). Planning support systems for smart cities. *City, Culture and Society, 12*, 13–24. https://doi.org/10.1016/j.ccs.2017.10.002.

Radoff, J. (12 November 2021). Clash of the metaverse titans: Microsoft, Meta and Apple. *Medium*. Retrieved 1st December 2021 from https://medium.com/building-the-metaverse/clash-of-the-metaverse-titans-microsoft-meta-and-apple-ce505b010376.

Roblek, V. (2019). 5—The smart city of Vienna. In L. Anthopoulos (Ed.), *Smart city emergence* (pp. 105–127). Elsevier. https://doi.org/10.1016/B978-0-12-816169-2.00005-5.

Rossner, M., & Tait, D. (2021). Presence and participation in a virtual court. *Criminology & Criminal Justice*, *23*(1), 135–157. https://doi.org/10.1177/17488958211017372.

Sá, M. J., & Serpa, S. (2023). Metaverse as a learning environment: Some considerations. *Sustainability*, *15*(3).

Sadowski, J. (2020). The internet of landlords: Digital platforms and new mechanisms of rentier capitalism. *Antipode*, *52*(2), 562–580. https://doi.org/10.1111/anti.12595.

Shakeri, S., & Ornek, M. (2022). *How metaverse evolves the architectural design*. Beirut, Lebanon: ASCAAD.

Shi, F., Ning, H., Zhang, X., Li, R., Tian, Q., Zhang, S., Zheng, Y., Guo, Y., & Daneshmand, M. (2023). A new technology perspective of the metaverse: Its essence, framework and challenges. *Digital Communications and Networks*. https://doi.org/10.1016/j.dcan.2023.02.017.

Theo. (5 August 2021). Digital twins, IoT and the metaverse. *Medium*. Retrieved 3rd December 2021 from https://medium.com/@theo/digital-twins-iot-and-the-metaverse-b4efbfc01112.

Trade Arabia. (11 September 2022). *Qatar airways website wins FTE award for VR experience*. Trade Arabia. Retrieved 11th February 2023 from https://tradearabia.com/news/TTN_400518.html.

Tsamados, A., Aggarwal, N., Cowls, J., Morley, J., Roberts, H., Taddeo, M., & Floridi, L. (2022). The ethics of algorithms: Key problems and solutions. *AI & SOCIETY*, *37*(1), 215–230. https://doi.org/10.1007/s00146-021-01154-8.

Wang, Y., & Lin, Y.-S. (2023). Public participation in urban design with augmented reality technology based on indicator evaluation [Original Research]. *Frontiers in Virtual Reality*, *4*. https://doi.org/10.3389/frvir.2023.1071355.

Yang, S. (2023). Storytelling and user experience in the cultural metaverse. *Heliyon*, *9*(4), e14759. https://doi.org/10.1016/j.heliyon.2023.e14759.

Chapter 8

The metaverse and real estate development

Introduction to metaverse in real estate development

The metamorphosis of the real estate industry across the world has been due to a myriad of factors, both instigated internally and externally. One of the key externalities that has been significantly influential in this industry is the emergence and subsequent adoption of digitization. The contribution of this has escalated to the current dispensation, where attention is now gradually turning toward the metaverse, an immersive virtual universe that is not restrained by physical limitations, but instead, allows for seamless integration of physical and virtual realms. The concept of metaverse was introduced by Stephenson in his 1992 novel dubbed Snow Crash. In the book, the metaverse is described as a virtual reality space where users can interact in a physically persistent virtual space, advanced through networked computing, sensors, and databases (Stephenson, 2003).

The ability to seamlessly integrate the physical and virtual realm promises a radical reshaping of the real estate industry, with substantive, transformative implications in areas such as conceptualization, architectural designs, and diverse transaction processes, et cetera (Dwivedi et al., 2022). The relevance of the metaverse in the real estate sector can be argued by considering its capacity to revolutionize traditional practices, just like it has successfully brought positive transformations in sectors like entertainment and e-commerce (Qi, 2022).

The digitization of physical spaces made possible by some elements of the metaverse, such as virtual reality (VR) and augmented reality (AR), has led to increasing attention on the Digital Twins (DT) technology that is characterized by the creation of digital duplicates of physical objects. The digital representation of physical objects is easily available in the virtual world. With such a technology, it then becomes possible to enhance visualization, planning, and decision-making processes in real estate (Bhattacharya et al., 2023). For instance, property investors and homebuyers now have the opportunity to take virtual tours of properties, breaking down geographic and temporal constraint barriers (Wong, 2020).

Given the earlier applicability potentials of the metaverse, it would be paramount to understand the lexicon associated with it. These are provided in Table 8.1 in the following.

Within the real estate industry, these three technologies have enabled numerous applications such as virtual property tours, AR-enhanced marketing materials, and digital twins of properties for improved project management. Their significance in real estate development is becoming increasingly undeniable, for both the developers and the buyers alike. Practically, it has been widely documented that VR can allow potential buyers to visualize their potential investments better and; hence, make informed decisions based on concrete information (Bibri et al., 2022). It is for this reason that the Forbes predicted the potential market for VR in real estate is anticipated to grow to approximately $252.16 billion by 2028 from the $27.96 billion reported in 2021 (Abaulzolof, 2022). With the current trends in the real estate industry, including the emergence of virtual real estate, it might turn out that the VR and AR market will even outgrow those predictions.

The chapter aims to explore the relationship between the metaverse and real estate development and elucidate the potential impacts, opportunities, and challenges that this integration presents. In addition, the chapter will also seek to provide insights into the possible future trends that may define and dominate this nexus. The expectation is that the outcome of this exploration will not only add to the academic discourse on the topic but will also benefit industry players who need to adapt to this evolving landscape.

Traditional real estate development: Challenges and limitations

Traditionally, real estate developments were characterized by a series of methodical stages, starting from land acquisition, strategic planning, construction, and

TABLE 8.1 Different terminology associated with the metaverse.

Lexicon	Association
Virtual reality	VR which offers a simulated experience that can be similar to or entirely different from the experience in the real world
Augmented reality	Associated with providing an interactive experience to users of a real-world environment where objects present in the physical world are augmented by computer-generated perceptual information
Digital twin (DT)	Represents a virtual replica of a physical entity (Juarez et al., 2021)

eventually sale or lease of properties. Whereas this conventional methodology may seem to be water-tight, it is argued to be marred with a litany of challenges that in reality impede the sector's capacity to meet evolving urban demands efficiently. For instance, attempts to access traditional real estate are frequently hurdled by barriers ranging from financial, geographical, locational, and some social barriers. As a result, a significant part of the global population, especially those at the lower-income order, struggles with the prohibitive cost of property ownership, rendering a sizable segment of urban dwellers homeless as depicted in Fig. 8.1 in the following (Immergluck & Law, 2014). In addition, relatively high property prices and stringent zoning regulations further exacerbate the property ownership challenges, making real estate investment quite daunting for most potential buyers.

The prohibitive costs are not only experienced by buyers alone but are even relatively higher when it comes to developers and investors. The cumulative costs are amassed at each stage of traditional real estate development. That is, from land acquisition to property management to insurance fees, government

FIG. 8.1 A shanty structure housing a homeless household in Los Angeles (Space, 2021).

taxation, et cetera. In addition, unforeseen expenses are also inevitable, due to dynamics such as construction delays, policy shifts, supply chain challenges, changing labor costs, and market fluctuations, to name a few. To put this into perspective, it has been established that in the course of developing a real estate project, there are possibilities that the cost overruns may average an alarming 80% of the initial cost (Steininger et al., 2021). In such situations, it would be impossible to stick to any of the projections, including the sale value of the properties.

Besides the cost implications, the real estate industry has been facing substantial challenges prompted by the global calls for environmental consciousness, sustainable extraction, and consumption of resources, et cetera (Allam, 2012; Allam, Bibri, Chabaud, & Moreno, 2022; Allam, Sharifi, Giurco, & Sharpe, 2022). Such demand has been prompted by rapid urban expansion, which in turn has led to habitat destruction and increased pollution (noise, water, and air pollution). Urbanization has further led to an escalation in greenhouse gas emissions contributing to climate change (cities contribute approximately 70% of all emissions, despite occupying less than 1% of the total habitable land mass) (Dasgupta et al., 2022). On its part, the buildings and construction industry is reported to account for an approximated 39% of global CO_2 emissions, underscoring the pressing need for more sustainable practices in the sector (World Green Building Council, 2019).

Another notable challenge that confronts and derails successful real estate development is the lack of effective stakeholder engagement, prompted by factors like power disparities, and insufficient or redundant platforms for such interactions. Insufficient engagement has often led to conflicts, legal entanglements, consequent project delays, and in worst-case scenarios, abandonment of projects (Fig. 8.2).

FIG. 8.2 An abandoned construction site (Nohassi, 2023).

In the recent past, the real estate industry has really embraced the use of different technologies. As a result, the industry has benefited in several ways including enhanced operations, increased efficiency, and improved customer experiences, et cetera. However, despite this, the traditional real estate models continue to suffer from challenges such as hidden cost considerations, data security concerns, and resistance to change within organizations, which point to the need for further interventions that the metaverse could address.

On another front, the traditional real estate industry continues to face substantial challenges in the form of market volatility and trends. Such are triggered by factors like supply chain disruption, as was the case during and post COVID-19 pandemic (Allam, 2020; Meyer et al., 2021). Other factors include financial crisis, inflation, and others, which, when cumulated spotlight the need for adaptability within the industry. Unfortunately, the traditional real estate model does not have the capacity for adaptability, especially with their protracted timelines and substantial capital investment requirements. This inability to respond swiftly and in tandem to shifts in the market landscape underscores the inherent limitations of traditional real estate development.

It is impossible to take away the role the traditional real estate development played especially in serving as the cornerstone of urban growth and development. However, the aforementioned limitations, spanning from accessibility and cost issues to environmental concerns and technological integration, present significant hurdles that require to be addressed, especially in the wake of rapid urbanization. In addition, the need to address these challenges becomes paramount to fostering sustainable, inclusive, and resilient urban landscapes.

The metaverse and virtual real estate

> The advent of the metaverse and its subsequent adoption in urban planning has given rise to new concepts including virtual real estate, which is expected to bring a total transformation in the sector.

Despite it being virtual, it is much like its physical counterpart, in that it encompasses trends such as ownership, sale, lease, and development. The only difference is that all those are accessible in the virtual realm; hence, only accessible to individuals with access to cybernetic spaces.

It has been argued that acquiring virtual real estate is akin to processes found in the physical world, only that this has a distinctive digital flavor. In the digital realm, virtual properties such as parcels of virtual land or space, can be purchased directly from platform providers. Further, they can also be traded between users in a digital marketplace or occasionally, won as consolation prizes in diverse competitions available in the virtual realm. A classic example is the case presented in the movie "Ready Player One" where the winner of the competition was to become the ultimate owner of the virtual realm "Oasis"

(Hudson, 2018). The interesting bit about virtual real estate is that once the borders of ownership are drawn, it becomes the prerogative of the developers to craft a variety of digital constructs on their virtual land. As such, it is not surprising to find constructs such as skyscrapers and parks built by leveraging tools provided by the platforms within the metaverse or using custom 3D modeling software (Sun, 2021).

To facilitate and foster security, transparency, and immutability of transactions, blockchain technology has become instrumental in underpinning these virtual universes (Gadekallu et al., 2022).

The economic potential of virtual real estate is unquestionable and has demonstrated an impressive growth trajectory over the years. A report by Vantage Market Research (2022) projects the market to continue expanding; from the current value of approximately $1139.55 million to a high of 15698.24 million by 2030 (Vantage Market Research). The growth will be spearheaded by the numerous investment opportunities in the virtual realm, which range from purchasing and leasing digital land to developing and marketing virtual constructs. After it became apparent that virtual real estate was viable and with unlimited potential, companies began to position themselves to possess potential spaces in this sphere, crafting branded virtual environments as novel venues for advertising and customer engagement.

When compared to traditional real estate, the virtual version offers a myriad of compelling advantages. To begin with, virtual real estate is very accessible and affordable compared to its physical counterparts. On this, it is without doubt that physical real estate is, by their very nature, geographically constrained; a factor that further makes them relatively expensive. On the contrary, virtual real estate is not subject to such limitations, and anyone, anywhere with access to the internet connection can navigate, acquire, and develop virtual properties. The entry costs for virtual real estate are also considerable and less expensive than physical real estate, broadening the potential investor base significantly.

The metaverse provides an unparalleled and unmatched platform for creative freedom. This is a serious departure from the setup in the physical realm, where numerous constraints abound, that prevent the creatives from exploiting their potential to the maximum. With the metaverse, such constraints are rendered irrelevant, and the designers, developers, and owners can imagine their environments in ways that defy reality. The lack of material constraints makes it possible for boundless architectural innovation and personal expression to abound, offering a playground for the imagination (Nicholson, 2022). Fig. 8.3 in the following showcases a 3D-rendered digital, creative creation that depicts a city in the metaverse.

As the metaverse continues to be imagined, several virtual real estate platforms and projects have emerged and continue to gain traction. A good example is the Decentraland, which is a virtual reality platform powered by the Ethereum blockchain (Decentraland, 2023). This platform offers users a limitless canvas where they can craft, experience, and monetize content and applications.

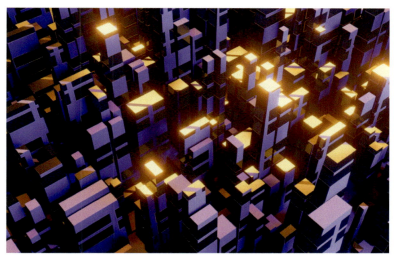

FIG. 8.3 A 3D-rendered digital work (Johnson, 2021).

Another similar platform that is equally important is the Sandbox, also powered by Ethereum. Within this platform, individuals can own, create, and monetize their gaming experiences.

Virtual real estate is not without a share of challenges, just like is the case with the metaverse at large. For instance, it is currently wrestling with a host of legal and regulatory issues, especially arising from the fact that there has not been established a governance structure for the metaverse that would help in controlling and regulating operations in the virtual world. As such, questions surrounding property rights, governance, and data privacy are of paramount importance and need to be addressed urgently. The quagmire on these issues is compounded by the fact that virtual spaces often extend beyond national boundaries, hence, it is unclear which jurisdiction's laws would apply in cases of disputes involving virtual property (Lubin, 2022). In the absence of established legal and regulatory frameworks, the potential for fraud and other malpractices remains significant (Cheong, 2022).

Beyond the aforementioned challenges, the processes for buying and developing virtual real estate bear striking similarities to the physical world. That is, once ownership is established, owners have the liberty to personalize their virtual spaces, using diverse digital tools and assets. This ability creates unique and immersive experiences for both the owners and the visitors. The small difference known when comparing the trading for real estate on the two distinctive dimensions is that for the virtual version, trading is done online, on various marketplaces. Another notable difference is that it is possible to include blockchain technology in the transactions to guarantee security and transparency (Huynh-The et al., 2023).

The metaverse and real estate visualization

> Architectural visualization refers to the process of creating visual representations, typically in the form of images or videos, that depict architectural designs, spaces, and structures before they are built or constructed.

Architectural visualization has in the recent past been made possible by the availability of numerous technologies. However, the metaverse can be argued to have added the icing by providing additional tools and dimensions. To begin with, it allows for an immersive experience allowing users to interact with unending computer-generated environments (Giang Barrera & Shah, 2023). The interplay between architecture and the metaverse changes the way individuals understand and represent built environments, particularly when such are enhanced by the power of Virtual Reality (VR) and Augmented Reality (AR) technologies. VR technology allows prospective buyers or tenants to undertake a remote virtual tour of a property from any location. They can explore every room, layout, space, and esthetic detail in a prospective building all from the comfort of their own home. With the AR, clients have access to enhanced physical property viewing; where digital information, such as property dimensions are overlaid onto the real-world environment. These advanced technologies elevate property viewings to a level of convenience and interactivity that traditional methods struggle to match.

The benefits of VR and AR property viewings are manifold. First, they offer unprecedented convenience to both buyers and sellers. In the traditional process, potential buyers or tenants often have to spend precious time traveling to various locations to view properties. However, with VR, it becomes possible for them to view properties virtually at any time, from any place (Lee et al., 2020). In addition, VR and AR enhance interactivity. That is, they allow users to navigate the property at their own pace, zooming in on specific features or aspects of the design that interest them. These technologies also offer a personalized experience. For instance, users can adjust lighting conditions, alter furniture arrangements, and even simulate different times of day to better understand how the property might suit their lifestyle (Nicholson, 2022).

The application of VR and AR technologies in virtual real estate extends beyond property viewings; they also offer potential for property marketing. They help reach a broader audience, given that anyone with a compatible device can access the virtual property viewings (Allam, Sharifi, Bibri, et al., 2022; Giang Barrera & Shah, 2023). Noting that the metaverse avails a global reach, it then significantly expands the pool of potential buyers or tenants that a seller can reach, regardless of their geographical location. The two technologies captivate users, opening them to an engaging and comprehensive understanding of the property being sold, which can inform their decision-making and potentially influence their readiness to invest.

Virtual staging is another powerful tool in the metaverse that is argued to assist potential buyers or tenants in visualizing and imagining a space. Unlike traditional staging, which involves physically furnishing a property, virtual staging utilizes digital assets to transform an empty property, making it more appealing and attractive. It allows users to visualize how a room might look with different furniture styles, color schemes, and layouts. In doing so, virtual staging helps buyers or tenants imagine how they might utilize the space, thus, enhancing their connection with the property (Virtually Staging, 2023).

However, the use of VR and AR technologies for property viewings attracts several limitations. First, for users to access the metaverse using these two technologies, they must have unmetered access to the internet. However, there is a segment of the population, especially those in the lower economic status that might not always have this access; thus, denying them the opportunity to enjoy the virtual benefits. In addition, VR and AR technologies require specific hardware and software, which may not be readily available to all users (Çöl et al., 2023). Furthermore, some users may experience disorientation or discomfort during VR viewings due to the simulated movement and the disparity between the virtual and real-world environments (Virtually Staging, 2023).

The advent of VR and AR property viewings has undeniably impacted decision-making and real estate transactions. These technologies provide a comprehensive understanding of the property, influencing users' perceptions and decisions (Virtually Staging, 2023). Furthermore, they enable real estate professionals to communicate architectural concepts and space functionality in a better way, enhancing the quality of information available to potential buyers or tenants. The depth of details and enhanced communication potentially lead to more informed decisions among individuals or businesses seeking rentals or ready-to-buy properties. The technology further facilitates more efficient real estate transactions, where both the buyer and seller feel satisfied with the process and outcome.

Another indisputable advantage of virtual and augmented realities is their potential to contribute to the reduction of the time properties spend on the market. By providing immersive, detailed, and interactive viewings, potential buyers can make quicker decisions, thus accelerating the sales process. Furthermore, by enabling viewings from anywhere in the world, VR expands the potential buyer pool, increasing the likelihood of a quick sale.

The impact of VR and AR on decision-making is not always positive. First, there are possibilities of incorrect perceptions about the property on sale due to the obvious disconnect between the virtual and the physical realities. Secondly, while virtual staging is argued to help users visualize a space better, it might however set unrealistic expectations, leading to dissatisfaction among some users when they physically encounter the property. Thirdly, the immersive nature of VR could potentially encourage and eventually lead to impulse buying, where the novelty and excitement of the technology could overshadow a careful evaluation of the property (Virtually Staging, 2023). The fourth challenge is that VR and AR can lead to some legal issues around international real estate transactions, especially noting that these two open the possibilities of global viewership. The two further raise concerns regarding data privacy and security, especially given the significant amount of personal and financial information involved in real estate transactions.

Despite these potential challenges, VR and AR are revolutionizing real estate visualization and transactions in the metaverse. They offer significant advantages, including convenience, interactivity, personalization, and enhanced marketing potential. Moreover, they provide a powerful tool for architectural visualization, enabling a depth of exploration and understanding that is not achievable at all in the case of traditional real estate marketing strategy. These benefits can be cemented even further by ensuring that the associated challenges discussed earlier are addressed amicably.

Smart technologies in real estate management

Smart property management signifies a transformative shift in the realm of real estate management, one that is informed by the rise of sophisticated technologies like Artificial Intelligence (AI), Blockchain, and the Internet of Things (IoT). Inextricably linked to this shift is the metaverse, which offers an interactive and immersive environment for developers and realtors to manage and monitor properties in real-time (De Regt et al., 2021). Both AI and IoT technologies have played a paramount role in this evolution, by acting as the conduits that facilitate comprehensive data collection and analysis. IoT devices, embedded throughout the property, provide real-time data on numerous variables, ranging from environmental parameters such as temperature and humidity to security features encompassing door locks and surveillance systems (Guo et al., 2018). The continuous flow of data allows property managers to analyze and draw actionable insights, thereby enabling them to respond promptly to emerging situations and ensure that the properties are well-maintained and secure.

Beyond real-time monitoring, smart technologies have also been instrumental in fundamentally reshaping the maintenance landscape within property management. The synergistic blend of AI algorithms with IoT sensors enables the implementation of predictive maintenance (Allam, Bibri, Jones, et al., 2022; Allam & Jones, 2021). This approach is made possible by the prospect of early detection and remediation of potential issues, preemptively addressing them before they escalate into significant problems. The ability to perform predictive maintenance helps to avert costly and disruptive repairs, extends the life span of the property, and drives down overall maintenance expenses (Cline, 2023). The two technologies also help to automate the course of property management, hence, streamlining several routine tasks such as scheduling maintenance and managing energy consumption. Automating these tasks liberates property managers, allowing them to divert and devote their energies towards strategic tasks that add value and improve the property's overall efficiency and profitability (Cline, 2023).

AI and IoT further enhance and empower data-driven decision-making which allows for optimized management strategies, and improvement in the overall outlook of the property and their use. Among insights drawn from such data include tenant behaviors, resource consumption, and property usage. Such enables property managers to customize and fine-tune services and amenities to match tenant preferences and to optimize consumption of resources.

In the realm of smart property management, the metaverse also instrumentally acts in promoting community interactions within residential properties. That is, it offers a platform where virtual spaces are curated to mirror physical common areas within a property, thus, fostering interactions in a digital setting. This digital interaction can engender a sense of community and togetherness, especially in large residential complexes where face-to-face interaction might not be practically possible. Moreover, the metaverse has the potential to facilitate virtual meetings, events, and social spaces, thereby nurturing an active and vibrant community.

The smart property management landscape also holds promising prospects for enhancing tenant satisfaction and retention. The improved maintenance procedures, bespoke services, and vibrant community interactions all collectively contribute to enriching the quality of living for tenants. Such an enhanced living experience invariably leads to improved tenant satisfaction and retention rates.

While celebrating the breakthrough that both AI and IoT have brought in property management, it is important not to lose sight of the possible concerns they raise. For instance, they spark privacy concerns, where personal information amassed could be potentially misused or fall into unauthorized hands. As such, it is paramount to adopt stringent data protection protocols and maintain transparent communication with tenants concerning the nature of the data collected and its usage. It is also crucial to strike a balance between leveraging the benefits of smart technologies and addressing the inherent privacy concerns to ensure a secure and comfortable living environment for the tenants.

The benefits and challenges of metaverse in real estate

From the discussions in the previous sections, it is evident that the advent of the metaverse opens up a plethora of possibilities within the realm of real estate, offering a notable boost towards increased accessibility and inclusivity. It helps reduce the disadvantages associated with geographical limitations by helping participants from across the globe to partake in property viewings, negotiations, and transactions in a virtual setting (Virtually Staging, 2023). This inclusivity in turn has helped in the emergence of vast new markets, promising a more equitable real estate landscape that transcends socioeconomic and geographic barriers. The metaverse further helps in cost reductions in real estate development and transactions, making them significantly attractive to a wider pool of buyers.

In a ground-breaking way, the metaverse opens possibilities to visualize and explore properties virtually before they are physically constructed, thus reducing costs and time associated with physical models and mock-ups. Additionally, the digital nature of transactions within the metaverse helps to streamline administrative processes, such as contract signing and property registration, which could translate into substantial cost savings and a quicker sale period compared to the brick-and-mortar approach.

On the environmental front, there is optimism that the metaverse will contribute significantly to reducing the real estate sector's carbon footprint. This could be through frontiers such as virtual property viewing and virtual transactions that could curtail travel-related emissions. In addition, the smart property management approaches facilitated by the metaverse could also help optimize energy consumption within properties, leading to considerable energy savings and reduced environmental impact.

The metaverse has been hailed for its potential to prompt unique innovation and creativity in real estate. In particular, its capacity to facilitate novel property visualization techniques and unique innovations such as virtual staging is lauded for the way it enables potential buyers to visualize spaces tailored to their tastes (Virtually Staging, 2023). Additionally, it opens platforms for developers to showcase avant-garde architectural designs and creative amenities in an immersive and interactive manner, spurring innovation within the industry (Bibri et al., 2022; Allam, Sharifi, Bibri, et al., 2022).

However, along with these promising prospects are some notable challenges that cannot be wished away. The concern of cybersecurity is particularly distinctive, as there has been an increase in threats ranging from data breaches to fraud. Breaches lead to compromise on private data and information, which frauds could entail issues such as manipulation of property transactions, et cetera. As a mitigation strategy for those, robust cybersecurity measures need to be implemented to safeguard the metaverse and its users from such threats (Chow et al., 2022). These measures may include robust encryption, two-factor authentication, and continuous monitoring and updating of security protocols. Furthermore, the metaverse attracts a complex array of legal and regulatory issues. The nature of property rights within the metaverse, the jurisdictional issues surrounding transnational transactions, and the enforceability of virtual contracts are some of the legal quandaries that need to be resolved. Those would require robust legal frameworks to be developed (after wide consultation) that consider the unique characteristics of the metaverse, and international cooperation needs.

Another concern that cannot be overlooked is the digital divide, or the disparity in access to technology, which has been cited to have the potential to derail the enjoyment of metaverse and associated benefits such as virtual real estate. While the metaverse promises inclusivity, this promise is contingent on users having access to relevant technology and stable internet connectivity. To ensure equity in access, concerted efforts between different stakeholders and players are needed to bridge this digital divide, through investment in digital infrastructure and promoting affordable access to technology, and also by ensuring there is standardization of protocols to allow devices to share common networks (Nicholson, 2022). Finally, it will be necessary to invest in and emphasize user education and awareness about metaverse technologies in real estate. The target information and education package should be customized to empower users to be able to navigate the metaverse, understand property rights within this virtual realm, and safeguard their data.

From a broader viewpoint, the metaverse does not only represent a technological innovation but signifies a new cultural paradigm in the way individuals will interact, work, and live in the near future (Allam, Sharifi, Bibri, et al., 2022). In the context of real estate, this paradigm shift extends beyond the transactional aspects to encompass the experiential elements of property ownership and residency. For instance, in the metaverse, property owners and residents can collaborate to create and customize communal spaces, reflecting their shared values and aspirations (Bruner, 2022). These virtual communities could foster a sense of togetherness and camaraderie that transcends the physical boundaries of traditional real estate. Consequently, through the metaverse, real estate developers have the opportunity to cocreate with potential buyers and tenants, integrating their preferences and feedback into the design process; thus, facilitating the creation of properties that are universally accepted by both the sellers and buyers. This collaborative approach could engender a more user-centric model of real estate development, leading to more sustainable and resilient communities.

Despite these potential benefits of metaverse integration in the real estate industry, it is crucial to recognize the ethical and societal implications that are imminent. For example, the proliferation of virtual real estate may reinforce existing socioeconomic inequalities, with affluent individuals and corporations dominating the virtual real estate market, as has been depicted in the movie, Ready Player One (Hudson, 2018). Furthermore, there is a risk of commodifying communal spaces within the metaverse, which may undermine the sense of community and social cohesion.

Therefore, in navigating the aforementioned complexities, it would be imperative to adopt a holistic and inclusive approach to policymaking and regulation, one that balances economic viability with social equity and environmental sustainability. This would involve multistakeholder dialogs, involving governments, private sector players, civil society, and users, to formulate policies and guidelines that ensure the metaverse serves the common good.

Case studies

Decentraland

Decentraland is considered to be the pioneer virtual real estate platform, that stands as a testament to the convergence of blockchain technology and metaverse possibilities (Decentraland, 2023). This digital ecosystem, built on the

Ethereum blockchain platform presents a marketplace for parcels of land that are uniquely identified as nonfungible tokens (NFTs). Through it, metaverse users can purchase, develop, and monetize the virtual parcels of land (Huynh-The et al., 2023). This platform has engendered a robust creator economy, with membership from all over the world. That is, individuals globally have the opportunity to harness their creative and entrepreneurial talents, establishing a myriad of experiences from gaming arcades to art galleries on their virtual plots, powered by Decentraland. These activities have prompted the emergence of new avenues of income streams, reshaping conventional concepts of real estate ownership and economic opportunity. Interestingly, Decentraland's decentralized framework offers a level playing field that allow people, irrespective of their geographic backgrounds or socioeconomic condition to engage, innovate, and prosper in this virtual landscape (Koohang et al., 2023). Decentraland underscores the potential of virtual real estate as a medium for expression and community-building. By owning land in Decentraland, users can shape their environment, cultivating a unique digital identity while participating in a broader collective narrative. This element of the metaverse emphasizes the significance of digital spaces not merely as platforms for economic transactions but as arenas of social and cultural interplay.

The promising benefits and openness associated with Decentraland however does raise questions of regulation and oversight, sparking intriguing debates on governance in the metaverse. As is the case with other virtual platforms, there is a need to address those concerns at the earliest opportunity to void their potential to derail future successes.

Sotheby's international realty

Sotheby's International Realty has embraced VR technology with notable success. It is characterized by a Curate app, which depicts an innovative integration of Virtual Reality in property marketing (Reynolds, 2022). Curate provides immersive, realistic VR tours of listed properties by transporting users into available homes without the need to step foot inside them. This capability has transformed the property viewing process, offering unprecedented convenience and flexibility (Sotherby's International Realty, 2018). Curate's VR environment goes beyond simple property tours. It enables potential buyers to visualize different interior designs and furnishings within the properties, adding a layer of personalization and interactivity, while reducing associated costs and saving on time (Reynolds, 2022). This feature empowers customers to envision themselves in the space, fostering emotional connections that have the potential to drive quick purchase decisions. In addition, Sotheby's implementation of VR has expanded its reach beyond geographical boundaries, opening its doors to international buyers who are also able to tour properties from their own homes, regardless of distance. As a result, the company has witnessed an increase in engagement and sales, validating the efficacy of VR in overcoming traditional real estate hurdles.

However, several concerns related to the integration of VR tools by Sotheby's International Realty have been identified. Some of those include the need to ensure the high quality of VR content, managing potential technical glitches, and facilitating user comfort. The journey of Sotheby's highlights that while VR can revolutionize real estate, its deployment must be thoughtful and user-centric.

WeWork

WeWork's deployment of smart technologies in its coworking spaces is another example that helps to offer insights into the transformative potential of the IoT and AI in property management. It has managed to achieve this by incorporating smart sensors and devices in its facilities, hence, enhancing building operations and user experience, and effectively addressing the dynamic needs of its clientele (Morey, 2022). It uses IoT sensors to monitor real-time building usage, which in turn assists in predictive maintenance and operational efficiency. To put this into perspective, the data collected from HVAC systems helps predict potential equipment failure and optimizes energy consumption. This data-driven, proactive approach to maintenance reduces downtime and costs while improving the occupants' comfort and experience.

Additionally, the integration of AI extends beyond facilities management to community engagement within WeWork spaces. The company uses AI algorithms to recommend networking opportunities and events to members based on their interests and professional domains, fostering a vibrant and interactive community (Morey, 2022). However, like in many such platforms, data collection and usage raise privacy concerns, making data security and transparent communication imperative. Ultimately, the WeWork case illustrates how smart technologies can create a responsive, interactive, and efficient built environment, paving the way for a new paradigm in property management.

Cryptovoxels

Cryptovoxels is another prominent virtual real estate platform that helps exemplify the complex legal and regulatory landscape of digital property. Built on the Ethereum blockchain which powers this tool, users buy, sell, and develop digital land, much like is the case in Decentraland (Weston, 2022). Users can leverage the platform to express creativity, conduct business, and generate wealth. This platform has made commendable efforts to self-regulate, establish community-led governance systems, and implement policies to address concerns such as intellectual property infringement. However, the absence of a standardized regulatory framework poses unique challenges including legal uncertainties around property rights, taxation, and dispute resolution. Like other metaverse platforms, Cryptovoxels must tread a careful pathway, advocating for user freedoms, while at the same time, ensuring legality and ethical behaviors are observed. In summary, it is worth noting that the case of Cryptovoxels underscores the need for concerted multistakeholder dialog, paving the way for robust, adaptable, and fair regulatory frameworks for virtual real estate.

Microsoft

Microsoft's "Campus of the Future" initiative is a further classic case that showcases the potential of metaverse technologies in promoting sustainable real estate development. The initiative leverages a digital twin of its Microsoft's Redmond headquarters to demonstrate how simulation, optimization, and predictive analytics can inform sustainable architectural design and resource management (Javier & Takeo, 2017). This digital twin allows for detailed energy consumption modeling and performance simulations, optimizing building design for energy efficiency. It can also predict the impact of climate change on the campus, informing resilient design strategies. This approach has the potential to reduce both the environmental impact and operational costs, thus, demonstrating the intersection of sustainability and profitability in smart real estate. It is therefore safe to argue that Microsoft's example underscores the transformative potential of the metaverse in fostering a sustainable real estate sector. It emphasizes the role of technology not only as a tool for efficiency and convenience but also as an agent of ecological stewardship.

Conclusion and future outlook

Reflecting upon the intricate discussions developed in the previous sections of this chapter, the transformative potential of the metaverse within the real estate domain is evidenced through an array of multitudinous possibilities. Such includes virtual property transactions, augmented property management paradigms, and overall sustainability in the real estate sector. These signal a more holistic, dynamic, and environmentally considerate future under the egis of metaverse technologies.

One of the most promising of those impending transformations is the rise of innovative virtual real estate platforms like Decentraland, WeWork, and Cryptovoxels. By facilitating the touring, acquisition, trading, and developmental processes of digital properties, these platforms are creating a myriad of entrepreneurial opportunities that would ultimately culminate into intricate legal and regulatory quandaries. Concurrently, metaverse technologies are pivotal in widening the spectrum of accessibility and inclusivity within the real estate industry, especially through employing VR and AR to provide an immersive property viewing experience, as exemplified by Sotheby's (Sotherby's International Realty, 2018). The incorporation of smart technologies, such as AI and IoT, in property management allows for enhanced real-time surveillance, predictive maintenance, and heightened automation (Allam, Bibri, Jones, et al., 2022). The amalgamation of digital twins and metaverse technologies is on the precipice of reducing the carbon footprint of the real estate sector, promoting energy-efficient building designs and operations as evidenced by Microsoft's "Campus of the Future" initiative (Javier & Takeo, 2017).

Going into the future, metaverse technologies are set to carve out new avenues in the real estate landscape. The gradually increasing usage of "smart contracts" within blockchain networks aims at automation, thus reducing costs and improving efficiency. Furthermore, advancements in 3D modeling and simulations, and the emergence of technologies such as 5G and 6G could enhance the authenticity of virtual property viewings, offering users immersive experiences of unmatched fidelity. This nascent field then invites exploration and research in multifarious dimensions to establish, among other things, the economic dynamics of virtual real estate markets, and how such could aid in informed decision-making for investors and policymakers. A holistic understanding of the societal implications of these technologies and the digital inequalities is essential for fostering an equitable virtual environment. Regulatory bodies and policymakers will need to steer these developments meticulously, establishing frameworks that cater to the unique challenges posed by virtual real estate such as property rights, taxation, and dispute resolution. Equally important is the need to strike a balance between safeguarding user freedoms while maintaining legal and ethical parameters. As we continue to embrace the metaverse in real estate, it is becoming crucial to address the critical concerns of accessibility, equity, and privacy. Such could be addressed through the formulation of policies that ensure that technological dividends are equitably distributed, thereby mitigating socioeconomic disparities. User education and awareness about these technologies are essential in facilitating lasting solutions to the earlier-mentioned challenges that are sought and implemented.

In envisioning the future of real estate within the metaverse, it is evident that there is unimaginable, untapped potential. The seamless integration of metaverse technologies in real estate transactions, efficient property management, and immersive property experiences appear within reach. However, such a vision is also a clarion call for responsible, ethical, and equitable adoption of these technologies. It calls upon all stakeholders—developers, users, policymakers, and researchers—to venture into this unchartered territory guided by principles of fairness, sustainability, and inclusivity.

References

Abaulzolof, P. (2022). *5 Ways to use virtual reality in your real estate business* [Online]. *Forbes*. Available: https://www.Forbes.Com/Sites/Forbestechcouncil/2022/10/05/5-Ways-To-Use-Virtual-Reality-In-Your-Real-Estate-Business/?Sh=4ea5477c7b1d. (Accessed 20 May 2023).

Allam, Z. (2012). Sustainable architecture: Utopia or feasible reality? *Journal of Biourbanism, 2*, 47–61.

Allam, Z. (2020). Underlining the role of data science and technology in supporting supply chains, political stability and health networks during pandemics. *Surveying The Covid-19 Pandemic Its Implications*, *129*.

Allam, Z., Bibri, S. E., Chabaud, D., & Moreno, C. (2022). The '15-Minute City' concept can shape a net-zero urban future. *Humanities and Social Sciences Communications*, *9*, 126.

Allam, Z., Bibri, S. E., Jones, D. S., Chabaud, D., & Moreno, C. (2022). Unpacking the 15-Minute City Via 6g, Iot, and digital twins: Towards a new narrative for increasing urban efficiency, resilience, and sustainability. *Sensors*, *22*, 1369.

Allam, Z., & Jones, D. S. (2021). Future (post-Covid) digital, smart and sustainable cities in the wake of 6g: Digital twins, immersive realities and new urban economies. *Land Use Policy*, *101*, 105201.

Allam, Z., Sharifi, A., Bibri, S. E., Jones, D. S., & Krogstie, J. (2022). The metaverse as a virtual form of smart cities: Opportunities and challenges for environmental, economic, and social sustainability in urban futures. *Smart Cities*, *5*, 771–801. https://doi.org/10.3390/smartcities5030040.

Allam, Z., Sharifi, A., Giurco, D., & Sharpe, S. A. (2022). Green new deals could be the answer to Cop26's deep decarbonisation needs. *Sustainable Horizons*, *1*, 100006.

Bhattacharya, P., Saraswat, D., Savaliya, D., Sanghavi, S., Verma, A., Sakariya, V., Tanwar, S., Sharma, R., Raboaca, M. S., & Manea, D. L. (2023). Towards future internet: The metaverse perspective for diverse industrial applications. *Mathematics [Online]*, *11*.

Bibri, S. E., Allam, Z., & Krogstie, J. (2022). The metaverse as a virtual form of data-driven smart urbanism: Platformization and its underlying processes, institutional dimensions, and disruptive impacts. *Computational Urban Science*, *2*, 24. https://doi.org/10.1007/s43762-022-00051-0.

Bruner, R. (2022). *Why investors are paying real money for virtual land* [Online]. *Time*. Available: https://Time.Com/6140467/Metaverse-Real-Estate/. (Accessed 10 February 2023).

Cheong, B. C. (2022). Avatars in the metaverse: Potential legal issues and remedies. *International Cybersecurity Law Review*, *3*, 467–494.

Chow, Y. W., Susilo, W., Li, Y., Li, N., & Nguyen, C. (2022). Visualization and cybersecurity in the metaverse: A survey. *Journal of Imaging*, *9*.

Cline, B. (2023). *Why predictive maintenance makes sense for healthy buildings* [Online]. *Buildings*. Available: https://www.Buildings.Com/Building-Controls/Article/21545613/Why-Predictive-Maintenance-Makes-Sense-For-Healthy-Buildings. (Accessed 21 May 2023).

Çöl, B. G., İmre, M., & Yıkmış, S. (2023). Virtual reality and augmented reality technologies in gastronomy: A review. *eFood*, *4*, E84.

Dasgupta, S., Lall, S., & Wheeler, D. (2022). *Cutting global carbon emissions: Where do cities stand?* [Online]. *The World Bank*. Available: https://Blogs.Worldbank.Org/Sustainablecities/Cutting-Global-Carbon-Emissions-Where-Do-Cities-Stand. (Accessed 2 February 2022).

De Regt, A., Plangger, K., & Barnes, S. J. (2021). Virtual reality marketing and customer advocacy: Transforming experiences from story-telling to story-doing. *Journal of Business Research*, *136*, 513–522.

Decentraland. (2023). *Welcome to decentraland [Online]*. Decentraland. Available: https://Decentraland.Org/. (Accessed 15 May 2023).

Dwivedi, Y. K., Hughes, L., Baabdullah, A. M., Ribeiro-Navarrete, S., Giannakis, M., Al-Debei, M. M., Dennehy, D., Metri, B., Buhalis, D., Cheung, C. M. K., Conboy, K., Doyle, R., Dubey, R., Dutot, V., Felix, R., Goyal, D. P., Gustafsson, A., Hinsch, C., Jebabli, I., ... Wamba, S. F. (2022). Metaverse beyond the hype: Multidisciplinary perspectives on emerging challenges, opportunities, and agenda for research, practice and policy. *International Journal of Information Management*, *66*, 102542.

Gadekallu, T., Huynh-The, T., Wang, W., Yenduri, G., Ranaweera, P., Pham, V., Costa, D. B., & Liyanage, M. (2022). *Blockchain for the metaverse: A review*.

Giang Barrera, K., & Shah, D. (2023). Marketing in the metaverse: Conceptual understanding, framework, and research agenda. *Journal of Business Research*, *155*, 113420.

Guo, K., Lu, Y., Gao, H., & Cao, R. (2018). Artificial intelligence-based semantic internet of things in a user-centric smart city. *Sensors (Basel)*, *18*.

Hudson, L. (2018). *If you want to know how we ended up in a cyber dystopia, read ready player one* [Online]. *The Verge*. Available: https://www.Theverge.Com/2018/4/19/17250892/Ready-Player-One-Book-Facebook-Internet-Dystopia. (Accessed 29 October 2021).

Huynh-The, T., Gadekallu, T. R., Wang, W., Yenduri, G., Ranaweera, P., Pham, Q.-V., Da Costa, D. B., & Liyanage, M. (2023). Blockchain for the metaverse: A review. *Future Generation Computer Systems*, *143*, 401–419.

Immergluck, D., & Law, J. (2014). Investing in crisis: The methods, strategies, and expectations of investors in single-family foreclosed homes in distressed neighborhoods. *Housing Policy Debate*, *24*, 568–593.

Javier, L., & Takeo, R. (2017). *Microsoft plans major 'Redmond campus of the future' expansion* [Online]. *Kin 5*. Available: https://Www.King5.Com/Article/Tech/Microsoft-Plans-Major-Redmond-Campus-Of-The-Future-Expansion/281-495379061. (Accessed 24 May 2023).

Johnson, S. (2021). *3D render [Online]*. Unsplash. Available: https://Unsplash.Com/Photos/Blkuln9vhwo. (Accessed 16 June 2023).

Juarez, M. G., Botti, V. J., & Giret, A. S. (2021). Digital twins: Review And challenges. *Journal of Computing and Information Science in Engineering*, *21*.

Koohang, A., Nord, J., Ooi, K.-B., Tan, G., Al-Emran, M., Aw, E., Baabdullah, A., Buhalis, D., Cham, T.-H., Dennis, C., Dutot, V., Dwivedi, Y., Hughes, L., Mogaji, E., Pandey, N., Phau, I., Raman, R., Sharma, A., Sigala, M., & Wong, L.-W. (2023). Shaping the metaverse into reality: A holistic multidisciplinary understanding of opportunities, challenges, and avenues for future investigation. *Journal of Computer Information Systems*, *63*, 1–31.

Lee, J., Seo, J., Abbas, A., & Choi, M. (2020). End-users' augmented reality utilization for architectural design review. *Applied Sciences*, *10*, 5363.

Lubin, A. (2022). *Governance in the metaverse* [Online]. *Datasphere*. Available: https://www.Thedatasphere.Org/News/Governance-In-The-Metaverse/. (Accessed 12 February 2023).

Meyer, A., Walter, W., & Seuring, S. (2021). The impact of the coronavirus pandemic on supply chains and their sustainability: A text mining approach. *Frontiers in Sustainability*, *2*.

Morey, S. (2022). *Creating a flexible world of work with technology* [Online]. *Wework*. Available: https://www.Wework.Com/En-Gb/Ideas/Workspace-Solutions/Creating-A-Flexible-World-Of-Work-With-Technology. (Accessed 23 May 2023).

Nicholson, C. (2022). *The current state of the real estate metaverse* [Online]. *Inman*. Available: https://www.Inman.Com/2022/06/10/The-Current-State-Of-The-Real-Estate-Metaverse/. (Accessed 20 May 2023).

Nohassi, M. (2023). *Summer camp 3D render [Online]*. Asilah, Morocco: Unsplash. Available: https://Unsplash.Com/Photos/Er3tnawvycw. (Accessed 14 June 2023).

Qi, W. (2022). The investment value of metaverse in the media and entertainment industry. *BCP Business & Management*, *34*, 279–283.

Reynolds, E. (2022). *One Sotheby's Is selling the first real-world home through the metaverse using NFT technology* [Online]. *Forbes*. Available: https://www.Forbes.Com/Sites/Emmareynolds/2022/01/05/One-Sothebys-Is-Selling-The-First-Real-World-Home-Through-The-Metaverse-Using-Nft-Technology/?Sh=39c7d4893471. (Accessed 22 May 2023).

Sotherby's International Realty. (2018). *Sotheby's international realty first real estate brand to launch augmented reality app: Introducing curate by Sotheby's international realty* [Online]. *Sotherby's International Realty*. Available: https://www.Sothebysrealty.Com/Extraordinary-Living-Blog/Sothebys-International-Realty-Launches-Augmented-Reality-App. (Accessed 23 May 2023).

Space, R. (2021). *Black plastic bag shanty [Online]*. Los Angeles: Unsplash. Available: https://Unsplash.Com/Photos/Zjgcxyzq_E4. (Accessed 15 June 2023).

Steininger, B. I., Groth, M., & Weber, B. L. (2021). Cost overruns and delays in infrastructure projects: The case of Stuttgart 21. *Journal of Property Investment & Finance*, *39*, 256–282.

Stephenson, N. (2003). *Snow crash: A novel*. New York, NY: Random House Publishing Group.

Sun, C. (2021). *Architecting the metaverse* [Online]. *Archi Daily*. Available: https://www.Archdaily.Com/968905/Architecting-The-Metaverse. (Accessed 23 May 2023).

Vantage Market Research. (2022). *Metaverse in real estate market—Global industry assessment & forecast [Online]*. Vantage Market Research. Available: https://www.Vantagemarketresearch.Com/Industry-Report/Metaverse-In-Real-Estate-Market-1516. (Accessed 23 May 2023).

Virtually Staging. (2023). *What is virtual staging* [Online]. *Virtually Staging*. Available: https://Virtuallystagingproperties.Com/Virtual-Staging-What-Is-Virtual-Staging/. (Accessed 20 May 2023).

Weston, G. (2022). *Cryptovoxels metaverse—Everything you need to know* [Online]. *101 Blockchains*. Available: https://101blockchains.Com/Cryptovoxels-Metaverse/. (Accessed 22 May 2023).

Wong, B. A. (2020). *How digital entrepreneurs will help shape the world after the Covid-19 pandemic* [Online]. *We Forum*. Available: https://www.Weforum.Org/Agenda/2020/06/Entrepreneurs-Must-Embrace-Digital-During-Pandemic-For-Society/. (Accessed 20 February 2022).

World Green Building Council. (2019). *Bringing embodied carbon upfront [Online]*. World Green Building Council. Available: https://Worldgbc.Org/Advancing-Net-Zero/Embodied-Carbon/#:~:Text=Buildings%20are%20currently%20responsible%20for,11%25%20from%20materials%20and%20construction. (Accessed 23 May 2023).

Chapter 9

The social implications of the metaverse in cities

Challenges of social interactions in urban environments

In modern urban setups, there are substantial social challenges that residents must put up with. Ranging from reduced social interactions to inequalities to housing scarcity, et cetera. Therefore, in contemplating them to come up with long-term solutions, it is imperative to consider the intricacies of the lived urban experience. It is also worth appreciating that the cityscape, in its complex grandeur, manifests assorted social complexities and paradoxes, wherein the same streets teeming with life may also serve as an epicenter for isolation, fragmentation, and polarization (Salingaros, 2014).

On the face value, the urban space, with its density and diversity, appears to be a fertile ground for diverse social connections. However, that has often been deceiving, especially noting that while cities might be deemed as a melting pot of cultures and experiences, they could also serve as battlegrounds for social dislocation and discontent. This paradox is at the heart of understanding social interactions in urban environments. It is important to understand that the issue of social isolation in cities is paradoxical, yet not entirely baffling when we examine it at close range. Despite the city's bustling ethos, it is surprising to meet individuals inhabiting these spaces who report feeling isolated or lonely. A recent study discovered that urbanites are 21% more likely to experience loneliness than their rural counterparts, despite being in crowds of people (Peen et al., 2010). That means that the anonymity that a city offers, although appealing for many, can often mutate into a feeling of invisibility or neglect. Fig. 9.1 shows an image of a person experiencing loneliness.

Another urban issue that is not conducive for social life in urban areas is that of fragmentation. Unfortunately, this is often deeply embedded within the structural and infrastructural aspects of cities, and not just refers to the physical separation of neighborhoods, but also to the socioeconomic and cultural disparities that splinter the city's populace (Bibri, 2022). Such schisms could negatively impact social interactions and community-building efforts, as people often tend to engage and closely relate with those who are perceived as similar to them.

FIG. 9.1 A picture depicting the impacts of loneliness (Khamseh, 2020).

As a result, the city becomes an amalgamation of isolated and detached enclaves rather than a unified (whole) social ecosystem (Allam, Moreno, et al., 2022; Allam, Sharifi, et al., 2022). The ideal urban ecosystem is further affected by the aspect of polarization, which could be viewed as an extension of fragmentation. Polarization emerges from the social and economic disparities within the city, resulting in an obvious juxtaposition of privilege and deprivation. In most cities, these disparities often manifest in the form of gentrification; where low-income populations are unceremoniously displaced by wealthier residents, as they are unable to cope with the high costs of living in such neighborhoods (Wilhelmsson et al., 2021). This fosters a climate of social tension, detracting from the inclusive essence of urban life.

The earlier cited issues significantly impact community-building efforts and sound social connections within cities. With those issues, the most obvious outcome is the destruction of the social fabric, where the sense of community and the notion of belonging are no longer pursued or seen as important. In the long term, instead of a city serving as a locus for social cohesion, it inadvertently harbors and promotes social disintegration.

A classic case that can be put forward to illustrate the earlier urban social dynamic is that of New York City (NYC). Despite its reputation as a global hub of connectivity, NYC has been grappling with social issues emblematic of modern urban environments. A 2022 survey revealed that approximately 57% of New Yorkers report feeling lonely, indicating the pervasiveness of social isolation within the city (Leland, 2022). Those statistics are not surprising as the geographic fragmentation in NYC is evident and true through the clear socioeconomic divisions between neighborhoods like the Bronx and Manhattan. Such contrasts make the city a patchwork of disparity, contributing to social polarization. The positive side amid these challenges is that while they may be deemed daunting, they are surmountable. In particular, with a forward-looking attitude, and openness to dialogues and inclusivity efforts, such challenges could be mitigated in a record time. Surmounting those challenges need not be an option, after all, the metropolis, with its ceaseless flux, provides the perfect backdrop for innovation and social reinvention. It is within these intricate challenges that the true potential of the city—as a dynamic nexus of humanity—may be fully realized.

Enhancing community building and social connections

> Social connections: Relationships and interactions that individuals have with others in their social networks.

There have been numerous approaches explored in the recent past all of which aimed at addressing the different urban challenges. The most recent approach is the adoption of the metaverse, which has shown immense potential in addressing some social issues such as interpersonal relationships among others. In the exploration of this universe and its possibilities for addressing urban social challenges, it is unsurprising that there is evidence of a paradigm shift in the way diverse issues are approached. This shift begins from our very understanding of the metaverse—a convergent space combining virtual reality (VR), augmented reality (AR), 3D immersive simulations, and more—and extends beyond mere technology. From a wider scope of view, the metaverse represents a new sociospatial context that is not constrained by traditional limitations, such as geographical boundaries, language barriers, or racial backgrounds to name a few. In the metaverse, those obstacles are renegotiated, and boundaries reimagined.

One of the most astounding characteristics of the metaverse is that in its grand, boundless expanse, it possesses unparalleled potential for immersive experiences that significantly enrich social connections and promote community-building efforts. It is not surprising that it has been considered a digital "third place," in other words, a realm beyond home and work where people congregate, socialize, and engage with one another in a unique and immersive way (George et al., 2021). Through the help of diverse technologies such as VR and AG, the metaverse has the capacity to recreate lifelike experiences and facilitate immersive interactions, unhindered by the diverse constraints that often crowd the fabric of physical urban landscapes. One notable transformative aspect of the metaverse lies in its ability to make the concepts of distance and time redundant. As such, users in the metaverse can engage in real-time with peers located thousands of miles away. This has been instrumental in effectively overshadowing geographical boundaries and overcoming the isolation occasioned by sprawling urban spaces (Dwivedi et al., 2022). This attribute signifies a considerable departure from conventional urban experience, where social connections are often dictated by proximity.

Beyond promoting a sense of community across different parts of the world, the metaverse has been hailed for its role in fostering unconstrained collaboration between people with shared interests. As a result, it is becoming a platform of choice for people eager to share experiences and promote collective problem-solving. That is, it plays a significant role in encouraging active user participation, fostering spaces that are not merely places of visitation, but environments of interaction and collective participation. As a result, there has been a substantial shift, away from passive consumption towards active and concerted cocreation and coexistence within the metaverse, engendering community engagement and social cohesion (Polyviou & Pappas, 2022). The metaverse's capacity to influence and restructure social relations finds expression in "virtual towns" and "digital cities" (Lv et al., 2022). These spaces which represent the digital reconstructions of physical environments, facilitate shared problem-solving approaches and dialogue, fostering a sense of shared responsibility. By providing opportunities for users to collectively pursue common strategies to address urban challenges, these spaces not only mimic physical cities but, in many ways, transcend them by fostering social connections that are often unfeasible in physical urban environments due to both socioeconomic and spatial disparities (Allam, Sharifi, et al., 2022).

The true measure of the metaverse's potential in community building can be expressed in successful initiatives that are already done within its confines. For instance, the Burning Man Multiverse concept epitomizes this potential by transporting a city's worth of people into a digital platform, where a unique fusion of shared experiences, collective creativity, and community building are showcased (BurningMan.Org, 2020). Another example is the virtual city of Oasis, in the movie "Ready Player One," which has demonstrated a degree of community engagement and collective problem-solving that mirrors—and often surpasses—that of real-world cities (Snowden, 2019).

Augmented reality for cultural experiences and diversity

The timely advent of augmented reality (AR) and its gradual acceptance and integration into urban environments presents an intriguing avenue to enrich cultural experiences and champion diversity. This transformative technology, which superimposes digital information onto our physical surroundings, provides a promising platform for cultural immersion, understanding, and exchange in urban environments (Allam & Jones, 2021; Wang & Lin, 2023). It holds an immense capacity to democratize cultural experiences and makes way for an equitable and inclusive cultural landscape in cities around the world. This technology has been hailed for its multilayered cultural narrative that allows it to enhance cultural understanding and facilitate cultural exchanges seamlessly and interactively. Through it, users can explore and interact with diverse cultural elements in an immersive and accessible manner, rendering distant cultures proximate and abstract cultural concepts tangible (Paulauskas et al., 2023).

For instance, AR-based language learning apps, make it possible for users to easily comprehend and engage in cultural exchanges regardless of the unfamiliar language landscapes.

Augmented reality has also been very instrumental in revitalizing and preserving cultural heritage in cities. It achieves this by empowering users to virtually interact with historical sites and artifacts, revealing hidden narratives and forgotten histories. The overlay of historical data onto physical sites is believed to prompt a deeper appreciation and understanding of a city's cultural heritage and uniqueness, which are most often lost in the hubbub of modern urban life. This has significant implications for cities with rich cultural heritages (including the forgotten history), as AR can bring the past alive, and consequently provide educational experiences to users. On the same, it can also foster a sense of shared history among citizens, prompting togetherness and community. Far and beyond, AR's interactive capabilities provide unprecedented opportunities for individuals to engage with their city's cultural heritage (Allam & Dhunny, 2019; Allam & Newman, 2018). A case to illustrate this can be made of the AR-powered museum exhibits, which enable visitors to interact with artifacts, discovering stories and historical contexts that might otherwise remain unnoticed, or may eventually be lost as new cultures arise. This not only enriches the visitors' cultural experience but also increases their engagement and connection with the artifact and its cultural narrative (İbiŞ & Cakici Alp, 2023).

Numerous real-world examples clearly showcase that the cultural impact of AR in urban environments is not merely speculative. One such example is the AR application dubbed "Pompeii Touch," which allows users to "time travel" history lane, back to the city of Pompeii before its ultimate destruction (Fig. 9.2

FIG. 9.2 The ruins of Pompeii (Holmes, 2018).

showcases a part of the city many years after destruction) (Esposito, 2014). Through this app, individuals can experience and explore this ancient city virtually though it is physically, totally different. This immersive experience facilitates a deeper understanding of the city's historical and cultural context.

Another interesting AR application worth mentioning is the "Streetmuseum" launched by the Museum of London in 2010. On the bare minimum, this app allows users to juxtapose historical images onto present-day London streets, thus creating a temporal fusion of past and present (Peyer, 2014). This experience provides users with an enriched understanding of their city's evolution over time, enhancing their appreciation of its cultural heritage. It is worth noting also that, AR applications are not limited to historical or cultural heritage sites only, but have also been effectively used to promote contemporary cultural experiences. For instance, the AR app "Invisible Cities" in Manchester, United Kingdom, offers users an immersive narrative experience that explores modern urban folklore and subcultures, thus demonstrating AR's potential to foster contemporary cultural understanding and diversity.

Smart technologies for efficient social service delivery

In the recent past, the world is experiencing unprecedented changes prompted by rapid urbanization and a high rate of urban population growth. Among the notable changes include the adoption of emerging technologies and digital devices as potent tools to revolutionize the delivery of social services. This emerging digital ecosystem, characterized by the increased convergence of advanced technologies such as artificial intelligence (AI), Internet of Things (IoT), mobile connectivity technologies such as 5G and 6G, data analytics, and virtual platforms, holds significant potential for efficient and personalized service delivery in cities (Allam & Jones, 2021). Virtual platforms, in particular, with their immersive, interactive, and accessible attributes, play a critical role in enhancing the accessibility and delivery of social services (Wang et al., 2023). Education, healthcare, and public assistance can be ubiquitously provided, beyond the physical location constraints or socioeconomic stratification. This potential to narrow the social service inequality and address exclusion is particularly profound in cities, where disparities in access to social services are often starkly visible.

Besides the virtual technologies, AI and Computing (data analytics) technologies also present an unparalleled level of sophistication to the virtualized service delivery. This brings the capability to process vast amounts of data in realtime, thus making it possible for customization and personalization of services according to individual needs and preferences (Allam & Dhunny, 2019; Chen et al., 2021). This personalization substantially enhances user experience, as services delivered almost mirror the unique user circumstances. On the other hand, data analytics have been found to foster efficiency in service provision by enabling data-driven decision-making and policy formulation, thus, complementing the powers of AI (Sarker, 2021). Analysis of user data allows for a better and comprehensive understanding of different individual needs and preferences, and their service demand trends, informing service design, allocation, and delivery. User data analysis paves the way for more responsive, timely, and efficient social services, effectively addressing the dynamic and complex needs of urban societies (Allam, 2020, 2021).

In the recent past, there has been a myriad of examples and case studies that help showcase the successful implementations of smart technologies in social service delivery, in cities, and also within the metaverse. One such example is "VirBELA," which is a virtual realistic school platform that facilitates interactive learning experiences in a manner far superior to traditional educational delivery (Virbela, 2023).

In the healthcare sector, there is the "VRHealth" platform that stands out as a pioneer in the industry in utilizing virtual reality for remote rehabilitation services. This environment makes it possible for patients to undergo therapy in the comfort of their homes under professional guidance, thus, increasing accessibility to healthcare services and personalizing treatment based on patient feedback and progress. Another example that has gained significant traction in the health sector is the "AidChain" platform which utilizes blockchain technology to enhance transparency and efficiency in the allocation and distribution of aid in the public assistance sector. This platform ensures that aid reaches its intended beneficiaries through real-time tracking of donations (Tracxn, 2023).

The earlier examples only represent a smart part of the "iceberg" that characterizes the expansive application of smart technologies not only in education, healthcare, and public assistance. In fact, smart technologies have infiltrated sectors such as environmental management, transportation, public safety, et cetera. To put this into perspective, it is not surprising that there is an astounding deployment of predictive algorithms in waste management to optimize resource extraction and consumption. Also, there has been an increased interest in smart transportation systems in the recent past, targeting to enhance mobility and traffic management in cities.

From the diverse areas in which smart technologies have been deployed, there is upbeat that even more application prospects will arise. In particular, there is excitement about how much the smart technologies deployment in the metaverse will influence the delivery of social services. The potential to redefine how services in sectors such as education, healthcare, transport, housing, and public assistance are provided could drastically improve the quality of life for urban dwellers. It is anticipated that as further exploration into immersive learning environments is pursued, there will be a significant transformation in different urban landscapes (Alfaisal et al., 2022). For instance, the potential for remote and virtualized learning platforms, like the aforementioned "VirBELA," could pave the way for more inclusive educational platforms and environments, that would ultimately break down geographical, financial, and physical barriers. This would be even more interesting as advancements in virtual reality and augmented reality continue to be realized; hence, fostering substantial interactive and engaging learning experiences as well as promoting better knowledge retention and comprehension.

In the healthcare sector, AI-powered virtual platforms like "VRHealth" are already making headwinds, and could be very instrumental in revolutionizing treatment delivery, especially in the case of mental health services. Also, it is expected to make it possible for services such as remote counseling or therapy sessions which could in turn, promote eliminating stigma associated with seeking help, further promoting the democratization of mental health services (Ahmadi Marzaleh et al., 2022). In addition, the deployment of AI in diagnosing and predicting certain health conditions could help in the prevention and management of diseases, hence, contributing to the overall well-being of urban populations.

The application of smart technologies extends beyond individual service to the realm of potentially revolutionizing the governance and administration of cities. By leveraging AI and data analytics, city administrators would have the potential to gain deeper insights into diverse urban issues, thus, make more informed decisions as well as increase the quality of responses to citizen needs. On other fronts, the integration of blockchain technology, as exemplified in the case of "AidChain," could enhance the transparency and accountability of public services, fostering trust in public institutions (Tracxn, 2023).

Whereas the aforementioned technologies and subsequent platforms are very promising, their success is subject to a thoughtful integration into the existing urban fabric environments to avoid potential challenges. Therefore, a holistic approach to their design and implementation is essential, which will allow for the diverse urban dwellers' needs, preferences, and capacities to be captured. This inclusivity is key to ensuring that the benefits of smart technologies are equitably distributed across all urban sections.

In addition to the aforementioned, it should not be lost that in the intersection of the digital and physical worlds lies the issue and concerns of privacy and security, of both humans, as well as the infrastructure. As a mitigation measure, it will be necessary to ensure that personal data and information that are increasingly becoming part of social service provision are guarded with robust cybersecurity policies and clear data governance protocols (Onwujekwe et al., 2019). There will also be a need to address the persistent digital divide that continues to mar digital spaces including the metaverse. Such could be addressed by emphasizing on initiatives fashioned towards improving digital literacy and access.

Privacy considerations in the metaverse

The recent gradual integration of the metaverse into urban environments presents real possibilities for the reconfiguration of the general livability status of residents as well as how they socialize, and access diverse services, et cetera. But beyond the myriad of goodies the metaverse avails, are a host of privacy and security concerns, mostly touching on areas such as data collection, surveillance, and the unauthorized use of personal information (Dencik et al., 2016). These challenges are subject to different parameters, given that they are fundamentally different in nature compared to their physical counterparts.

One of the critical privacy concerns associated with the metaverse pertains to data collection and subsequent usage (Falchuk et al., 2018). It has been established that within the metaverse, vast amounts of personal information could be collected, most often without explicit user consent or knowledge. Such data could entail diverse transactional records, communication logs, individuals' behavioral patterns, and even biometric data. Whereas these are similar to those in the physical realm, the metaverse's immersive environments can generate data points that are more intimate and revealing than traditional digital platforms, given their ability to mimic and capture real-world behaviors and interactions (Canbay et al., 2022). Besides concerns about data collection, the metaverse is also being viewed as a platform for potential, extensive surveillance, especially with no clear governance structure. Concerns are that the metaverse could increase the pervasiveness and intrusion, with users constantly being monitored and their data being analyzed and leveraged in real-time (Gupta et al., 2023). Those concerns could even be exacerbated by the integration of AI and data analytics technologies within the digital spaces especially due to their ability to automate processing of collected data (Huynh-The et al., 2023). The potential for "dataveillance," or the systematic monitoring of people's actions or communications through the application of information technology, poses significant threats to individual privacy (Clarke, 1988).

Another significant privacy concern that has the potential to derail the adoption of the metaverse is the unauthorized use of personal information. This challenge is particularly exacerbated by the notable lack of proper regulations and safeguards for the personal data collected within the metaverse. For this reason, there are fears that data generated therein could be used for malicious purposes, such as identity theft, online harassment, terrorism (Debuire, 2022), or targeted advertising (Du et al., 2022). These risks underscore the urgent need for robust privacy protections within the metaverse, balancing the advantages of immersive digital experiences with the imperative to safeguard user privacy.

The importance of privacy protection in the metaverse cannot be overstated, especially noting that it is a fundamental human right, integral to individual autonomy and dignity. As such, it behooves all players to be cognizant of the negative consequences of the proliferation of digital platforms and the consequent erosion of privacy boundaries; hence, make it an urgent agenda to formulate and implement stringent policies and regulations for the metaverse. In addition, it would be imperative to explore various potential solutions and best practices that could complement the policies and regulations. One such solution could be the implementation of "Privacy by Design" principles, which involve embedding privacy considerations into the design and operation of technologies. In summary, this approach includes limiting the amount of personal data to be collected and ensuring transparency in data collection and usage. It also entails prioritizing user consent in data-related actions. Another solution to strengthen the policies would entail the formulation and adoption of stringent data protection regulations, akin to the General Data Protection Regulation (GDPR) in the European Union (Hoofnagle et al., 2019). This would thus serve as a legal framework to safeguard privacy in the metaverse.

The aforementioned regulations need to be fashioned such that they provide clear consent mechanisms, data minimization, and the right to erasure, among other privacy-enhancing provisions. In addition to these, the adoption and subsequent application of advanced encryption technologies and anonymization techniques can protect personal data from unauthorized access and misuse. Such could be achieved by relying on technologies such as blockchain technology, which over the years have proven to be superior in promoting immutability and transparency (Arun et al., 2021).

Inclusivity and accessibility in the metaverse

The numerous positive aspects of the metaverse cannot be wished away at the behest of a few surmountable challenges that have been cited as potential to derail its success. Among such are the concerns of inclusivity and accessibility that it brings to the fore. With such introspection is important, as the metaverse might inadvertently accentuate social disparities and foster exclusivity (Dwivedi et al., 2022). One key obstacle to achieving a more equitable and inclusive metaverse is the persistence of digital divides, often underpinned by factors such as socioeconomic status, education, housing, and geographical location. These contribute significantly to inequality in access to digital resources and benefits and the associated literacy. The concern with these is that if the metaverse is not judiciously designed and managed, it could widen the disparity gap, thus, perpetuating differences in access to the virtual spaces it creates. To illustrate this, a case could be made of a low-income individual without a reliable internet connection. The lack of access could exclude them from digital service delivery within the metaverse, further solidifying existing socioeconomic divides.

While the challenges associated with the metaverse can be termed as universal, affecting individuals across the wider spectrum, they are more accentuated in the case of individuals with disabilities. As such, the design of the metaverse must prioritize accessibility, ensuring that all users, irrespective of their physical or cognitive abilities, can effectively be accommodated. For instance, it would be critically important to ensure that the standard user interfaces for the metaverse do not amplify the challenges visually or hearing-impaired individuals already face. For such reasons, it could be imperative to incorporate assistive technologies and inclusive design principles into the fabric of the metaverse (Felix, 2022).

Language barriers form another significant obstacle that could exacerbate the challenge of achieving inclusivity and accessibility in the metaverse for all. The dominance of a particular dialect or language, for instance, English, within digital spaces can marginalize those who are nonnative speakers or speak less globally prevalent languages. Therefore, the provision of robust multilingual support systems such as the use of AI and efficient translation services within the metaverse will be vital to fostering inclusivity and accessibility (Li & Yu, 2023).

The aspects of equal access and representation in the metaverse necessitate the adoption of comprehensive strategies and long-term solutions. One potent strategy is the incorporation of universal design principles, with the objective of making the environments as accessible as possible to all, irrespective of their demographic profiles. These principles emphasize the need for flexibility, simplicity, and intuitiveness in design, thus, broadening the accessibility of the metaverse. In addition, it could be critical to incorporate digital literacy programs to help bridge digital divides. By emphasizing on skills and knowledge necessary for individuals to navigate digital spaces, such programs could democratize access to the metaverse. Ultimately, those programs foster an understanding of and confidence in, the use of digital platforms, which is crucial for effective participation in the metaverse. To sum it all up, regulatory measures to ensure fair and affordable access to digital infrastructure need to be prioritized at these earliest stages of the metaverse. Such need to be complemented by progressive policies that fully support digital inclusion, especially for marginalized populations.

Projects and initiatives also need to be pursued targeting to address the issue of inclusivity and accessibility in the metaverse. A good example of such is the "Open Metaverse Accessibility Initiative" which champions the development of guidelines and standards to make the metaverse more accessible to people with disabilities (Sghaier et al., 2022). Another one is the "Internet-in-a-Box" project whose aim is to bridge digital divides by providing offline access to digital resources and can facilitate access to the metaverse even in areas with unreliable internet connectivity (Missen, 2005). In an effort to address the language barrier, "TranslAide" software that helps in translation could be integrated into digital platforms, enabling multilingual communication and interaction within the metaverse (Jaworski & Ziemlińska, 2014).

Cultural sensitivity in virtual environments

Cultural sensitivity involves recognizing and appreciating the unique beliefs, values, customs, languages, traditions, and practices that shape the identities and experiences of different cultures.

The expansive and immersive digital landscapes that characterize the metaverse offer an entirely new milieu for social interaction and engagement. However, the creation of these virtual environments has the potential to raise concerns regarding cultural sensitivity. An understanding of this truth is paramount for developers and users alike to ensure a harmonious coexistence within this new ecosystem. From the onset, it is important to appreciate that cultural sensitivity needs to play a critical role when designing and populating virtual environments. This truth is pegged on the fact that the global reach and the multicultural nature of the metaverse is currently unmatched, hence it would be crucial for these spaces to respect cultural diversity, prevent misinterpretation, and promote intercultural understanding. In right to that, failing to account for cultural diversity in design, might ultimately lead to a monolithic environment that neither represents nor respects the rich tapestry of human cultures.

Despite the metaverse still being in the infancy stage of its development, the challenge of cultural misrepresentation looms large. The foretelling for this is how cultural symbols (Fig. 9.3), narratives, and practices are often misunderstood, misrepresented, or commodified, leading to harmful stereotypes and cultural appropriation, especially due to the lack of a defined ownership or governance of these spaces. A case in point is the use of sacred cultural symbols within the metaverse as mere esthetic elements. While this may seem interesting and attractive to some people, it can equally translate to disrespect and offensive to the communities from which they originate.

Buying from this example, it is important to note that the potential of the metaverse to inadvertently perpetuate harmful cultural stereotypes is an issue that requires careful attention and effective remediation. It would then be important to adopt user-generated content and community moderation, which

FIG. 9.3 A sacred cultural symbol—Tibetan Prayer Flag (Kychan, 2016).

plays a significant role in ensuring cultural sensitivity within the metaverse. Another remedy for that would be to empower users to create original content, which allows for the representation of a diverse range of cultural perspectives, without invoking negative connotations (George et al., 2021). Users, provided they are respectful and educated about different cultures, can ensure the metaverse becomes a space for cultural exchange and mutual respect.

Another approach that needs to be accorded maximum attention is community moderation to further bolster cultural sensitivity in the metaverse. In pursuit of this, moderation teams need to come up with guidelines and enforcement rules that prohibit disrespectful or offensive content, foster a culture of respect, and encourage learning and understanding among users. With such, it is anticipated that the harmful cultural misrepresentation and appropriation would be mitigated, while at the same time promoting a more inclusive and respectful metaverse.

In line with the earlier discussion, various projects have made strides in addressing cultural sensitivity issues in the metaverse. For instance, "the Indigenous Metaverses Project," which collaborates with indigenous communities to create virtual spaces that accurately and respectfully represent their cultures, thus combating cultural appropriation and misrepresentation is aiming for recognition, even by UNESCO (Glendon York University, 2022). Another initiative is the "Cultural Exchange Metaverse Initiative" which encourages users to learn about different cultures and share their cultural heritage, as they promote a respectful and diverse metaverse.

At every stage and phase of designing and application of the metaverse, the aspect of cultural sensitivity should be a central tenet that can never be overlooked. Also, respect for diversity, proactive steps against misrepresentation and appropriation, and user empowerment need to be given priority if a culturally sensitive and responsive metaverse is to be created. Not only will this foster a more inclusive and respectful environment, but it will also contribute to the metaverse's role as a platform for cultural exchange and learning, reflective of the diverse world it serves.

Discussions and conclusions

The challenge of privacy in the metaverse, as has been comprehensively discussed in the preceding sections, is of paramount concern, that cannot be wished away. While privacy concerns may arise at any stage in the development of the metaverse, it has been observed to start right from the data collection point. The extensive data collection and subsequent surveillance in the metaverse's infrastructure, just like is the case in the physical realm, have the potential to infringe on individuals' privacy rights. The emphasis, therefore, must be on the need to develop robust regulations and policies that protect personal data and establish clear boundaries around its usage (Allam, 2020, 2021). This behooves the tech industry, regulatory bodies, civic societies, and other stakeholders to collaborate on this front, devising innovative solutions and best practices that can serve as guidelines for ensuring privacy in the metaverse (Kitchin, 2016). At the same time, considerations of inclusivity and accessibility in the metaverse also call for maximum attention and consideration. This could be addressed by focusing on reducing the digital divides prevalent in all societies, which have the potential to be mirrored and even exacerbated within the metaverse.

As has been discussed earlier, several initiatives and platforms such as the universal design principles, digital literacy programs, and regulatory measures that have emerged over the years need to be considered to guarantee the fair access that the digital infrastructures can contribute towards a more inclusive metaverse (Dwivedi et al., 2022; Gupta et al., 2023). Notably, the various initiatives and projects highlighted in this chapter indicate a positive trajectory towards promoting inclusivity and accessibility in the metaverse.

In relation to cultural sensitivity, this chapter has underscored the crucial role it plays in designing virtual environments (Allam & Newman, 2018). However, there are fears of cultural misrepresentation and appropriation within the metaverse that pose significant challenges making it essential for user-generated content and community moderation to be cognizant of these issues. These notwithstanding, the successful implementation of diverse projects as well as providing relevant education on different cultures could help address cultural sensitivity issues in the metaverse now and in the future. These explorations, however, are not exhaustive, especially given the infancy stage at which the metaverse is; therefore, this study urges future research to delve deeper into these issues. It should not also be lost that the intersection of the metaverse with smart cities is a burgeoning field that is rapidly evolving. Therefore, the understanding of different players in the urban planning field on these concepts must evolve concurrently to anticipate challenges and seize opportunities. Furthermore, it is believed that a key area for future inquiry could be the examination of how the metaverse's growth affects urban development and planning (Allam, Sharifi, et al., 2022). Questions such as how virtual spaces influence physical urban spaces, or how the metaverse can be leveraged to enhance urban services and citizen engagement, are ripe for investigation. Similarly, the role of governance in the metaverse is an area that warrants examination.

As the metaverse becomes an integral part of urban life, establishing frameworks for its governance, such as regulations around virtual real estate, businesses, or digital rights, will be imperative.

References

Ahmadi Marzaleh, M., Peyravi, M., & Shaygani, F. (2022). A revolution in health: Opportunities and challenges of the metaverse. *EXCLI Journal, 21*, 791–792. https://doi.org/10.17179/excli2022-5017.

Alfaisal, R., Hashim, H., & Azizan, U. H. (2022). Metaverse system adoption in education: A systematic literature review. *Journal of Computers in Education, 1*. https://doi.org/10.1007/s40692-022-00256-6.

Allam, Z. (2020). Data as the new driving gears of urbanization. In *Cities and the digital revolution* (pp. 1–29). Cham: Palgrave Pivot.

Allam, Z. (2021). Big data, artificial intelligence and the rise of autonomous smart cities. In *The rise of autonomous smart cities* (pp. 7–30). Cham: Palgrave Macmillan.

Allam, Z., & Dhunny, Z. A. (2019). On big data, artificial intelligence and smart cities. *Cities*, *89*, 80–91. https://doi.org/10.1016/j.cities.2019.01.032.

Allam, Z., & Jones, D. S. (2021). Future (post-COVID) digital, smart and sustainable cities in the wake of 6G: Digital twins, immersive realities and new urban economies. *Land Use Policy*, *101*, 105201. https://doi.org/10.1016/j.landusepol.2020.105201.

Allam, Z., Moreno, C., Chabaud, D., & Pratlong, F. (2022). Proximity-based planning and the "15-Minute City": A sustainable model for the city of the future. In *The Palgrave handbook of global sustainability*.

Allam, Z., & Newman, P. (2018). Redefining the smart city: Culture, metabolism and governance. *Smart Cities*, *1*(1), 4–25.

Allam, Z., Sharifi, A., Bibri, S. E., Jones, D. S., & Krogstie, J. (2022). The metaverse as a virtual form of smart cities: Opportunities and challenges for environmental, economic, and social sustainability in urban futures. *Smart Cities*, *5*(3), 771–801. https://www.mdpi.com/2624-6511/5/3/40.

Arun, N., Mathiyalagan, R., & Suchithra. (2021). Authentication and identity validation blockchain application. *Journal of Physics: Conference Series*, *1979*(1), 012017. https://doi.org/10.1088/1742-6596/1979/1/012017.

Bibri, S. (2022). The social shaping of the metaverse as an alternative to the imaginaries of data-driven smart cities: A study in science, technology, and society. *Smart Cities*, *5*. https://doi.org/10.3390/smartcities5030043.

BurningMan.Org. (2020). Burning Man in the multiverse. *Burning Man*. Retrieved 25th May from https://burningman.org/about/history/brc-history/event-archives/2020-event-archive/virtual-brc-2020/.

Canbay, Y., Utku, A., & Canbay, P. (2022). *Privacy concerns and measures in metaverse: A review*. https://doi.org/10.1109/ISCTURKEY56345.2022.9931866.

Chen, T., Guo, W., Gao, X., & Liang, Z. (2021). AI-based self-service technology in public service delivery: User experience and influencing factors. *Government Information Quarterly*, *38*(4), 101520. https://doi.org/10.1016/j.giq.2020.101520.

Clarke, R. (1988). Information technology and dataveillance. *Communications of the ACM*, *31*(5), 498–512.

Debuire, D. (12 April 2022). Terrorist use of the metaverse: New opportunities and new challenges. *Security Distillery*. Retrieved 30th May 2022 from https://thesecuritydistillery.org/all-articles/terrorism-and-the-metaverse-new-opportunities-and-new-challenges.

Dencik, L., Hintz, A., & Cable, J. (2016). Towards data justice? The ambiguity of anti-surveillance resistance in political activism. *Big Data & Society*, *3*(2). 2053951716679678.

Du, H., Niyato, D., Miao, C., Kang, J., & Kim, D. I. (2022). Optimal targeted advertising strategy for secure wireless edge metaverse. In *GLOBECOM 2022-2022 IEEE global communications conference*.

Dwivedi, Y. K., Hughes, L., Baabdullah, A. M., Ribeiro-Navarrete, S., Giannakis, M., Al-Debei, M. M., Dennehy, D., Metri, B., Buhalis, D., Cheung, C. M. K., Conboy, K., Doyle, R., Dubey, R., Dutot, V., Felix, R., Goyal, D. P., Gustafsson, A., Hinsch, C., Jebabli, I., … Wamba, S. F. (2022). Metaverse beyond the hype: Multidisciplinary perspectives on emerging challenges, opportunities, and agenda for research, practice and policy. *International Journal of Information Management*, *66*, 102542. https://doi.org/10.1016/j.ijinfomgt.2022.102542.

Esposito, P. (2014). From accounting to accountability at the virtual museums in Pompeii and Herculaneum. In *Handbook of research on management of cultural products* (pp. 245–256). IGI Global.

Falchuk, B., Loeb, S., & Neff, R. (2018). The social metaverse: Battle for privacy. *IEEE Technology and Society Magazine*, *37*(2), 52–61. https://doi.org/10.1109/MTS.2018.2826060.

Felix, A. (19 December 2022). An accessible, disability-inclusive metaverse? *European Disability Forum*. Retrieved 27th May 2023 from https://www.edf-feph.org/an-accessible-disability-inclusive-metaverse/.

George, A. S., Fernando, M., George, A. S., Baskar, D., & Pandey, D. (2021). Metaverse: The next stage of human culture and the internet. *International Journal of Advanced Research Trends in Engineering and Technology (IJARTET)*, *8*(12), 1–10. https://doi.org/10.20247/IJARTET.2021.0812001.

Glendon York University. (14 November 2022). *Indigenous Metaverse project joins UNESCO campaign to promote and protect Indigenous languages*. Glendon Campus. Retrieved 27th May 2023 from https://www.yorku.ca/glendon/2022/11/14/indigenous-metaverse-project-joins-unesco-campaign-to-promote-and-protect-indigenous-languages/.

Gupta, A., Khan, H. U., Nazir, S., Shafiq, M., & Shabaz, M. (2023). Metaverse security: Issues, challenges and a viable ZTA model. *Electronics*, *12*(2), 391. https://doi.org/10.3390/electronics12020391.

Holmes, A. (10 July 2018). *Pompeii ruins*. Unsplash. Retrieved 21st June 2023 from https://unsplash.com/photos/h5cYy5OHDWM.

Hoofnagle, C. J., van der Sloot, B., & Borgesius, F. Z. (2019). The European Union general data protection regulation: What it is and what it means. *Information & Communications Technology Law*, *28*(1), 65–98. https://doi.org/10.1080/13600834.2019.1573501.

Huynh-The, T., Pham, Q.-V., Pham, X.-Q., Nguyen, T. T., Han, Z., & Kim, D.-S. (2023). Artificial intelligence for the metaverse: A survey. *Engineering Applications of Artificial Intelligence*, *117*, 105581. https://doi.org/10.1016/j.engappai.2022.105581.

IbiŞ, A., & Cakici Alp, N. (2023). *Augmented reality used in cultural heritage: A systematic review*. https://doi.org/10.21203/rs.3.rs-2482925/v1.

Jaworski, R., & Ziemlińska, R. (2014). *The translaide.pl system: An effective real world installation of translation memory searching and EBMT*.

Khamseh, S. M. (13 September 2020). *Loneliness*. Unsplash. Retrieved 21st June 2023 from https://unsplash.com/photos/gH5yrgiw4Xw.

Kitchin, R. (2016). The ethics of smart cities and urban science. *Philosophical Transactions of the Royal Society A: Mathematical, Physical and Engineering Sciences*, *374*(2083), 1–15. https://doi.org/10.1098/rsta.2016.0115.

Kychan. (11 June 2016). *Tibetan prayer flag*. Unsplash. Retrieved 19th June 2023 from https://unsplash.com/photos/QU7EJulPh0A.

Leland, J. (20 April 2022). How loneliness is damaging our health. *New York Times*. Retrieved 26th May 2023 from https://www.nytimes.com/2022/04/20/nyregion/loneliness-epidemic.html.

Li, M., & Yu, Z. (2023). A systematic review on the metaverse-based blended English learning [systematic review]. *Frontiers in Psychology*, *13*. https://doi.org/10.3389/fpsyg.2022.1087508.

Lv, Z., Shang, W.-L., & Guizani, M. (2022). Impact of digital twins and metaverse on cities: History, current situation, and application perspectives. *Applied Sciences*, *12*(24).

Missen, C. (2005). Internet in a box: The eGranary digital library serves scholars lacking internet bandwidth. *New Review of Information Networking*, *11*. https://doi.org/10.1080/13614570600573367.

Onwujekwe, G., Thomas, M., & Osei-Bryson, K.-M. (2019). *Using robust data governance to mitigate the impact of cybercrime.* https://doi.org/10.1145/3325917.3325923.

Paulauskas, L., Paulauskas, A., Blažauskas, T., Damaševičius, R., & Maskeliūnas, R. (2023). Reconstruction of industrial and historical heritage for cultural enrichment using virtual and augmented reality. *Technologies, 11*(2).

Peen, J., Schoevers, R. A., Beekman, A. T., & Dekker, J. (2010). The current status of urban-rural differences in psychiatric disorders. *Acta Psychiatrica Scandinavica, 121*(2), 84–93. https://doi.org/10.1111/j.1600-0447.2009.01438.x.

Peyer, R. D. (26 February 2014). Streetmuseum app creates a stunning picture of you in a London scene from a bygone era. *Evening Standard.* Retrieved 25th May 2023 from https://www.standard.co.uk/news/london/streetmuseum-app-creates-a-stunning-picture-of-you-in-a-london-scene-from-a-bygone-era-9153842.html.

Polyviou, A., & Pappas, I. O. (2022). Chasing metaverses: Reflecting on existing literature to understand the business value of metaverses. *Information Systems Frontiers.* https://doi.org/10.1007/s10796-022-10364-4.

Salingaros, N. A. (2014). Complexity in architecture and design. *Oz, 36,* 18–25.

Sarker, I. H. (2021). Data science and analytics: An overview from data-driven smart computing, decision-making and applications perspective. *SN Computer Science, 2*(5), 377. https://doi.org/10.1007/s42979-021-00765-8.

Sghaier, S., Elfakki, A. O., & Alotaibi, A. A. (2022). Development of an intelligent system based on metaverse learning for students with disabilities. *Frontiers in Robotics and AI, 9,* 1006921. https://doi.org/10.3389/frobt.2022.1006921.

Snowden, A. (2019). From lawnmower man to ready player one: A cultural history of virtual reality. In C. Deprez, & K. Gough (Eds.), *New directions in mobile media and performance* (pp. 57–69). Routledge.

Tracxn. (2023). *Aidchain.* Tracxn. Retrieved 26th May 2023 from https://tracxn.com/d/companies/aidchain/___JSRUx1JEgAJKdWEvVkVCkwVWuMUEarcBk2ASA4x6AQ.

Virbela. (2023). *Bring your online class to life with Virbela's virtual learning environments.* Virbela. Retrieved 25th May 2023 from https://www.virbela.com/go/education.

Wang, Y., & Lin, Y.-S. (2023). Public participation in urban design with augmented reality technology based on indicator evaluation [original research]. *Frontiers in Virtual Reality, 4.* https://doi.org/10.3389/frvir.2023.1071355.

Wang, X.-N., Young, G., Plechatá, A., Mc Guckin, C., & Makransky, G. (2023). Utilizing virtual reality to assist social competence education and social support for children from underrepresented backgrounds. *Computers & Education,* 104815. https://doi.org/10.1016/j.compedu.2023.104815.

Wilhelmsson, M., Ismail, M., & Warsame, A. (2021). Gentrification effects on housing prices in neighbouring areas. *International Journal of Housing Markets and Analysis.* https://doi.org/10.1108/IJHMA-04-2021-0049 (ahead-of-print).

Chapter 10

The economic implications of the metaverse in cities

Economic challenges in traditional urban settings

The conventional urban setting has been at the heart of human civilization since ancient days, serving as the crux of economic, social, and political interaction. Despite those eons of years in existence, these intricate urban landscapes have continued to endure diverse economic challenges, prompted by dynamics in population growth, changes in human consumption and production behaviors, et cetera. Changes in economic activities, livability status, and other frontiers have always been the boiling point for urban challenges.

One key factor to consider in how the cities have continued to evolve, and why they still face diverse challenges is the lack of job opportunities, which ultimately exacerbates the issue of underemployment, and other major issues ranging from economic to social challenges. According to the International Labor Organization (ILO), global unemployment was estimated at 205 million in 2021, a figure higher than prepandemic levels by approximately 25 million (International Labour Organization, 2022). Undeniably, this situation had caused untold challenges for the urban residents, given the denser population. It has rightly been argued that limited job opportunities catalyze the rise of informal economies, which, due to their nature, are sometimes characterized by precarious work conditions, income insecurity, and a lack of social benefits. Unfortunately, postpandemic, and with the escalation of the sociopolitical tension between Russia and Ukraine, this employment quandary intertwines with the escalating cost of living in cities (Allam, 2020a, 2020b, 2020c, 2020d; Allam & Jones, 2020; International Labour Organization, 2022). It also comes at a time when urban land and housing prices have consistently outpaced wage growth, leaving over 200 million people homeless across the globe as of 2020 (Bezgrebelna et al., 2021).

High costs of housing and essential commodities, juxtaposed with static or minimally growing wages, have engendered a critical paradox of urban life, including in developed economies such as those in Europe (The World Bank, 2023). In an era where cities have become primary drivers of economic

FIG. 10.1 A homeless man in the streets of London (Fewings, 2018).

growth, the inability of numerous city dwellers to afford a decent standard of living (as depicted in Fig. 10.1 in the following) is a poignant paradox.

Given the earlier background, economic inequality within urban locales remains an inescapable predicament, that would require serious consideration. According to data from Census Bureau, the average Gini coefficient for cities worldwide between 2020 and 2021 was 0.488 and 0.494, where 0 represents perfect equality and 1 indicates maximal inequality (Semega & Kollar, 2022). This level of economic disparity has had deleterious effects, undermined social cohesion, and fanned the flames of social discontent and alienation.

The socioeconomic fragmentation noted previously can be tied to a broader issue such as the lack of economic mobility. This lack of mobility within urban areas is especially amplified in cities with a reputation for racial segregation, known educational disparities, and income inequality (Chetty & Hendren, 2018). The socioeconomic inequality, exacerbated by the absence of sufficient opportunity for upward mobility, threatens to ossify these disparities, engendering a deeply entrenched socioeconomic hierarchy.

All the challenges bear significant implications for urban communities. To start with, it has been recorded that income distribution in urban areas has over the years been dramatically skewed by the earlier issues, contributing to a widening wealth gap. Unfortunately, when unchecked, income inequality dampens social cohesion, with individuals and communities feeling increasingly disassociated from the broader urban fabric. This disassociation has the potential to compromise the collective feeling required to tackle other social challenges and may undermine overall urban vitality. Economic disparities also adversely affect the quality of life, especially when viewed through the lens of housing instability, food insecurity, and limited access to essential services, thereby casting a long shadow over the urban living experience.

While those challenges have persisted for centuries, traditional economic models have never been able to address them amicably. In fact, these models have instead demonstrated their limited capacity to offer solutions to the urban economic challenges adequately. Even to neoclassical economists, the complexity and dynamism of contemporary urban issues often assume homogeneity and perfect rationality of economic actors (Storper, 2020). These assumptions fail to consider the diversity and intricacies of urban economic behavior, rendering the models ineffective in resolving urban economic challenges.

With traditional models failing, innovative approaches are thus required to offer solutions to these urban economic problems. One qualification for the right approach would be the capacity to allow for a more inclusive economic model that emphasizes broad-based growth, equitable wealth distribution, and enhanced social mobility (Allam, 2019, 2021; Raworth, 2017). On this, the implementation of smart city technologies and the advent of the metaverse may turn out to be the solutions to these challenges, hence, necessitating further exploration and consideration. However, it should be noted that in the rush to embrace innovation, the guiding principle must be to ensure that the solutions are grounded within the context of human-centric urban development. That is, the ethos of creating "people-centric" cities that cater to the well-being of all urban inhabitants must prevail at every stage of these innovations. It has been argued that if smart city technologies are harnessed appropriately, they can provide unprecedented opportunities for increased economic participation, flexible work arrangements, and more efficient delivery of essential services (Allam & Newman, 2018). On its part, the metaverse can offer platforms and spaces for fostering economic inclusivity, increased economic activities, and unlimited opportunities for people to interact. Therefore, by enabling a virtual space where people can work, learn, and interact, the metaverse might offer new solutions to problems like underemployment and lack of job opportunities (Cheng et al., 2022).

It is however important not to view such technological and economic innovations as silver bullets for all the urban challenges. Instead, those advances need to be integrated within a broader strategy of economic and social policy reform, driven by a commitment to reducing inequality, promoting social mobility, and enhancing the standard of living for all urban inhabitants.

Economic opportunities of the metaverse in cities

The prospect of the conception of new industries within the metaverse is one of the most compelling economic breakthroughs we might experience since a long time. To put this into perspective, the virtual real estate within the metaverse, for instance, where digital environments are bought, sold, and leased, has seen considerable growth, with transactions exceeding $500 million in 2022 alone, and expected to double by end of 2023 (Frank, 2022). Such a phenomenon suggests a burgeoning industry that is likely to expand even further as the metaverse takes shape. For instance, the transactions are anticipated to grow by a further $5.37 trillion by 2030, depicting a remarkable growth projection (Kamin, 2023). Furthermore, with the metaverse comes the prospect of entirely new sectors such as virtual tourism, digital art trading, virtual fashion shows, new entertainment domains, and metaverse infrastructure development, all contributing to an enriched and diverse urban economy. The revenue from live entertainment in the metaverse is projected to increase from the current $0.24 billion to about $105.40 billion by 2030 (Statista, 2023).

> NFTs are type of digital assets that represents ownership or proof of authenticity of a unique item or piece of content, typically on a blockchain network.

On the other hand, revenues from games and nonfungible tokens (NFT) are expected to increase by approximately $300 billion by 2030, representing a 10% of the luxury market in the metaverse (Canny, 2021). These new industries are anticipated to inevitably bring about fresh job opportunities, for developers, gamers, creators, et cetera. The emergence of roles such as virtual reality architects, metaverse content creators, and blockchain technologists is imminent (Faraboschi et al., 2022). Such roles will not only create new employment avenues but may also catalyze a shift in the traditional job market, fostering new skills and challenging existing notions of work and professional interaction.

At the core of the metaverse are virtual and augmented reality (VR/AR) technologies which form the backbone of this new economic paradigm. These technologies have enabled and will continue to enable the creation of immersive, interactive digital environments that can foster innovation and entrepreneurship (Dimov & Dimov, 2022). For instance, VR/AR technologies can provide platforms for developing virtual marketplaces, where businesses can engage customers in novel and immersive ways, far surpassing the limitations of traditional digital commerce (Bhattacharya et al., 2023). In addition, VR/AR technologies could allow for the creation of virtual incubators and accelerators, fostering entrepreneurial activity and innovation within the metaverse. Such environments can provide resources, mentorship, and community engagement for entrepreneurs, enabling them to develop and refine their ideas, and thus drive economic growth and job creation within urban settings (Kulkov et al., 2021).

The metaverse is also argued to hold the potential to reshape urban economic transactions and financial systems through its ability to allow increased activities touching on virtual currencies and blockchain technology. Virtual currencies are an important component in the virtual realm as they facilitate seamless transactions across digital spaces, allowing for trade and commerce that defies geographical and political boundaries (Roy, 2021). On the other hand,

FIG. 10.2 Blockchain 3D illustration (Shubham Dhage, 2022).

blockchain technology (Fig. 10.2) is anticipated to ensure the transparency, security, and immutability of these transactions, fostering trust within the metaverse economy (Gadekallu et al., 2022; Huynh-The et al., 2023).

The adoption of blockchain technologies is also projected to facilitate tokenization within the metaverse, enabling the creation of unique digital assets that can be traded or used as a store of value (Huynh-The et al., 2023). This could lead to the development of a vibrant and diverse virtual economy, presenting city residents with new income streams where they can generate more wealth and partake in economic activity. The adoption of the metaverse in the urban ecosystems is also likely to attract significant investment, talent, and tourism, further stimulating urban economic revitalization. The allure of the metaverse lies in its untapped potential, drawing investors keen to capitalize on this new frontier. As such, cities that embrace the metaverse could attract top-tier digital talent, eager to work in a cutting-edge environment, and ready to explore the uncharted pathways in the digital economic landscapes.

In addition to the prospective economic frontiers within the metaverse, virtual tourism which is an emerging concept promises to provide a fresh perspective on urban exploration, as well as a new way of revenue generation. With these new digital platforms, tourists could experience city landmarks, cultural events, and historical narratives in immersive reality, far much better than is offered within the traditional setup. As such, they could stimulate the attraction of virtual visitors, who might never have the opportunity, time, or resources to visit certain places in the physical setup. As more new tourism attraction products and dimensions continue to emerge within the virtual world, it is anticipated that revenue for urban economies will also continue to increase. For instance, in a report by McKinsey, it is projected that the travel industry, which is a constituent of the tourism industry is expected to experience a $20 billion growth by 2030.

Urban economic planning and development with the metaverse

As the advent of the metaverse continues to reshape the economic fabric of cities, it is also expected to stimulate unprecedented urban planning and development by offering powerful new tools and platforms for different stakeholders. In particular, it provides a realistic opportunity for cities to leverage virtual simulations, data analytics, and artificial intelligence to envision, test, and optimize strategies for urban design, land use planning, infrastructure development, and resource management. With such, it then becomes possible to foster "smart" economic zones within the cities that drive innovation and economic growth. With the metaverse, urban planning in its totality stands to benefit considerably, including in areas like transportation, housing, and in the provision of different services such as education, health, waste management, and others. At the core of these transformations is the ability to perform virtual simulations and modeling, which serve as tools to visualize and examine the potential impact of various economic strategies and urban designs (Hudson-Smith, 2022). By creating intricate, realistic simulations of cities within the metaverse, urban planners can evaluate different scenarios and outcomes, making data-driven decisions that optimize the usage of urban spaces and resources.

Besides simulation and modeling, the metaverse could greatly influence how urban land is used, especially regarding development projects. Traditionally, land use decisions have always been based on static maps and demographic data. As such, the scope for understanding the multifaceted impacts of different land use scenarios has always been limited and not congruent with real urban demands and challenges. However, with virtual simulations within the metaverse, planners can now gain a deep, dynamic, and nuanced understanding of these impacts, aiding them in making informed decisions that balance economic growth, sustainability, and social equity, as well as aligned with prevailing global agendas, especially on the environment and reduction of emissions. Virtual simulations in the metaverse also offer a platform for prototyping and refining infrastructure development projects, in line with emerging urban demands and changes. For instance, in the recent past, particularly after the dreadful impacts of COVID-19, there has been a rush by cities to adopt the 15-Minute City planning model (Allam, Bibri, Chabaud, & Moreno, 2022a; Allam, Bibri, Jones, et al., 2022; Allam, Nieuwenhuijsen, Chabaud, & Moreno, 2022). However, with most cities already built, with existing infrastructure and systems, it would need proper planning and substantial resources. Therefore, before initiating costly construction projects and initiatives such as the 15-Minute City concept, planners can use the metaverse to simulate the project, evaluating its design, cost-effectiveness, and potential impact on the city's economic vitality and residents' quality of life (Allam, Bibri, Chabaud, & Moreno, 2022b). This approach could not only lead to a more efficient allocation of resources but also reduce the risk of project failures and cost overruns as well as promote near-universal acceptance by locals, who also get the opportunity via the metaverse to contribute in the planning and decision-making.

One advantage of the metaverse as a tool for economic planning and development is the ability to integrate advanced technologies such as Artificial Intelligence (AI), Data Computing, Big data, and Machine Learning among others. It should be appreciated that the metaverse generates vast amounts of data from user interactions and transactions, which, when analyzed, could offer valuable insights into urban economic trends and behaviors. With the power of AI, it could be possible to automate and enhance the data analysis processes, hence, fostering real-time predictions and recommendations that inform city planning and economic decision-making (Sun et al., 2022). A classic example to illustrate this is to consider how data-driven insights can guide the creation of "smart economic zones" within the metaverse. Like their physical counterparts, these zones can serve as hotspots for innovation and economic growth, attracting businesses and talent with a favorable regulatory environment, advanced infrastructure, and opportunities for collaboration. Such a zone (dubbed Japanese Metaverse Economic Zone or "Ryugukoku") has already been created in Japan, through the help of Fujitsu, Mitsubishi, and Japan Credit Bureau (JCB) (Liu, 2023). The Japanese version seeks to create an enabling environment by focusing on areas such as interoperability, gamification, fintech, and information communication technology (ICT), thereby, providing end users with immersive experiences in their virtual quests.

By capitalizing on data analytics, it could be possible to identify and stimulate sectors that are likely to thrive in the anticipated "smart economic zones." Data analytics would help such by identifying the skills that will be in demand, and the optimal scale and location for these zones. Such could further be enhanced by integrating AI, to help monitor those zones in real-time, hence, allowing for continuous adjustment of the plans and strategies based on the changing dynamics of the metaverse economy. This agility can ensure that these smart economic zones remain competitive and adaptive to emerging trends and challenges.

However, while leveraging the metaverse for urban economic planning and development, it would be important to be cognizant of the obvious issues and challenges, to ensure they are addressed at the earliest opportunity. On this, the metaverse has been accused of exacerbating issues related to data privacy, cyber-security, digital divide, as well as raising sustainability concerns. These have the potential to derail the implementation pace of the metaverse, or projects and initiatives such as the "smart economic zone," and hence, must be addressed proactively. It would also be critical to address the governance concerns, which would help solve issues such as ownership and control in this realm, to ensure that the metaverse contributes to equitable and sustainable urban development.

Implications of the metaverse for urban employment and skills

The increased attention on the emergence came at a time when the world was in dire need for profound transformations in the urban employment landscape, redefining job roles, creating new industries, and recasting the skills required for economic success. This is after the devastating impacts of COVID-19 that prompted a massive global economic downturn (Fig. 10.3), prompting massive job losses in most sectors (Allam, 2020a, 2020c, 2020d; Wong, 2020). However, as noted in the previous sections, technologies, including the metaverse are not a silver bullet to the socioeconomic challenges that confront the world. This is because, despite the numerous positives associated with it, it poses the risk of job displacement and exacerbating inequality if not harnessed with a vigilant eye towards upskilling, reskilling, and inclusive growth. A case on this can be made by considering the scope of job creation that the metaverse portends. As a convergent platform of various technologies including virtual reality, augmented reality, AI, and blockchain, the metaverse will spur the birth of several new occupations and industries (Roy, 2021). Examples of such include virtual reality architects, digital asset creators, new forms of realtors, and AI ethicists, which are roles that could raise the demand as the metaverse evolves. That notwithstanding, the metaverse can potentially create millions of new jobs globally, contributing significantly to urban employment.

Alongside job creation, the metaverse may also lead to job displacement. Traditional roles, particularly those that can be digitized or automated, may face

FIG. 10.3 A deserted street in Amsterdam during lockdown (de Vos, 2020).

obsolescence as attention shifts from the physical to the virtual realm; thus, displacing workers who lack the necessary skills to adapt. Such shifts would not only cause displacement of a certain cadre of jobs, but also instigate labor market disruptions and necessitate substantial occupational shifts, which might be expensive as people would be required to invest in education, time, and other resources to acquire relevant knowledge and skills.

The new skill set and competencies required to navigate this transformative phase may include digital literacy, the ability to use, understand, and create digital technology, and the ability to use diverse digital devices, et cetera. There will also be a need for a paradigm shift in terms of creativity, critical thinking, adaptability, and problem-solving skills to thrive in the dynamic, uncertain landscape of the metaverse (Sá & Serpa, 2023). Such "21st-century skills" are not merely technical but encompass cognitive, interpersonal, and intrapersonal dimensions. In addition to those needs, upskilling and reskilling initiatives emerge as critical policy imperatives to ensure a smooth transition to a metaverse-based economy. Governments, educational institutions, and businesses need to collaborate in a concerted manner on comprehensive lifelong learning curricula and systems that can equip individuals with the skills needed for the metaverse (Zhang et al., 2022). Without such initiatives, there would be concerns that the metaverse could widen socioeconomic inequality, as those with the necessary skills prosper while others are left behind to scrabble for the few job opportunities that will be available.

The metaverse is also changing the job market landscape by offering an opportunity to transcend geographical barriers and democratize economic opportunities through remote work and entrepreneurship. The concepts of "working from anywhere" and "work-from-home" could reach their zenith in the metaverse, where physical presence is no longer a prerequisite for economic participation (Choudhury, 2020). Such concepts have the potential to enhance workforce flexibility, reduce commuting costs, and enable individuals to access job opportunities far beyond their physical geographical locations.

On other frontiers, the metaverse could enable entrepreneurship by providing a low-cost, accessible platform for launching and growing new products and businesses. Startups could also leverage virtual storefronts, digital marketing, and global customer bases that have been rendered possible through the removal of some of the geographical constraints that traditionally limit business opportunities (Dwivedi et al., 2022).

Despite its potential benefits, this shift to remote work and entrepreneurship in the metaverse is not devoid of challenges. Issues related to the digital divide, work-life balance, and virtual collaboration need to be addressed to ensure that these opportunities are equitably and sustainably harnessed. There will also be a need to ensure that everyone has the opportunity to access education and relevant skill sets to enable them to participate successfully in this virtual realm.

Equity and inclusivity considerations in metaverse-based economies

The advent of the metaverse ushers in a distinctive opportunity to reimagine economic equity and inclusivity within urban landscapes. These potentials harbor wide-reaching implications yet are layered with challenges that require careful and comprehensive analysis.

The unprecedented market value growth of the metaverse since it came into the limelight to the anticipated over $900 billion by 2030 showcases that it holds considerable potential to significantly prompt (Thomas, 2022). In conventional reality, establishing a business demands substantial capital investment, and forms a formidable barrier for many aspiring entrepreneurs. However, the metaverse is seen to be slowly bringing some changes in the form of democratized entrepreneurship. For instance, setting up a virtual store in the metaverse could potentially cost substantially less than its physical counterpart, thereby enabling a broader spectrum of individuals to venture into entrepreneurship.

In addition to enabling entrepreneurship, the metaverse could also provide new routes to employment such as introducing remote and digital work opportunities that are not constrained by geographical boundaries or by the traditional employment limitations. However, the promise of equitable economic opportunities presented by the metaverse is directly proportional to the prospect of achieving equal access and participation by all. This caveat is based on the fact that as it stands, the metaverse has shown signals of having the potential to exacerbate the existing digital divides. Such has appeared in many forms, such as disparities in access to digital infrastructure, differences in digital literacy, and gaps in affordability (Nijman & Wei, 2020). As we tread towards metaverse-based economies, addressing these digital divides effectively becomes a pressing imperative.

For the metaverse to be considered successful, comprehensive strategies to combat the aforementioned divides are inevitable. These call for a collective effort involving both the public and private players. For the public, governments must prioritize investments in digital infrastructure, especially in underserved areas, to ensure affordable and universally accessible internet services. In addition, it must ensure that educational systems are restructured to incorporate digital literacy into their curricula and nurture lifelong learning opportunities to facilitate continuous digital skills development (Sá & Serpa, 2023). On the other hand, the private sector needs to play its role such as developing affordable digital devices and offering employee training programs (World Economic Forum, 2023).

In the course of democratizing economic landscapes, the metaverse prompts a positive transformation and empowerment of marginalized communities stimulating increased social mobility. This happens as the members of the marginalized groups are also able to participate and engage via the virtual spaces for commerce, cultural expression, and social interaction. Such spaces afford them platforms to voice their perspectives, market their products, and build social capital. This potential is not merely theoretical, for a growing number of individuals are already earning considerable income from digital and creative work in existing virtual spaces, indicating the potential of metaverse economies to foster inclusive growth (McKinsey, 2022).

Despite these promises, the metaverse also bears potential risks of exacerbating existing inequalities and plunging a sizable number of the population into much poverty. As societies transition towards digital economies, individuals lacking the necessary digital skills may find themselves increasingly marginalized. In addition, issues of representation in the metaverse also need to be carefully considered. Challenges such as gender and racial bias in virtual avatars and AI systems must be proactively addressed to ensure that all individuals feel valued, seen, and adequately represented within the digital landscape (Dwivedi et al., 2022). Moreover, ensuring that people with disabilities are part and parcel of the metaverse presents a crucial equity consideration (Felix, 2022). Developers of metaverse technologies must consider a diverse range of access needs to ensure that all users can participate fully in metaverse experiences. This demands a proactive commitment to design that privileges inclusivity and access for all users.

Ethical and legal implications of metaverse-based economies

The deployment of the metaverse in urban economic contexts ushers in some ethical and legal challenges, that might overshadow the aforementioned benefits if not comprehensively addressed. The tangible implications of these challenges cut across issues related to personal privacy, security (of both humans and infrastructure), data ownership concerns, intellectual property rights, fair competition, and the overarching need for regulatory frameworks and governance models.

Regarding privacy and security, the metaverse could engender unprecedented invasions of personal privacy and security, as well as expose some digital installations to security threats if unchecked. The immersive and interactive nature of the metaverse implies that enormous amounts of data would be collected, tracked, and potentially exploited for diverse purposes, including commercialization, and in worse-case scenarios, for terrorism activities (Debuire, 2022). Among personal data that could be compromised include biometric data, behavioral patterns, and personal communications details and trends. Beyond privacy, the digital realm is equally fraught with cybersecurity risks, such as data breaches and identity thefts, which necessitates robust security measures to protect users and their data within the metaverse.

Ownership of data in the metaverse is another area that is attracting numerous ethical questions. As users interact within the metaverse, the vast trove of data they generate is consciously or otherwise utilized for various purposes, including personalized advertising to improve user experience (Ahmad &

Corovic, 2022). However, without clear guidelines on data ownership, users could be deprived of their right to control how their data is used or shared. Policymakers and technologists, therefore, must engage in forward-looking discussions about who should own and govern, as well as profit from such data, and ensure users' rights are adequately safeguarded (Canbay et al., 2022).

Unlike in the physical realm, the concept of intellectual property rights takes on an entirely new dimension in the context of metaverse-based economies. The creation and exchange of virtual assets, such as real estate, avatars, digital art, et cetera, have become lucrative activities in the emerging digital economy. However, without clear rules governing intellectual property rights for such assets, creators may find themselves answering questions such as copyright infringement and asset theft. This then behooves the need to develop fair and enforceable intellectual property guidelines for the metaverse, which would be critical in protecting creators and fostering innovation (Vig, 2022).

Similarly, the rise of metaverse-based economies could raise issues related to fair competition. Normally, such concerns would be prompted by the dominant players who could potentially monopolize digital spaces and use their competitive advantage to stifle new entrants; hence, limiting the scope of choices for consumers. Such trends however could be mitigated by implementing competition law within the metaverse which also targets to maintain market fairness, ensuring a diverse and competitive economic landscape (Smaili & de Rancourt-Raymond, 2022). These emerging challenges underscore the need for robust regulatory frameworks and governance models to not only guide the metaverse but also associated tools and technologies. Metaverse-based economic activities, with their novelty and complexity, need to be anchored on a strong regulatory framework that guarantees consumer protection, prevents abuses, and fosters trust (Shi et al., 2023). Crafting these regulations, however, calls for a delicate balance—they must provide adequate safeguards without stifling the innovation and potential benefits of metaverse economies. As such, international collaborations are necessary in shaping ethical and legal frameworks for the metaverse. Therefore, international standards-setting bodies, intergovernmental organizations, and multinational corporations will have no other option than to collaborate in the development of universal norms and standards that uphold the principles of fairness, inclusivity, and transparency within the metaverse.

Discussions and conclusions

This chapter has comprehensively explored the metaverse's transformative implications for urban economic planning, employment, and skills. It has also delved into issues of equity and inclusivity, and ethical and legal aspects, culminating in a plethora of compelling insights, opportunities, challenges, and directions for future research and policymaking.

In the course of analyzing the diverse potentials of the metaverse for urban economic planning and development, it has been evidently clear that this new digital frontier will revolutionize urban economic activities, and also planning processes. It is expected to stimulate the emergence of new economic frontiers that have the potential to address various urban challenges such as unemployment and reduce revenue streams for individuals and government at large.

In urban planning and development, it is anticipated that the metaverse will catalyze the evolution of smarter, more resilient, and adaptable cities. For instance, virtual simulations and modeling could provide city planners and designers with a detailed understanding of the urban milieu and a sandbox environment for testing and refining strategies. Meanwhile, technologies such as data analytics and AI have the potential to drive efficient resource management and informed decision-making (Batty, 2013). However, as exciting as these prospects may be, the actualization of these potentials is contingent on access to robust data infrastructure and the availability of technical expertise among city planners and urban developers.

In relation to employment and skills, that would allow individuals to capitalize on the metaverse's based economic frontiers, the metaverse represents a double-edged sword. On one end, it harbors the potential to disrupt traditional employment patterns and prompt the need for a new set of skills. On the other end, it presents opportunities for remote work, entrepreneurship, and the creation of new digital professions. Regarding new skill sets, such are prompted by the emergence of these new forms of work which underscores the need for robust upskilling and reskilling initiatives to prepare workers for the transition to a metaverse-driven economy. While it is still early in relation to the development of the metaverse and understanding fully what it might hold in the future, it behooves policymakers and educators to rethink current approaches to skills development and lifelong learning to ensure that they align with the evolving demands of the digital age (World Economic Forum, 2023).

The metaverse will serve as a powerful platform for economic activity, hence, its potential to foster economic equity and inclusivity cannot be underestimated. By reducing barriers to entry and promoting equal economic opportunities, it could serve as a tool for social mobility and economic empowerment. However, as has clearly been argued in the discussions earlier, caution must be exercised to prevent the existing digital divide from translating into a metaverse divide, where access and benefits are unevenly distributed. Such a tragedy could be avoided by ensuring that best practices such as digital literacy, affordability, and connectivity are ubiquitous to ensure broad-based participation in metaverse-based economic activities.

Ethical and legal concerns touching on the metaverse should also not be left to spread unchecked. These present a labyrinth of complex issues, including privacy, security, data ownership, intellectual property rights, fair competition, and the need for comprehensive regulatory frameworks. These issues underscore the need for proactive measures to protect users' rights and interests in the metaverse, safeguard the integrity of digital economies, and foster an environment of trust and fairness. Here, international cooperation will be key in developing globally accepted norms and standards that underpin the ethical and legal frameworks of the metaverse.

In sum, this chapter has provided a comprehensive exploration of the potential implications of the metaverse for urban economies, and how such would be transformed going into the future. Therefore, it is agreeable that as the metaverse evolves, so will its impact on various aspects of urban life; hence, the need for all players to be proactive. Policymakers, urban planners, educators, and other stakeholders will need to remain vigilant and responsive, proactively addressing emerging challenges and capitalizing on the opportunities presented by this new frontier. This necessitates continuous research, dialog, and collaboration among diverse stakeholders to navigate the uncharted territory of metaverse-based economies and build a future that is inclusive, equitable, and sustainable.

References

Ahmad, I., & Corovic, T. (25 January 2022). *Privacy in a parallel digital universe: The metaverse*. Norton Rose Fulbright. Retrieved 30th May 2022 from https://www.dataprotectionreport.com/2022/01/privacy-in-a-parallel-digital-universe-the-metaverse/.

Allam, M. Z. (2019). *Urban resilience and economic equity in an era of global climate crisis*. University of Sydney.

Allam, Z. (2020a). The first 50 days of COVID-19: A detailed chronological timeline and extensive review of literature documenting the pandemic. *Surveying the Covid-19 Pandemic its Implications, 1*.

Allam, Z. (2020b). Oil, health equipment, and trade: Revisiting political economy and international relations during the COVID-19 pandemic. *Surveying the Covid-19 Pandemic its Implications, 119*.

Allam, Z. (2020c). The second 50 days: A detailed chronological timeline and extensive review of literature documenting the COVID-19 pandemic from day 50 to day 100. *Surveying the Covid-19 Pandemic its Implications, 9*.

Allam, Z. (2020d). The third 50 days: A detailed chronological timeline and extensive review of literature documenting the COVID-19 pandemic from day 100 to day 150. *Surveying the Covid-19 Pandemic its Implications, 41*.

Allam, Z. (2021). On global capitalism and autonomous smart cities: A view on the economic engines of tomorrow. In *The rise of autonomous smart cities* (pp. 49–60). Cham: Palgrave Macmillan.

Allam, Z., Bibri, S. E., Chabaud, D., & Moreno, C. (2022a). The '15-Minute City' concept can shape a net-zero urban future. *Humanities and Social Sciences Communications, 9*(1), 126. https://doi.org/10.1057/s41599-022-01145-0.

Allam, Z., Bibri, S. E., Chabaud, D., & Moreno, C. (2022b). The theoretical, practical, and technological foundations of the 15-Minute City model: Proximity and its environmental, social and economic benefits for sustainability. *Energies, 15*(16), 6042. https://doi.org/10.3390/en15166042.

Allam, Z., Bibri, S. E., Jones, D. S., Chabaud, D., & Moreno, C. (2022). Unpacking the 15-Minute City via 6G, IoT, and digital twins: Towards a new narrative for increasing urban efficiency, resilience, and sustainability. *Sensors, 22*(4), 1369. https://doi.org/10.3390/s22041369.

Allam, Z., & Jones, D. S. (2020). Pandemic stricken cities on lockdown. Where are our planning and design professionals [now, then and into the future]? *Land Use Policy, 97*, 104805.

Allam, Z., & Newman, P. (2018). Redefining the smart city: Culture, metabolism and governance. *Smart Cities, 1*(1). https://doi.org/10.3390/smartcities1010002.

Allam, Z., Nieuwenhuijsen, M., Chabaud, D., & Moreno, C. (2022). The 15-minute city offers a new framework for sustainability, liveability, and health. *The Lancet. Planetary Health, 6*(3), e181–e183.

Batty, M. (2013). Big data, smart cities and city planning. *Dialogues in Human Geography, 3*(3), 274–279. https://doi.org/10.1177/2043820613513390.

Bezgrebelna, M., McKenzie, K., Wells, S., Ravindran, A., Kral, M., Christensen, J., Stergiopoulos, V., Gaetz, S., & Kidd, S. A. (2021). Climate change, weather, housing precarity, and homelessness: A systematic review of reviews. *International Journal of Environmental Research and Public Health, 18*(11). https://doi.org/10.3390/ijerph18115812.

Bhattacharya, P., Saraswat, D., Savaliya, D., Sanghavi, S., Verma, A., Sakariya, V., Tanwar, S., Sharma, R., Raboaca, M. S., & Manea, D. L. (2023). Towards future internet: The metaverse perspective for diverse industrial applications. *Mathematics, 11*(4).

Canbay, Y., Utku, A., & Canbay, P. (2022). *Privacy concerns and measures in metaverse: A review*. https://doi.org/10.1109/ISCTURKEY56345.2022.9931866.

Canny, W. (22 November 2021). *Metaverse gaming, NFTs could account for 10% of luxury market by 2030: Morgan Stanley*. Coin Desk. Retrieved 30th May 2023 from https://www.coindesk.com/business/2021/11/22/metaverse-gaming-nfts-could-account-for-10-of-luxury-market-by-2030-morgan-stanley/.

Cheng, X., Zhang, S., Fu, S., Liu, W., Guan, C., Mou, J., Ye, Q., & Huang, C. (2022). Exploring the metaverse in the digital economy: An overview and research framework. *Journal of Electronic Business & Digital Economics, 1*(1/2), 206–224. https://doi.org/10.1108/JEBDE-09-2022-0036.

Chetty, R., & Hendren, N. (2018). The impacts of neighborhoods on intergenerational mobility II: County-level estimates. *The Quarterly Journal of Economics, 133*(3), 1163–1228. https://doi.org/10.1093/qje/qjy006.

Choudhury, P. (2020). Our work-from-anywhere future. *Harvard Business Review*. Retrieved 1st June 2023 from https://hbr.org/2020/11/our-work-from-anywhere-future.

de Vos, S. (5 April 2020). *Silent Amsterdam*. Unsplash. Retrieved 21st June 2023 from https://unsplash.com/photos/oBGimThy-mU.

Debuire, D. (12 April 2022). Terrorist use of the metaverse: New opportunities and new challenges. *Security Distillery*. Retrieved 30th May 2022 from https://thesecuritydistillery.org/all-articles/terrorism-and-the-metaverse-new-opportunities-and-new-challenges.

Dimov, R., & Dimov, D. (2022). *Metaverse implementation in real life. Augmented and virtual reality*.

Dwivedi, Y. K., Hughes, L., Baabdullah, A. M., Ribeiro-Navarrete, S., Giannakis, M., Al-Debei, M. M., Dennehy, D., Metri, B., Buhalis, D., Cheung, C. M. K., Conboy, K., Doyle, R., Dubey, R., Dutot, V., Felix, R., Goyal, D. P., Gustafsson, A., Hinsch, C., Jebabli, I., … Wamba, S. F. (2022). Metaverse beyond the hype: Multidisciplinary perspectives on emerging challenges, opportunities, and agenda for research, practice and policy. *International Journal of Information Management, 66*, 102542. https://doi.org/10.1016/j.ijinfomgt.2022.102542.

Faraboschi, P., Frachtenberg, E., Laplante, P., Milojicic, D., & Saracco, R. (2022). Virtual worlds (metaverse): From skepticism, to fear, to immersive opportunities. *Computer, 55*(10), 100–106. https://doi.org/10.1109/MC.2022.3192702.

Felix, A. (19 December 2022). An accessible, disability-inclusive metaverse? *European Disability Forum*. Retrieved 27th May 2023 from https://www.edf-feph.org/an-accessible-disability-inclusive-metaverse/.

Fewings, N. (16 November 2018). *Homelessness in London*. Unsplash. Retrieved 21st June 2023 from https://unsplash.com/photos/4OFU9yxUvLc.

Frank, R. (1 February 2022). *Metaverse real estate sales top $500 million, and are projected to double this year*. CNBC. Retrieved 1st June 2023 from https://www.cnbc.com/2022/02/01/metaverse-real-estate-sales-top-500-million-metametric-solutions-says.html.

Gadekallu, T., Huynh-The, T., Wang, W., Yenduri, G., Ranaweera, P., Pham, V., Costa, D. B., & Liyanage, M. (2022). *Blockchain for the metaverse: A review*.

Hudson-Smith, A. (2022). Incoming metaverses: Digital mirrors for urban planning. *Urban Planning*, 7(2). https://doi.org/10.17645/up.v7i2.5193. (2022): Gaming, simulations, and planning: Physical and digital technologies for public participation in urban planning https://www.cogitatiopress.com/urbanplanning/article/view/5193.

Huynh-The, T., Gadekallu, T. R., Wang, W., Yenduri, G., Ranaweera, P., Pham, Q.-V., da Costa, D. B., & Liyanage, M. (2023). Blockchain for the metaverse: A review. *Future Generation Computer Systems*, 143, 401–419. https://doi.org/10.1016/j.future.2023.02.008.

International Labour Organization. (31 October 2022). *Global labour market to deteriorate further as Ukraine conflict and other crises continue*. ILO. Retrieved 5th April 2023 from https://www.ilo.org/global/about-the-ilo/newsroom/news/WCMS_859191/lang- -en/index.htm#:~:text=In%20addition%20to%20the%20terrible%2C%20pre%2Dconflict%2C%20level.

Kamin, D. (19 February 2023). The next hot housing market is out of this world. It's in the metaverse. *New York Times*. Retrieved 30th May 2023 from https://www.nytimes.com/2023/02/19/realestate/metaverse-vr-housing-market.html.

Kulkov, I., Berggren, B., Hellström, M., & Wikström, K. (2021). Navigating uncharted waters: Designing business models for virtual and augmented reality companies in the medical industry. *Journal of Engineering and Technology Management*, 59, 101614. https://doi.org/10.1016/j.jengtecman.2021.101614.

Liu, B. (27 February 2023). Japan gets its own 'metaverse economic zone,' with help from Fujitsu. *Blockworks*. Retrieved 1st June 2023 from https://blockworks.co/news/japan-metaverse-economic-zoneQ.

McKinsey. (24 May 2022). *Marketing in the metaverse: An opportunity for innovation and experimentation*. McKinsey & Company. Retrieved 10th February 2023 from https://www.mckinsey.com/capabilities/growth-marketing-and-sales/our-insights/marketing-in-the-metaverse-an-opportunity-for-innovation-and-experimentation.

Nijman, J., & Wei, Y. D. (2020). Urban inequalities in the 21st century economy. *Applied Geography*, 117, 102188. https://doi.org/10.1016/j.apgeog.2020.102188.

Raworth, K. (2017). *Doughnut economics: Seven ways to think like a 21st-century economist*. Random House.

Roy, A. (2 December 2021). Doing business in the metaverse: Opportunity or threat? *XR Today*. Retrieved 8th February 2023 from https://www.xrtoday.com/virtual-reality/doing-business-in-the-metaverse-opportunity-or-threat/.

Sá, M. J., & Serpa, S. (2023). Metaverse as a learning environment: Some considerations. *Sustainability*, 15(3).

Semega, J., & Kollar, M. (13 September 2022). *2021 Income Inequality Increased for first since 2011*. United States Census Bureau. Retrieved 1st June 2023 from https://www.census.gov/library/stories/2022/09/income-inequality-increased.html#:~:text=Using%20pretax%20money%20income%2C%20theindex%20had%20increased%20since%202011.

Shi, F., Ning, H., Zhang, X., Li, R., Tian, Q., Zhang, S., Zheng, Y., Guo, Y., & Daneshmand, M. (2023). A new technology perspective of the metaverse: Its essence, framework and challenges. *Digital Communications and Networks*. https://doi.org/10.1016/j.dcan.2023.02.017.

Shubham Dhage. (2022). *3D illustration of tezos coin, bitcoin, and ethereum.* Unsplash. Retrieved 21st June 2022 from https://unsplash.com/photos/HyxJ0yqa_8Q.

Smaili, N., & de Rancourt-Raymond, A. (2022). Metaverse: Welcome to the new fraud marketplace. *Journal of Financial Crime.* https://doi.org/10.1108/JFC-06-2022-0124 (ahead-of-print).

Statista. (2023). *Metaverse live entertainment—Worldwide.* Retrieved 1sth June 2023 from https://www.statista.com/outlook/amo/metaverse/metaverse-live-entertainment/worldwide#:~:text=In%20the%20Metaverse%20Live%20Entertainment%20market%2C%20the%20number%20of%20usersto%20amount%20to%20US%24105.40.

Storper, M. (2020). *Keys to the city: How economics, institutions, social interaction, and politics shape development.* Princeton University Press. https://books.google.co.ke/books?id=NZmzDwAAQBAJ.

Sun, J., Gan, W., Chen, Z., Li, J., & Yu, P. (2022). *Big data meets metaverse: A survey.*

The World Bank. (6 April 2023). *Weak growth and a cost-of-living crisis in emerging Europe and Central Asia region.* The World Bank. Retrieved 1st June 2023 from https://www.worldbank.org/en/news/feature/2023/04/06/weak-growth-and-a-cost-of-living-crisis-in-emerging-europe-and-central-asia-region.

Thomas, A. (23 August 2022). *Metaverse market size worldwide 2021-2030.* Statista. Retrieved 10th February 2023 from https://www.statista.com/statistics/1295784/metaverse-market-size/.

Vig, S. (2022). Intellectual property rights and the metaverse: An Indian perspective. *The Journal of World Intellectual Property, 25*(3), 753–766. https://doi.org/10.1111/jwip.12249.

Wong, B. A. (4 June 2020). How digital entrepreneurs will help shape the world after the COVID-19 pandemic. *We Forum.* Retrieved 20/2/22 from https://www.weforum.org/agenda/2020/06/entrepreneurs-must-embrace-digital-during-pandemic-for-society/.

World Economic Forum. (2023). Putting skills first: A framework for action. *World Economic Forum.* https://www3.weforum.org/docs/WEF_CNES_Putting_Skills_First_2023.pdf.

Zhang, X., Chen, Y., Hu, L., & Wang, Y. (2022). The metaverse in education: Definition, framework, features, potential applications, challenges, and future research topics [review]. *Frontiers in Psychology, 13.* https://doi.org/10.3389/fpsyg.2022.1016300.

Chapter 11

The environmental implications of the metaverse in cities

Energy efficiency and resource management

The emergence of the metaverse in this era is very timely as it has the potential to provide a compelling frontier in the quest to reduce energy consumption in cities. Before the metaverse started to gain traction, maximum attention was accorded to the smart cities concept which also has showcased unquestionable capability to help in addressing environmental sustainability concerns. The ability of the smart cities concept is tied to how it is undergirded by technologies such as the Internet of Things (IoT), Artificial intelligence (AI), Data Analytics, and others (Allam, 2021a, 2021b). After the emergence of the metaverse, which perfectly augmented the smart cities concept, the ability of cities to optimize energy use and resource management is no longer questionable (Petkov, 2023). In the metaverse, the amalgamation of virtual and augmented reality through technologies such as Digital Twins (DT) enables immersive simulations that can assist urban designers in creating energy-efficient infrastructures.

It has been argued that applying virtual simulations to urban design has the potential to yield tangible benefits. A recent study by Athienitis and Karava (2007) indicated that simulations could be instrumental in the optimal placement of buildings to exploit natural sunlight and airflows, thus reducing reliance on artificial lighting and cooling. Simulations are also gradually becoming popular in planning, especially in the transport sector where it is being used to plan for efficient public transport routes, thus, contributing to reduced fossil fuel consumption. To cap this all, the continuous digital footprint in the metaverse allows for real-time data collection, analytics, and feedback, hence, fostering the creation of "living labs" where urban design strategies are perpetually refined and adapted to promote energy efficiency.

The metaverse is also becoming very instrumental in the sustainability efforts, especially regarding Sustainable Development Goal (SDGs) number 12 which advocates for sustainable consumption and production as shown in Table 11.1 in the following (United Nations Development Programme (UNDP), 2015). For instance, in managing scarce resources, the metaverse is

TABLE 11.1 The main objectives of SDG 12.

i.	Sustainable consumption	Encourage individuals, businesses, and industries to adopt sustainable consumption practices, including resource efficiency, waste reduction, and responsible consumption of goods and services
ii.	Sustainable production	Promote the adoption of sustainable production methods, technologies, and practices across all sectors, aiming to minimize the environmental impact, resource depletion, and pollution associated with production processes
iii.	Resource efficiency	Improve resource efficiency, including energy efficiency, water efficiency, and material efficiency, to reduce waste generation, minimize resource depletion, and promote sustainable use of natural resources
iv.	Waste management	Implement sound waste management systems, including recycling, reuse, and proper disposal of waste, to reduce the amount of waste generated, prevent pollution, and promote the circular economy
v.	Sustainable supply chains	Encourage the development of sustainable and ethical supply chains, ensuring responsible sourcing, fair trade practices, and safe working conditions throughout

poised to revolutionize traditional practices, by ensuring that some resource-intensive practices shift to the virtual realm, hence, reducing consumption.

A case in point is the use of IoT-enabled sensors in the energy sector to allow for accurate, real-time monitoring and analysis of energy consumption (Allam, Sharifi, et al., 2022). With such sensors, it could be possible to shift to smart grids that rely on different data on issues such as consumer behavior, weather conditions, and energy price fluctuations to optimize the supply-demand balance. When such are integrated into the metaverse, it could add another dimension by facilitating predictive analysis based on these simulations, aiding in strategic decision-making and potentially averting resource crises.

Another significant avenue where the metaverse may impact energy efficiency is in the promotion of sustainable behaviors among producers and also diverse consumers. This is because it offers a wide range of platforms that could be leveraged to foster an acute awareness of energy usage and conservation. On this, it has been argued that if individuals were to witness the effects of their energy consumption habits when it is simulated, they could be more inclined to adopt sustainable behaviors in reality.

Renewable energy refers to energy derived from sources that are naturally replenished and have a minimal impact on the environment.

Another prospect to optimize energy production and consumption to align with a sustainable agenda could be through the integration of renewable energy sources into the virtual environment. Here, the metaverse could offer cities platforms for renewable energy sources into their infrastructures. Such efforts have always been hindered by numerous physical limitations. The metaverse offers an environment where such could be counteracted by simulating different renewable energy scenarios, offering cost-effective testing grounds. After different scenarios have been simulated and tested, the insights gained could guide the efficient and effective integration of renewable energy sources in real urban environments (Fig. 11.1).

While the integration of renewable energy in the virtual environment promises an array of benefits, it will be critical to pursue equitability regarding access to energy-efficient solutions within the metaverse. This caveat is based on the fact that the metaverse has been accused of having the potential to exacerbate the digital divide and, hence, widen socioeconomic disparities that already exist (Massally et al., 2022).

In addition to ensuring there is mitigation of the digital divide, it will also be important to ensure that the metaverse does not contribute to the increased demand for energy, especially from nonrenewable sources. This argument is based on the fact that several challenges and limitations stand in the path of leveraging the metaverse for energy efficiency. One of these is the energy-intensive nature of some of the information and communication (ICT) systems. On this, a study by McKenzie (2021), highlighted that the ICT sector's energy consumption is set to exceed 20% of the total global electricity consumption by 2025 due to factors like an increase in the amount of data being generated.

FIG. 11.1 Sustainable energy farm in the United Kingdom (Doherty, 2019).

To ensure that the metaverse does not exacerbate this issue, energy-efficient technologies, infrastructure, and practices should be prioritized in its development.

Environmental monitoring and analysis

The metaverse offers numerous benefits and advantages to the environmental sustainability efforts. Among such is the real-time environmental monitoring made possible by the availability of diverse virtual environments in the metaverse. In addition, as noted in the previous section, the integration of advanced smart technologies such as remote sensing and IoT, which can generate vast real-time data allows for immersive visualization (Fig. 11.2), which is key in taking care of the environment (Allam, Sharifi, et al., 2022). The data comes from smart establishments and devices such as traffic sensors and weather stations which are ubiquitous in smart cities (Allam & Dhunny, 2019; Allam & Newman, 2018; Hashem et al., 2016). When the data generated is analyzed using advanced technologies such as data analytic technologies, and in an advanced environment such as the metaverse, it becomes possible to visualize different scenarios, thus, enabling stakeholders to track environmental changes and formulate responsive, evidence-based strategies to counter the impacts (Batty, 2013). Notably, diverse data feeds increase the potential for stakeholders to access informed insight on various environmental parameters such as air and water quality, urban heat island effect, waste generation and management, et cetera.

FIG. 11.2 A smart home monitoring device (Getty Images, 2022).

Moreover, the metaverse is slowly proving to be a fertile ground for predictive modeling in urban environmental planning. Its strength here is anchored on the ability to allow simulations of various scenarios and their respective environmental impacts, thus, giving urban planners an edge to anticipate potential challenges and devise appropriate measures in advance. According to a study by Cao et al. (2023), predictive modeling in the metaverse can optimize urban planning for environmental sustainability, from reducing carbon emissions to promoting biodiversity in urban areas.

Another astounding potential of the metaverse is its ability to enhance urban resilience by simulating natural disasters and the diverse impacts of climate change. On this, it is without doubt that accurate, detailed simulations of potential disaster scenarios, such as floods, drought, or heatwaves, can help city authorities test and refine emergency response strategies (Merz et al., 2020). Furthermore, simulations of anticipated or possible long-term climate change impacts can inform proactive adaptations in urban design, ensuring that cities are correctly designed to adapt and become resilient in the face of anticipated future changes.

From diverse studies, it has been established that urban residents seldom participate in decision-making on matters of the environment. Notably, because of the lack of platforms that afford them to be involved in such discourses. However, the metaverse has been lauded for offering a potent platform for such citizens to engage in environmental initiatives. Through technologies such as virtual reality (VR) and augmented reality (AR), urban residents can be immersed in simulated environments, witnessing the effects of climate change or the benefits of sustainable practices firsthand (Yavo-Ayalon et al., 2023). Such immersive experiences can significantly enhance their environmental consciousness and motivate them to actively participate in environmental conservation efforts.

The metaverse is also being seen as a platform that has the potential to promote environmental justice and inclusivity which is considered very important in protecting vulnerable communities and states such as the Small Island Developing States (SIDS) and less polluting countries, especially in the global south. On this, the metaverse is hailed for offering spaces that promote virtual experiences to foster empathy and understanding of how different environmental actions and inactions affect the vulnerable. This is done through the creation of virtual narratives that highlight environmental disparities and injustices that exist in the world, especially between the developed economies which are higher polluters and less developed economies, whose contribution to global emissions is arguably less than 1% of the total emissions (Beusch et al., 2022). The metaverse can then be argued to be championing the cause of environmental justice, urging equitable access to environmental benefits and protections.

The metaverse can also facilitate collaboration between stakeholders for effective environmental management. By offering a shared virtual space, the metaverse can facilitate real-time dialog and cooperation among city planners, environmental scientists, and citizens. This collaborative approach, supported by digital tools such as shared data repositories and virtual meetings, can promote consensus-driven and inclusive environmental management.

To ensure that the momentum established by the metaverse in enhancing diverse environmental sustainability efforts is not distracted, it will be important to address some concerns, especially on privacy and security. Particularly, it will be critical to ensure that the massive data collected is utilized only for the intended purposes. Whereas the metaverse, through technologies such as the blockchain, has the capacity for anonymization and secure data handling, the ownership of different data-collecting devices raises concerns about individual privacy and data security (Zuboff, 2019). Careful governance would need to be established to facilitate a balance between the benefits of environmental data and the protection of citizens' privacy.

Sustainable transportation and mobility

> Sustainable Transportation: Transportation systems and practices that minimize environmental impacts, promote social equity, and support economic viability.

Cities across the globe have been facing unimaginable challenges because of increased traffic congestion, and unprecedented levels of emissions from automobiles. It is only in 2020, during the height of the COVID-19 pandemic that this situation was seen to have been reversed due to the health protocols and restrictions that had been instituted, warranting very minimal automobile transportation (Allam, 2020a, 2020b, 2020c). During the pandemic and after, certain best practices such as the work-from-home concept became popular, further compounding the reduction in automobile use (Fig. 11.3). However, the situation is still dire in most cities, and the emergence of the metaverse is a welcome relief, as it carries immense potential for reducing congestion and emissions from transportation. By digitally replicating the physical environment, it offers a robust platform for comprehensive traffic simulations, laying the groundwork for effective traffic management strategies. It has been argued that such simulations can revolutionize different facets of the transportation sectors including traffic light control systems by optimizing signal timing, thereby reducing waiting times and associated carbon emissions.

In addition to facilitating traffic management, the metaverse also presents realistic opportunities for urban mobility planning and design. Through it, urban planners can utilize virtual simulations to model the impacts of different strategies and interventions, thereby prompting the design of efficient and sustainable mobility systems (Hudson-Smith, 2022). By emphasizing on simulations, it is possible to plan pedestrian-friendly zones, cycle routes, and public transit networks (Kitchin, 2015).

The environmental implications of the metaverse in cities **Chapter | 11** **197**

FIG. 11.3 A bicycle land provision in Paris, France (Edouard, 2018).

The transport management does not only benefit from the adoption of the metaverse but also through the active integration of smart technologies which have been there even before the metaverse became popular. The wide-ranging use of IoT devices and sensors in smart cities has given rise to a wealth of real-time mobility data (Bibri & Krogstie, 2019). When collected, analyzed, and visualized within the metaverse, this data can provide nuanced insights into transportation dynamics, enabling the design of adaptive, demand-responsive transportation systems. Through the metaverse immersive experiences instigated by virtual reality technologies, it is argued that there can be a significant influence on human behaviors prompting a positive change toward sustainable mobility (Pamucar et al., 2022). Thus, by encouraging the users to virtually experience the benefits of sustainable practices, showcased during simulations, the metaverse can potentially stimulate shifts towards environmentally friendly modes of transportation, such as cycling.

Enhancing accessibility and inclusivity in mobility systems is yet another domain where the metaverse is seen to be gaining maximum attention due to the valuable contributions it promises. The truth on this is that the virtual simulations made possible by the metaverse and technologies such as DT could help understand and subsequently mitigate the barriers faced by different user groups, including those with mobility impairments (Garaj et al., 2022). This implies that by trying and testing and refining designs in a virtual environment, it would be possible to ensure that physical mobility systems are accessible and inclusive to all.

As is the case in all other frontiers, it would be grave not to consider the issues of privacy and security concerns surrounding the collection and analysis of mobility data, even though the benefit is vivid and massive. It then behooves all players in the transportation sector to consider it urgent to strike a balance between gathering sufficient data to improve mobility services and safeguarding the privacy of individuals. Technologies such as blockchain that allow for active anonymization, encryption, and secure data handling protocols must be leveraged to protect user data (Gadekallu et al., 2022). It will also be important to engage in proactive discourses and efforts that would help to bridge the "digital divide" associated with the metaverse and ensure that the benefits of the digital benefits are accessible to all city residents, irrespective of their socioeconomic status (Massally et al., 2022). The metaverse can also foster collaborative approaches to multimodal transportation planning and implementation. By offering a shared, interactive platform, the metaverse can facilitate dialog and cooperation among city planners, transport operators, and citizens. This collaborative approach can pave the way for the cocreation and implementation of sustainable and equitable transportation strategies.

Waste management and circular economy

Circular Economy: An economic system that aims to eliminate waste and promote the continual use of resources.

Different forms of metaverse already exist and others are in the pipeline, but one convergent truth about them is that their potential is immeasurable. That is, in sum, the potential of the metaverse extends into almost all facets of the urban fabric. In the previous section, the discussion was focused on the environment and then on transportation. In this section, attention is drawn to how the metaverse is influencing waste management systems and its potential to influence the adoption of the circular economy concept. In the recent past, it has clearly been demonstrated that with increased urbanization, economic growth, population increase, and consumerism behaviors, waste generation has reached unprecedented levels and will continue to increase. For instance, it is anticipated that by 2050, the amount of waste per year will reach 3.4 billion metric tons, which is a 70% increase from the current amount being produced (Alves, 2023). The metaverse provides realistic opportunities to tackle this by stimulating behavioral changes, especially of the urban residents. By exposing users to the different environmental impacts of waste in an immersive, experiential manner, the metaverse could instigate a paradigm shift toward sustainable waste disposal practices.

Furthermore, through virtual simulations, the metaverse can enhance waste management systems and infrastructure. For instance, by creating a digital twin of a city's waste management system, it could become possible for urban planners to test different waste collection routes and schedules, thereby reducing operational inefficiencies and environmental footprint. In addition, the metaverse could become invaluable in helping design and simulate the operation of recycling facilities, leading to optimal configurations that maximize waste recovery rates (Sahota, 2023).

One of the platforms that could be used within the metaverse to increase awareness and the need for waste reduction is public education. The metaverse is ideal for this purpose due to several reasons, including its interactive nature, its global scope which transcends any geographical limitation and barriers, et cetera. In the course of public education, an immersive virtual environment can vividly demonstrate the lifecycle of waste and the environmental consequences of improper disposal, inculcating a stronger sense of environmental stewardship.

As a way of reducing the environmental footprint of the economy, a substantial number of countries across the world have embraced the concept of circular economy (Fig. 11.4). This concept emphasizes several principles including, reduction of waste, reuse of products to keep them in the system to the maximum, and recycling, when the life span cannot be extended (Nañez Alonso et al., 2021). These principles can further be enforced by the metaverse. This could be achieved through immersing users in a virtual world where resources reused or recycling is extensive; hence, prompting the desire for sustainable

FIG. 11.4 People promoting the concept of circular economy (Pestano, 2021).

consumption patterns. On this, it is anticipated that experiencing a virtual world that thrives on the circular economy could inspire users to replicate such practices in the real world.

Smart technologies, particularly the Internet of Things (IoT) via different devices offer opportunities to enhance waste collection and sorting in both virtual and physical spaces. For instance, connecting devices such as sensors on waste bins could provide real-time data on waste levels, facilitating dynamic collection schedules that save time and energy. Efficiency could further be enhanced through algorithms fashioned to help in sorting different types of digital waste more efficiently, thus, potentially informing strategies for physical waste sorting (Mohd Yusof et al., 2018). In addition to influencing sorting and efficient collection, the metaverse can also facilitate collaborative waste management efforts. For instance, by fostering interaction and communication between different stakeholders, such as local governments or municipal authorities, waste management companies, the local communities, and individual citizens, it can lead to more effective and inclusive waste management strategies. While at a nascent stage, the notion of recycling digital assets, such as 3D models and textures, could promote more sustainable digital consumption habits.

Despite the many benefits of the metaverse in addressing the problem of waste management, a few challenges related to inclusivity and accessibility persist. Such are particularly exacerbated by the digital divide which has extensively been shown that it could hamper universal access to the metaverse. This could in turn disrupt waste management efforts and solutions, thus, widening existing socioeconomic disparities. Overcoming this requires addressing digital literacy and infrastructure gaps, as well as promoting universal access to education for all, especially within digital platforms such as the metaverse.

Green spaces and urban biodiversity

The ability to integrate the metaverse into the urban green spaces presents an intriguing potential to enrich and protect urban biodiversity. While the "green" aspect be it green cover or green spaces in cities globally continue to decline rapidly, as a result of phenomenon such as rapid population growth and unprecedented urbanization continue to rise, the metaverse could be leveraged for its potential to augment physical green spaces. This would allow individuals to virtually connect with nature, even in densely built urban areas, and cities with little or no room for physical green spaces to be created. Through virtual simulations of physical cities, the metaverse could greatly benefit urban planners and designers by providing them the ability to accurately prioritize green infrastructure. Also, through simulating the ecological impacts of diverse urban designs, planners could better understand the trade-offs between urban development and biodiversity (Allam, Sharifi, et al., 2022). This facilitates informed decision-making that upholds the crucial balance between urban growth and ecological sustainability.

Citizen engagement in urban greening efforts is another potential application of the metaverse, that was anticipated to have significant positive impacts. Through the metaverse, users can actively participate in activities such as virtual gardening and urban farming initiatives which would not only educate the public about sustainable practices but also nurture a sense of ownership towards urban green spaces. The metaverse can also simulate the outcomes of these actions, providing an immediate feedback loop that reinforces the value of such efforts.

Another aspect of the urban green space that would benefit greatly from the adoption of the metaverse in urban planning is ecological restoration and conservation. In conventional cities, the ecology has been declining at an alarming rate following activities such as expansion of infrastructure, increased construction initiatives, pollution, and others. As such, most of those have been in dire need of rehabilitation, restoration, and conservation. As such, the metaverse came at the right time, since via its virtual platforms, it is possible to simulate and predict the impacts of restoration efforts, assisting in the strategic deployment of resources. In addition to simulation, the metaverse can be utilized for virtual biodiversity surveys, thus aiding in the identification and protection of urban habitats, that would be otherwise destroyed. The conservation fete would not only be achieved by urban managers and planners but also by individual urban dwellers, who through the immersive experiences in the metaverse could acquire maximum knowledge and a profound connection with nature, which would in turn stimulate appreciation for their environment. The virtual experience could further inspire individuals to contribute towards the preservation of the physical world.

It is common knowledge that urban areas in particular have been very unequal in matters of accessibility to green spaces. In particular, the situation is always worse for those in lower income status, and those with diverse mobility challenges. However, the metaverse is providing some glimpse of hope, by providing opportunities for democratization and access to green spaces, allowing individuals with mobility constraints or those living in green-space-deficient areas to virtually experience nature. It also provides platforms for dialog and consensus-building between different urban players such as planners, ecologists, community leaders, and citizens, leading to holistic and effective conservation strategies (Zhang et al., 2022).

However, the existing digital divide characterized by skewed access to infrastructure, unaffordability of devices and tools, and others could limit the inclusivity and ultimate democratization of green spaces. This necessitates proactive approaches and measures to increase digital literacy and infrastructure, which are prerequisites for bridging the digital divide. Privacy and ethical fears that crowd the metaverse, especially regarding data collection and usage warrant special attention, with the focus being to address them amicably, within the earliest possible opportunity. Further, it should be appreciated that the virtual realm can never, in reality, replace the physical realm. In the same vein, the pursuit of real-world urban greening should never be supplemented by the virtual realm.

Sustainable lifestyles and behaviors

The role of the metaverse in urban sustainability efforts cannot be overstated, for as it has been shown earlier, it can impact almost all sectors within the urban realm. Regarding those different aspects, its capacity to simulate real-world environments and interactions in unprecedented detail presents an innovative platform to foster sustainable lifestyles and behaviors (de Regt et al., 2021). Virtual experiences in the metaverse hold the potential for raising awareness and fostering behavior change, not only in those spaces but also in the physical realm. The users of the metaverse are motivated to adopt a paradigm shift in their lifestyles by the myriad of immersive, realistic simulations of different environmental scenarios, e.g., as is the case in the movie "The Matrix" (Wachowski & Wachowski, 1999). Such experiences could evoke empathy towards the environment and encourage more subtle, sustainable behaviors. A case in point to affirm this argument could be derived from the study conducted by Stanford University's Virtual Human Interaction Lab which highlighted that people who chopped down a virtual tree were 20% more likely to conserve paper in real life (Pietrobon, 2020). This then underscores the efficacy of the metaverse in triggering cognitive and emotional shifts that can lead to sustainable behavior change.

The metaverse also presents unique possibilities for the achievement of the SDG 12 that underscores the need for sustainable consumption and production patterns. The virtual marketplace aspect that is made possible by the metaverse could be at the fore in promoting environmentally friendly products and services as opined in a study by Hennig-Thurau et al. (2022) suggesting that immersive product presentations can significantly influence consumer purchasing decisions. Buying from this understanding, it would then imply that the metaverse could also influence sustainable production practices through virtual manufacturing and fabrication simulations. In other words, the numerous virtual experiences in the metaverse could be used to influence both consumer preferences and producer practices in shifting towards more sustainable consumption and production patterns. Furthermore, the metaverse also holds significant promise for shaping the agenda toward sustainable education and training. This is particularly critical, as the metaverse's ability transcends a myriad of the traditional pedagogical methods limitations by delivering interactive, experiential learning on sustainability topics, and by reaching a wider scope of audience (users) from any part of the world (Alfaisal et al., 2022). By immersing learners in realistic simulations of environmental phenomena and sustainability solutions, the metaverse can foster a deeper understanding and commitment to sustainability.

As the global population slowly transitions towards sustainable lifestyles, the principles of accessibility and inclusivity must be made central, especially regarding digital environments, devices, and infrastructure. This must be emphasized by ensuring that the metaverse is equally accessible to all, irrespective of their socioeconomic, cultural, or demographic profiles. The design of digital platforms must by all means be culturally sensitive to ensure that sustainability initiatives reach all segments of the population and that they respect the rich heritage possessed by different communities around the world. This would ensure that community-driven sustainability initiatives are significantly enhanced through, and in the metaverse in an immersive way. It has been rightly argued that virtual community platforms can facilitate the exchange of best practices, collaborative problem-solving, and concerted action towards sustainability goals, and such could include different issues that have been discussed in this chapter.

In addition to using virtual platforms to promote culturally sensitive practices, they could also be used to empower urban residents, regardless of their demographic backgrounds to participate in the codesign and implementation of local sustainability initiatives. On this, it has been found that online collaboration greatly increases the success rate of local sustainability initiatives. Collaborative approaches to sustainable behavior change are also critical. The metaverse can integrate perspectives and actions from the virtual and physical environments by promoting active collaboration between multiple stakeholders. This multistakeholder relationship can result in comprehensive, informed, and effective strategies for promoting sustainable behaviors, both in the virtual and physical realms. However, the metaverse's application especially for its ability for personalization must be balanced with privacy considerations. While personalized sustainability recommendations could motivate individual behavior change, they need to be carefully managed to respect users' privacy and data rights. Clear data governance protocols and ethical standards that play a pivotal role in addressing these concerns must be pursued, and strictly enforced.

Ethical considerations and future challenges

The emergence and rise of the metaverse came at an era where there have been profound ethical and moral concerns concerning the diverse use of technology in influencing normal human lives and their ecosystems. It is not surprising therefore that even in a pertinent and sensitive discourse about the environment, ethical concerns continue to emerge. It has therefore been argued that while the metaverse fuses virtual and physical realities in an immersive way in championing the environmental sustainability agenda, it attracts several pertinent ethical and moral concerns. First, a significant number of people are concerned about the equitability aspect, especially regarding the accessibility of metaverse-based environmental solutions. The concerns are exacerbated by an outright digital divide that exists and seems to be expanding across socioeconomic, geographic, and demographic boundaries, even with the rise of the metaverse (Bosworth & Gregg, 2021). Because of this, to effectively capitalize on the metaverse's environmental potential, everyone, including those with limited resources, unstable financial sources, or physical abilities, must be able to participate and benefit. Therefore, there is no ubiquity that inclusivity, accessibility, and digital literacy need to be prioritized in the design and implementation of metaverse solutions.

Privacy and security considerations must also be given maximum attention, particularly if the advocates of the metaverse are to expect universal support. On this, it has been widely documented that the vast quantity of environmental data collected and analyzed within the metaverse could easily inform sustainability strategies, but at the same time, pose risks related to data protection and privacy (Ahmad & Corovic, 2022). Hence, robust data governance frameworks need to be established, ensuring transparency, security, and user consent, just like is the case with other technologies being deployed in different facets of the urban fabric.

Another ethical consideration that should not escape the attention of the diverse stakeholders involved in building different virtual environmental initiatives is the sensitive issue of rights and representation quests of marginalized communities. It has rightly been recorded that historically, most of those communities have often been left out of environmental decisions that affect them; and projects and programs are forced on them. The apprehension of such faces could befall the metaverse if it were to perpetuate such exclusion, and close doors for diverse voices and perspectives (Adegoke, 2022). This underscores the need for equitable, participatory design in metaverse initiatives.

While the metaverse does not model the physical entities in silos but does so with the help of technologies such as DT, AI, and others, issues of biases and limitations in virtual environmental modeling and simulations keep on arising, thus prompting ethical concern. One of the biases is that the models may not perfectly replicate real-world environmental processes, thereby potentially leading to inaccurate predictions or interpretations. Such could be addressed by emphasizing on continuous improvement of virtual models, taking into account diverse environmental factors and contexts.

It has also been reported that metaverse-based environmental interventions have the potential to prompt unintended consequences. In most cases, which is the primary objective of the metaverse is for these interventions to instigate positive environmental benefits, however, they may also result in unforeseen negative effects, such as increased energy use from data centers hosting the metaverse (McKenzie, 2021). This calls for a cautious, balanced approach, assessing both the benefits and potential adverse impacts of these interventions.

Such assessments also need to be put into practice regarding attempts to scale up metaverse-based environmental solutions, for this too presents diverse future challenges. While those targeted solutions may work well at a small scale or in specific contexts, they may face difficulties when scaled up due to variations in environmental conditions, technological infrastructure, geographical profile differences, economic status, and user behaviors. Thus, context-sensitive strategies for scaling up, such as adaptive management and continual learning would be inevitable.

Interdisciplinary collaboration and stakeholder engagement would also be crucial for navigating these ethical and future challenges (Koohang et al., 2023). That is, the complexities of the metaverse and environmental sustainability pursuits require insights from diverse disciplines, including computer science, environmental science, sociology, et cetera. Engaging a broad range of stakeholders, from policymakers (both at national and local government levels) to community members, can also ensure that the development and implementation of metaverse-based solutions are inclusive, responsive, and accountable. Such would also help in devising strategies that translate to an agreeable balance between technological advancements and environmental sustainability in the metaverse. That is, such ensures that while technological innovations drive the evolution of the metaverse, they do not exacerbate environmental degradation. Instead, technology should be harnessed to promote sustainable resource use, reduce environmental impacts, and support ecological regeneration in the metaverse and beyond.

Despite the comprehensive discussion extended in this chapter, we appreciate that the long-term impacts of the metaverse on urban environmental sustainability are still unfolding. Therefore, it becomes imperative that the ongoing research and monitoring need to be continuous to assess the effectiveness and sustainability of metaverse-based environmental initiatives. This should involve longitudinal studies, real-time monitoring systems, and participatory evaluation mechanisms to capture the multifaceted impacts of these initiatives over time and across different contexts.

References

Adegoke, D. (2022). Youth digital exclusion, big data divide and the future of work. In Q. Àkànle (Ed.), *Youth exclusion and empowerment in the contemporary global order: Existentialities in migrations, identity and the digital space* (pp. 33–47). Emerald Publishing Limited. https://doi.org/10.1108/978-1-80382-777-320221004.

Ahmad, I., & Corovic, T. (25 January 2022). *Privacy in a parallel digital universe: The metaverse*. Norton Rose Fulbright. Retrieved 30th May 2022 from https://www.dataprotectionreport.com/2022/01/privacy-in-a-parallel-digital-universe-the-metaverse/.

Alfaisal, R., Hashim, H., & Azizan, U. H. (2022). Metaverse system adoption in education: A systematic literature review. *Journal of Computers in Education, 1*. https://doi.org/10.1007/s40692-022-00256-6.

Allam, Z. (2020a). The first 50 days of COVID-19: A detailed chronological timeline and extensive review of literature documenting the pandemic. *Surveying the Covid-19 Pandemic its Implications*, *1*.

Allam, Z. (2020b). The second 50 days: A detailed chronological timeline and extensive review of literature documenting the COVID-19 pandemic from day 50 to day 100. *Surveying the Covid-19 Pandemic its Implications*, *9*.

Allam, Z. (2020c). The third 50 days: A detailed chronological timeline and extensive review of literature documenting the COVID-19 pandemic from day 100 to day 150. *Surveying the Covid-19 Pandemic its Implications*, *41*.

Allam, Z. (2021a). The case for autonomous smart cities in the wake of climate change. In *The rise of autonomous smart cities* (pp. 61–74). Cham: Palgrave Macmillan.

Allam, Z. (2021b). Global tourism and the risks of cultural homogeneity in smart and future cities. In *The rise of autonomous smart cities* (pp. 75–90). Cham: Palgrave Macmillan.

Allam, Z., & Dhunny, A. Z. (2019). On big data, artificial intelligence and smart cities. *Cities*, *89*, 80–91.

Allam, Z., & Newman, P. (2018). Redefining the smart city: Culture, metabolism and governance. *Smart Cities*, *1*(1), 4–25.

Allam, Z., Sharifi, A., Bibri, S. E., Jones, D. S., & Krogstie, J. (2022). The metaverse as a virtual form of smart cities: Opportunities and challenges for environmental, economic, and social sustainability in urban futures. *Smart Cities*, *5*(3), 771–801.

Alves, B. (2 June 2023). *Global waste generation—Statistics & facts*. Statista. https://www.statista.com/topics/4983/waste-generation-worldwide/#topicOverview.

Athienitis, A., & Karava, P. (2007). Simulation of façade and envelope design options for a new institutional building. *Solar Energy*, *81*, 1088–1103. https://doi.org/10.1016/j.solener.2007.02.006.

Batty, M. (2013). Big data, smart cities and city planning. *Dialogues in Human Geography*, *3*(3), 274–279. https://doi.org/10.1177/2043820613513390.

Beusch, L., Nauels, A., Gudmundsson, L., Gütschow, J., Schleussner, C.-F., & Seneviratne, S. I. (2022). Responsibility of major emitters for country-level warming and extreme hot years. *Communications Earth & Environment*, *3*(1), 7. https://doi.org/10.1038/s43247-021-00320-6.

Bibri, S., & Krogstie, J. (2019). Towards a novel model for smart sustainable city planning and development: A scholarly backcasting approach. *Journal of Futures Studies*, *24*(1), 45–62. https://doi.org/10.6531/JFS.201909_24(1).0004.

Bosworth, A., & Gregg, N. (2021). Building the metaverse responsibly. *Meta*. (27th September 2027). Retrieved 22nd April 2022 from https://about.fb.com/news/2021/09/building-the-metaverse-responsibly/.

Cao, W., Cai, Z., Yao, X., & Chen, L. (2023). Digital transformation to help carbon neutrality and green sustainable development based on the metaverse. *Sustainability*, *15*(9), 7132. https://www.mdpi.com/2071-1050/15/9/7132.

de Regt, A., Plangger, K., & Barnes, S. J. (2021). Virtual reality marketing and customer advocacy: Transforming experiences from story-telling to story-doing. *Journal of Business Research*, *136*, 513–522. https://doi.org/10.1016/j.jbusres.2021.08.004.

Doherty, N. (24 January 2019). *Offshore wind farm, UK*. Unsplash. Retrieved 25th June 2023 from https://unsplash.com/photos/pONBhDyOFoM.

Edouard, G. (28 May 2018). *Bicycle lane, Paris*. Unsplash. Retrieved 24th June 2023 from https://unsplash.com/photos/LzwcTpH9KTY.

Gadekallu, T., Huynh-The, T., Wang, W., Yenduri, G., Ranaweera, P., Pham, V., Costa, D. B., & Liyanage, M. (2022). *Blockchain for the metaverse: A review*.

Garaj, V., Dudley, J., & Kristensson, P. O. (31 August 2022). Five ways the metaverse could be revolutionary for people with disabilities. *The Conversation*. Retrieved 2nd June 2023 from https://theconversation.com/five-ways-the-metaverse-could-be-revolutionary-for-people-with-disabilities-183057.

Getty Images. (24 August 2022). *Smart home devices*. Unsplash. Retrieved 25th June 2023 from https://unsplash.com/photos/ckPCV5cy-6A.

Hashem, I. A. T., Chang, V., Anuar, N. B., Adewole, K., Yaqoob, I., Gani, A., Ahmed, E., & Chiroma, H. (2016). The role of big data in smart city. *International Journal of Information Management*, 36(5), 748–758. https://doi.org/10.1016/j.ijinfomgt.2016.05.002.

Hennig-Thurau, T., Aliman, D. N., Herting, A. M., Cziehso, G. P., Linder, M., & Kübler, R. V. (2022). Social interactions in the metaverse: Framework, initial evidence, and research roadmap. *Journal of the Academy of Marketing Science*. https://doi.org/10.1007/s11747-022-00908-0.

Hudson-Smith, A. (2022). Incoming metaverses: Digital mirrors for urban planning. *Urban Planning*, 7(2). https://doi.org/10.17645/up.v7i2.5193. (2022): Gaming, simulations, and planning: Physical and digital technologies for public participation in urban planning https://www.cogitatiopress.com/urbanplanning/article/view/5193.

Kitchin, R. (2015). *Data-driven, networked urbanism*. (The programmable city, issue).

Koohang, A., Nord, J. H., Ooi, K.-B., Tan, G. W.-H., Al-Emran, M., Aw, E. C.-X., Baabdullah, A. M., Buhalis, D., Cham, T.-H., Dennis, C., Dutot, V., Dwivedi, Y. K., Hughes, L., Mogaji, E., Pandey, N., Phau, I., Raman, R., Sharma, A., Sigala, M., ... Wong, L.-W. (2023). Shaping the metaverse into reality: A holistic multidisciplinary understanding of opportunities, challenges, and avenues for future investigation. *Journal of Computer Information Systems*, 1–31. https://doi.org/10.1080/08874417.2023.2165197.

Massally, K. N., Samuel, N., & Fukagawa, K. (19 July 2022). *Traversing the metaverse whilst managing risks with opportunities*. UNDP. Retrieved 2nd June 2023 from https://www.undp.org/blog/traversing-metaverse-whilst-managing-risks-opportunities.

McKenzie, J. (13 January 2021). *Powering the beast: Why we shouldn't worry about the Internet's rising electricity consumption*. Physics World. Retrieved 2nd June 2023 from https://physicsworld.com/a/powering-the-beast-why-we-shouldnt-worry-about-the-internets-rising-electricity-consumption/#:~:text=20%25%20of%20the%20worlds%20totalby%20the%20Internet%20by%202025.

Merz, B., Kuhlicke, C., Kunz, M., Pittore, M., Babeyko, A., Bresch, D. N., Domeisen, D. I. V., Feser, F., Koszalka, I., Kreibich, H., Pantillon, F., Parolai, S., Pinto, J. G., Punge, H. J., Rivalta, E., Schröter, K., Strehlow, K., Weisse, R., & Wurpts, A. (2020). Impact forecasting to support emergency management of natural hazards. *Reviews of Geophysics*, 58(4). https://doi.org/10.1029/2020RG000704. e2020RG000704.

Mohd Yusof, N., Zulkifli, M. F., Mohd Yusof, N., & Azman, N. (2018). Smart waste bin with real-time monitoring system. *International Journal of Engineering & Technology*, 7, 725. https://doi.org/10.14419/ijet.v7i2.29.14006.

Nañez Alonso, S. L., Reier Forradellas, R. F., Pi Morell, O., & Jorge-Vazquez, J. (2021). Digitalization, circular economy and environmental sustainability: The application of artificial intelligence in the efficient self-management of waste. *Sustainability*, 13(4). https://doi.org/10.3390/su13042092.

Pamucar, D., Deveci, M., Gokasar, I., Tavana, M., & Koppen, M. (2022). A metaverse assessment model for sustainable transportation using ordinal priority approach and Aczel-Alsina norms. *Technological Forecasting and Social Change*, 182. https://doi.org/10.1016/j.techfore.2022.121778.

Pestano, S. (11 August 2021). *Single-use trash bags pollute!*. Unsplash. Retrieved 22nd June 2023 from https://unsplash.com/photos/kgKWPEj_EvA.

Petkov, M. (1 February 2023). The metaverse economy: Vision, interoperability, challenges. *LinkedIn*. Retrieved 2nd June 2023 from https://www.linkedin.com/pulse/metaverse-economy-vision-interoperability-challenges-martin-petkov.

Pietrobon, A. (19 April 2020). "VR can feel indistinguishable from the real-world"—Tobin Asher (Stanford's VHIL). *XR Must*. Retrieved 4th June 2023 from https://www.xrmust.com/xrmagazine/interview-tobin-asher-stanford-vhil/.

Sahota, N. (2 May 2023). *Industrial metaverse: A new frontier for sustainability*. LinkedIn. Retrieved 3rd June 2023 from https://www.linkedin.com/pulse/industrial-metaverse-new-frontier-sustainability-neil-sahota-%E8%90%A8%E5%86%A0%E5%86%9B-?trk=article-ssr-frontend-pulse_more-articles_related-content-card.

United Nations Development Programme (UNDP). (2015). *Sustainable development goals*. UNDP. https://www.undp.org/content/dam/undp/library/corporate/brochure/SDGs_Booklet_Web_En.pdf.

Wachowski, L., & Wachowski, L. (1999). *Matrix trilogy*. W. B. Entertainment. Imports.

Yavo-Ayalon, S., Joshi, S., Zhang, Y., Han, R., Mahyar, N., & Ju, W. (2023). Building community resiliency through immersive communal extended reality (CXR). *Multimodal Technologies and Interaction*, *7*(5).

Zhang, X., Yang, D., Yow, C. H., Huang, L., Wu, X., Huang, X., Guo, J., Zhou, S., & Cai, Y. (2022). Metaverse for cultural heritages. *Electronics*, *11*(22).

Zuboff, S. (2019). *The age of surveillance capitalism: The fight for a human future at the new frontier of power: Barack Obama's books of 2019*. Profile Books Publishers. https://books.google.co.ke/books?id=W7ZEDgAAQBAJ.

Chapter 12

Reflections and prospects: The metaverse and cities

Introduction

> The metaverse is expected to revolutionize how individuals experience and interact with the digital realm, shaping various aspects of daily life.

The inception of the metaverse is highly tied to the evolution of digital technology, as well as the speculative nature of science fiction (like in the case of a book—Snow Crash, or the movie, Matrix et cetera) and the potential to transition into the realms of reality through the exponential growth of virtual and augmented reality (VR and AR), blockchain technology, and Artificial Intelligence (AI) (Allam, Bibri, et al., 2022). As such, the metaverse can be argued to be an integrative concept conceptualized as a conglomerate of interconnected, immersive digital spaces, forming a parallel universe that coexists and interfaces with the physical world (Dwivedi et al., 2022). In sum, it would be right to conclude that the genesis of the metaverse lies in the technological advancements experienced in the late 20th century and early 21st century, particularly with the advent of the internet and virtual worlds.

Today, the metaverse is no longer a hypothetical construct, but a reality made possible by advancements in technologies such as AR, VR, and AI. It has also gained substantial traction because of quests by different technology enthusiasts to explore and test the limits of different digital solutions. It has been predicted that approximately 25% of global internet users will in one way or another have interacted with metaverse elements by 2026 (Gartner, 2022). In the United Kingdom (UK) alone, a 2023 report posits that at least 47% of the population will have had some experience with the metaverse by 2032 (KPMG, 2023). This evolution underscores the expanding influence of the metaverse, as it continues to influence various aspects of society, including the gaming, entertainment, and social media industries. Its ability to create engaging, immersive experiences has revolutionized the way people interact, communicate, and form communities (Bailenson, 2021).

On significant area that the metaverse have shown immense potential is in the context of smart cities, where it has prompted various transformative pathways to drive urban development and improve quality of life. For instance, it has been argued that integrating physical and virtual environments has the potential to bolster sustainability and resource optimization, as endeared in Sustainable Development Goal 12. In particular, data from virtual simulations could become invaluable in informing and optimizing the management of city resources, thereby enhancing the overall urban ecosystem (Hudson-Smith, 2022). Moreover, the metaverse offers platforms to create and foster more inclusive and accessible city services. It is also true that with digital twins—digital replicas of physical assets in a city—urban planners get the opportunity to test and deploy solutions in the metaverse before the actual implementation of the same in the physical world (Allam, Sharifi, et al., 2022). This has the potential to save time, resources, and even lives (Batty, 2013).

The digital advancements discussed above are not without challenges. For instance, the complexities related to privacy, security, equity, identity, and representation in the metaverse underscore the need for comprehensive regulations and ethical guidelines. Regarding privacy and data protection, it has been expressed that such are at the core of smart cities, and the same would be true in the metaverse. Thus, it is paramount to design robust digital rights frameworks that strictly align with the principles of transparency, fairness, and accountability (Kitchin, 2016).

On another front, the emergence of the metaverse has brought to light complex issues related to identity and representation, especially of the minority and vulnerable groups. On this, it has been noted that as users traverse and explore the virtual and physical spaces, their digital identities become extensions of their physical selves. However, issues of identity theft and misrepresentation are likely to arise, necessitating stringent identity verification processes (Cheong, 2022). There is also a need to ensure the issues of representation of diverse communities in the metaverse are addressed to warrant equitable access and avoid replicating existing physical, and societal inequalities in the virtual world (Noble, 2018).

Analyzing the metaverse in the context of smart cities, therefore, provides an incredible lens to understand the intersections between this emerging technology and urban development. If cities were to perfectly harness the metaverse's transformative power, they could leapfrog towards more sustainable, inclusive, and efficient futures. However, as expressed above, there needs to be caution when implementing the metaverse in cities, to ensure that the challenges that this digital revolution poses are amicably addressed.

Future developments in the metaverse

In the future, the trajectory of the metaverse's success is envisaged to be influenced by innovative technological advancements, emerging trends, adoption into the mainstream, and their synergistic interplay. In addition, three key technologies, Augmented Reality (AR), blockchain, and Artificial Intelligence (AI) are anticipated to be the transformative forces in the metaverse's eventual evolution.

Unlike VR which immerses users in entirely digital environments, AR overlays digital elements onto the physical world, providing a unique blend of both realms. As such, it is anticipated that AR can offer a realistic, tangible, interactive metaverse experience which greatly reduces the boundaries between virtual and real worlds. Therefore, it is the hope that as AR matures, it could prompt more realistic and intuitive interactions within the metaverse, moving beyond the confines of traditional screen-based interfaces to more holistic, contextually integrated experiences.

However, Blockchain technology is argued to serves as a foundational component for the metaverse by providing the architecture for decentralized virtual spaces and digital ownership. The immutability and transparency characteristics of blockchain could facilitate increased peer-to-peer transactions, enabling users to own and trade in diverse things such as virtual assets, such as virtual land, with real-world value (Gadekallu et al., 2022). Furthermore, blockchain could enable the adoption of more democratic governance structures within the metaverse, opening possibilities for user-driven development and evolution (Allam, 2018).

AI is expected to play a crucial role in the future development of the metaverse, powering intelligent virtual environments, personalized experiences, and dynamic interactions, thereby enhancing user engagement, and expanding the possibilities of this digital realm.

On its part, AI is observed to bring dynamism to the metaverse, allowing for more personalized and interactive experiences. Ture to its nature, it is anticipated to continue creating a context-aware environments, thus, responding to users' behavior trends and preferences in real-time. It can also facilitate the creation of Nonplayer Characters (NPCs) with increasingly sophisticated behavioral algorithms, enhancing social interactions within the metaverse (Multiverse, 2021).

The above developments, in addition, have had and will continue to have profound implications on cities. For instance, AR could allow for transformations of urban spaces into interactive platforms, layering digital information onto physical locations and enhancing urban exploration and experience (Kaji et al., 2018). However, Blockchain could continue to catalyze the development of a "virtual real estate market," affecting urban development in both parallel universes, and also by creating new economic opportunities and challenges (Huynh-The et al., 2023). AI, meanwhile, could enhance smarter city systems by utilizing metaverse data to influence diverse urban frontiers such as resource, traffic management, and public services deliveries (Batty, 2018).

The anticipation going into the future is that the metaverse could catalyze transformative changes across diverse sectors, including education, health, entertainment, tourism, culture and creative art, transport, environment, and others. In education, anticipation is that it will actualize the provision of immersive, interactive learning environments and enhance interpersonal engagement thus enabling new pedagogical approaches (Alfaisal et al., 2022). In healthcare, the metaverse is expected to stimulate different aspects through virtual simulations. For instance, it is expected to be instrumental in promotion training, telemedicine, and therapy, thus, extending the reach and effectiveness of health services (Benrimoh et al., 2022). In entertainment, the metaverse could revolutionize content production and eventual consumption, especially by creating immersive, participatory experiences that push the boundaries of traditional media (Qi, 2022) (Fig. 12.1).

Noting that the metaverse is still in the infancy stages of its development, and adoption in different sectors of the global economy, ongoing research and development will be the driving force behind which the anticipated feats will be achieved. This means that interdisciplinary collaboration will be very critical in catalyzing the metaverse's successful integration into cities. This means that all players and stakeholders within the urban planning and development realm including computer scientists, urban planners, sociologists, economists, and others, will need to understand and navigate the intricacies of the metaverse. A harmonious synthesis of these disciplines could guide the evolution of the metaverse, ensuring it is aligned with societal needs and values, and geared towards the creation of smart, inclusive, and sustainable cities.

FIG. 12.1 Illustration of virtual immersion with a VR headset (Studio, 2024).

Challenges and limitations of the metaverse

The numerous advancements and possibilities associated with the metaverse integration into urban life attracts a set of assorted challenges and limitations that cannot be overlooked. For instance, the metaverse's demand for robust technological infrastructure and pervasive connectivity represents a considerable obstacle for many urban areas. First, indeed most of these cities may not measure up to such infrastructural demands. Secondly, the financial implication of such infrastructural investments may not be tenable, especially, with the current states of a global economy which have been greatly affected by the COVID-19 pandemic (Allam & Jones, 2021), the Russia-Ukraine conflict and other challenges like climate change (Allam et al., 2020a, 2020b; Allam & Jones, 2019). As such, the basic requirements in the metaverse such as high-speed internet and advanced hardware, may derail its universal adoption, as such are inaccessible to a substantial part of the population, thus widening the digital divide. While those challenges are a reality, it is incumbent upon policymakers to strive for digital equity, ensuring that no demographic is left behind in this technological leap.

Another set of concerns associated with the metaverse include privacy, security, and data protection issues that, in reality are not unique to the virtual realm, but have been a bother since the emergence of the digital revolution. However, it is appreciated that the metaverse, by its nature, captures vast amount of personal data, and in the course of this maps user behaviors and preferences in a detailed, real-time manner (Ahmad & Corovic, 2022). Therefore, even as the push for an increased infiltration of the metaverse in different urban realm continues, it is deemed critical to ensure sensitive information is guarded from misuse and ensuring robust user consent mechanisms become paramount. That goes in hand with ensuring stringent security measures are in place to guard against cyberattacks, identity theft, and virtual vandalism are in place to maintain the metaverse as a safe and trustworthy environment (Gupta et al., 2023). In addition to those, it will be also important to address the multifaceted ethical questions on culture and heritage for different people. The metaverse could also amplify existing societal biases and inequalities if not designed inclusively. For example, the portrayal and representation of diverse cultures, genders, and identities within the metaverse is a complex issue that requires careful attention to avoid stereotyping or marginalization (George et al., 2021).

The reality of the above challenges should not over shadow the fact that the metaverse has the potential to disrupt social dynamics, offering new forms of interaction that may reshape cultural norms and societal structures (Allam, Sharifi, et al., 2022).

The metaverse's immersive and ubiquitous nature also poses risks related to misinformation, cyberbullying (Pooyandeh et al., 2022), addictive behaviors (Bojic, 2022; Lee et al., 2021), and in the extreme, the ability to aid antisocial behaviors like terrorism (Debuire, 2022). The potential for the high degree of user engagement in the metaverse can potentially act as a potent amplifier for misinformation and propaganda, exacerbating the challenges already faced in our information societies (Multiverse, 2021). As a counter to this, it will be paramount to develop special digital tools to authenticate information and curb the spread of harmful content within the metaverse. Likewise, it will be important to fast track the formulation of policies and mechanisms to prevent cyberbullying, protect user wellbeing, and promote healthy usage habits within the metaverse to prevent it from becoming an environment conducive to addictive, or other antisocial behaviors (Fig. 12.2).

> Addressing risks and ethical concerns: the metaverse's immersive nature poses risks of misinformation, cyberbullying, and addictive behaviors. Policymakers and industry leaders must develop digital tools to authenticate information and protect users' well-being, while fostering policies to prevent harmful content spread. Striking a balance between the metaverse's potential benefits and ethical concerns is essential to uphold individual rights, inclusivity, and social progress. Collaborative engagement among diverse stakeholders is critical for responsible metaverse implementation.

It should also be noted that the need to strike a balance between the metaverse's potential benefits and the associated concerns is a complex undertaking that demands careful and robust intervention. The allure of enhanced urban experiences, innovative digital applications, and new economic opportunities promised by the metaverse should not overcrowd the necessity of upholding individual rights, societal values, and sustainable practices. That is, the metaverse should not become a new platform for surveillance, exclusion, or

FIG. 12.2 An image representation of a cyberbully (Patterson, 2019).

exploitation, but should instead be fashioned to enhance collective wellbeing, inclusivity, and social progress (Massally et al., 2022).

The collaborative engagement of diverse stakeholders such as the policymakers, industry leaders, and user communities, is instrumental in addressing the above-mentioned challenges and ensuring a responsible trajectory for metaverse implementation. Policymakers need to provide a regulatory oversight framework to protect user rights, while industry leaders have a responsibility to develop ethical and inclusive technologies and digital tools. Meanwhile, users and communities would also need to play a crucial role in shaping the metaverse from the ground up, ensuring it reflects the diverse needs, cultural diversities, and aspirations of all.

The future of the metaverse and cities

The envisioned future metaverse within the context of urban life heralds a transformative convergence of physical and virtual worlds, engendering manifold opportunities, yet bringing about notable challenges. Amongst the most notable opportunities that the metaverse has brought forth is the capacity to revolutionize urban planning and design approaches. On this, through the lens of the metaverse, city planners could harness immersive simulations to facilitate a new dimension of spatial understanding, enabling predictive modeling of urban changes and scenario testing (White et al., 2021). The shift towards a data-driven approach in city planning, catalyzed by metaverse technologies, promises a precise understanding of urban phenomena, and may result in more responsive urban design.

At the nexus of the metaverse and smart cities is the increased promise for a notable paradigm shift in civic engagement, which has often hindered by physical constraints and participation inequality. The metaverse could potentially democratize access to civic participation, enabling remote attendance at public meetings, virtual town halls, and interactive policy discussions (Bingöl, 2022). In other fronts, but related to civic engagement, the metaverse could ignite new forms of cultural experiences, allowing users to engage with digitized artefacts, explore virtual heritage sites, and actively participate in digitally-enhanced cultural festivals and events. With these examples, it is true that if the metaverse is harnessed judiciously, it could serve as a tool for fostering equity, inclusivity, and accessibility within cities. This is because it has the potential to overcome physical barriers and bridge social divides by providing digital access to public services, cultural events, and civic participation (Paulauskas et al., 2023).

Another key advantage that the metaverse is making possible is the ability to reduce the physical distance or mobility constraints that have often inhibited individuals' quests to participate in urban life, thus, offering an inclusive platform for social interaction and cultural expression. In the urban setting still, the metaverse could contribute significantly to sustainable resource management, efficient and affordable mobility solutions, and optimized service delivery in future cities. By employing real-time data and advanced analytics, the metaverse could enhance the management of city resources such as water, energy, public spaces, and services, ensuring their optimal utilization. It could also enable smart mobility solutions (such as the use of bicycles), providing real-time traffic updates, route optimization, and demand-responsive transport services (Paiva et al., 2021).

Despite these promising prospects, prospective challenges will require a conscientious and concerted effort to mitigate, and if possible, to overcome. It will be inevitable to guarantee data privacy, digital rights, and equitable access stand for the realization of a fair and inclusive metaverse. Solutions that provide strong privacy protections, uphold user rights, and promote digital inclusivity must be a cornerstone of the metaverse's development.

Recommendations for policy and decision-makers

As the metaverse continues to elicit hope for a pivotal framework in human collective digital future, it invites a conscious relook into the policy formulation and decision-making practices, to ensure that those align with the anticipated changes. This then calls for a spirited and concerted stakeholders engage to proactively provide the way forward in this emergent reality.

One of the priorities for policymakers and urban planners would be to comprehend the intricate landscape of the metaverse, given its transformative potential and far-reaching possibilities and implications. It would then be of great importance if this understanding is pursued through multifaceted strategies, embracing rigorous academic research, innovative pilot projects, and comprehensive stakeholder engagement (Wang & Lin, 2023). Such approaches should aim to identify opportunities, anticipate challenges, and generate the knowledge necessary to guide the responsible integration of the metaverse into urban ecosystems.

Central to these strategies is the need to consider social, economic, and environmental factors and implications, as the metaverse is not merely a technological construct, but is inherently intertwined with diverse societal dimensions. Economic factors such as job creation, wealth distribution, and business models need to be investigated about metaverse technologies, especially in view of the recent trends where most activities are shifting to the digital realm. It should also be appreciated that environmentally, the metaverse could provide platforms for virtual meetings and events, potentially reducing travel and infrastructure building related carbon emissions. On the social level, the metaverse could enhance social connectivity (Fig. 12.3) but may also exacerbate digital divides if not implemented equitably. Therefore, an integrated approach that considers these interconnected dimensions is pivotal in steering the metaverse's pathway towards positive urban outcomes.

However, the complex, cross-cutting nature of the metaverse necessitates fostering robust collaborations between diverse sectors. Governments in particular should actively seek to build partnerships with private industry, academic

FIG. 12.3 People socializing in the virtual environment (Ava Calvar, 2023).

institutions, and civil society to enable inclusive and responsible metaverse implementation (Bosworth & Gregg, 2021). Such collaborations can facilitate knowledge exchange, resource pooling, and consensus-building, crucial components in navigating the multifaceted challenges of the metaverse.

Policy and decision-makers must also be privy and ready to act in relation to the critical issues of privacy, security, and ethics in the metaverse. Developing comprehensive guidelines, frameworks and robust regulations will be integral in addressing these concerns. These regulatory frameworks should aim to ensure transparency in data handling, protect user rights, and address ethical dilemmas, such as misinformation, cultural heritage abuse, addictions, and cyberbullying.

To ensure that the existing digital divide challenges are not rolled over into the metaverse, it will be critical to emphasize on investments in digital infrastructure, connectivity, and digital literacy initiatives. In the future, access to the metaverse should not be treated as a privilege confined to certain sections of society, but it needs to be viewed as it should be; a right accessible to all (Trunfio & Rossi, 2022). Therefore, initiatives aimed at enhancing digital literacy, improving connectivity, and expanding digital infrastructure will need to be integral in bridging the digital divide and ensuring equitable access to the metaverse.

To cap all the above, policymakers should be ready to actively support interdisciplinary research and innovation in metaverse applications. Such research could yield insights into its potential uses in diverse fields such as education, healthcare, urban sustainability, and beyond. Policy support—through funding, collaboration, or facilitation will also need to be given priority as it could accelerate the development and adoption of innovative metaverse applications that contribute to improving urban living conditions and achieving sustainability goals.

Final thoughts and closing remarks

The metaverse which is a digital universe envisioned as a true replica and extension of our physical world, has emerged as a powerful concept with the potential to significantly transform urban environments and enhance the quality of life for urban residents. The integration of this digital entity with physical environments in cities posits an unparalleled opportunity for societal progression, beyond what existing technological applications have so far offered.

Reflecting on the takeaways from this extensive and comprehensive exploration of the metaverse's intersection with smart cities, one can discern that the impact of the metaverse extends overwhelmingly beyond mere technological advancements. It permeates the complex layers of society, culture, and human interactions and interrelations, redefining the way people live, work, learn, enjoy recreation activities, and socialize (Allam, Sharifi, et al., 2022). The dynamics of the metaverse holds significant implications for our understanding of public and private spaces, democratic participation, social inclusion, and cultural representation (Multiverse, 2021). The intricate and multifaceted nature of the metaverse necessitates a commitment to continued research, experimentation, and exploration. While this book has started to unravel some of the metaverse's complexities and potentials, the journey towards fully understanding and optimizing this new reality may have just started, as the metaverse is still in its early stages. A continuation of this work will be inevitable as navigating the complexities of the metaverse, from technological hurdles to ethical quandaries will require a robust academic and practical inquiry grounded in interdisciplinary perspectives (Allam, Sharifi, et al., 2022).

One critical lesson that has emerged from this extensive examination is the need to embrace the metaverse, not in silos, but as a collective effort. The study has clearly unraveled that the onus of ensuring equity, inclusivity, and sustainability in the metaverse does not rest solely on policymakers, industry leaders, or individual users. Instead, it is a shared responsibility that requires concerted efforts from all stakeholders. For instance, it has come out clear that promoting digital literacy, safeguarding user rights, and mitigating the risk of the digital divide are among the numerous shared objectives that need undivided, collective attention and action.

Without a doubt, this study has confirmed that the metaverse holds the promise to significantly shape the cities of the future, offering platforms that allows for the integration of physical and virtual environments. When fully exploited, the metaverse could usher in a new era of innovation, hyperconnectivity, and enhanced urban experiences. But it should be appreciated that such transformative potential, should not overshadow the need for vigilance against possible adverse effects, such as privacy infringements, social isolation, and misinformation (Bosworth & Gregg, 2021).

After the extensive exploration of the metaverse and how it could be integrated into smart cities, we are left with a sense of cautious optimism. This is based on the fact that the promises of the metaverse are profound, but so too are the challenges it presents. The way forward then, it to encourage further investigation, interdisciplinary dialogue, and collaboration. The aim is to encourage the creation of cities that are not just smarter and more efficient, but also more sustainable, equitable, and inclusive. The metaverse, as envisioned today, stands at the threshold of a new frontier. Therefore, as we step into this future, we should carry with us the lessons learned from the past and the aspirations we hold for our collective urban future. It is with this thought that we close, acknowledging the journey ahead in understanding and navigating the metaverse in our urban landscapes. It is a voyage that we undertake not in isolation but in unity, with the shared goal of creating cities that embody the principles of sustainability, inclusivity, and humanity in the era of the metaverse.

References

Ahmad, I., & Corovic, T. (2022). *Privacy in a parallel digital universe: The metaverse* [Online]. *Norton Rose Fulbright*. Available: https://www.Dataprotectionreport.Com/2022/01/Privacy-In-A-Parallel-Digital-Universe-The-Metaverse/. (Accessed 30 May 2022).

Alfaisal, R., Hashim, H., & Azizan, U. H. (2022). Metaverse system adoption in education: A systematic literature review. *Journal of Computers in Education, 1*.

Allam, Z. (2018). On smart contracts and organisational performance: A review of smart contracts through the blockchain technology. *Review Of Economic Business Studies, 11*, 137–156.

Allam, Z., Bibri, S. E., Jones, D. S., Chabaud, D., & Moreno, C. (2022). Unpacking the 15-Minute City via 6g, Iot, and digital twins: Towards a new narrative for increasing urban efficiency, resilience, and sustainability. *Sensors, 22*, 1369.

Allam, Z., & Jones, D. (2019). Climate change and economic resilience through urban and cultural heritage: The case of emerging small island developing states economies. *Economies, 7*, 62.

Allam, Z., & Jones, D. S. (2021). Future (post-Covid) digital, smart and sustainable cities in the wake of 6g: Digital twins, immersive realities and new urban economies. *Land Use Policy, 101*, 105201.

Allam, Z., Jones, D., & Thondoo, M. (2020a). Climate change mitigation and urban liveability. In *Cities and climate change*. Cham: Palgrave Macmillan.

Allam, Z., Jones, D., & Thondoo, M. (2020b). Urban resilience and climate change. In *Cities and climate change*. Cham: Palgrave Macmillan.

Allam, Z., Sharifi, A., Bibri, S. E., Jones, D. S., & Krogstie, J. (2022). The metaverse as a virtual form of smart cities: Opportunities and challenges for environmental, economic, and social sustainability in urban futures. *Smart Cities, 5*, 771–801.

Ava Calvar. (2023). *VR headset* [Online]. *Unsplash*. Available: https://Unsplash.Com/Photos/Ts5kj02bfli. (Accessed 28 June 2023).

Bailenson, J. N. (2021). Nonverbal overload: A theoretical argument for the causes of zoom fatigue. *Technology, Mind, And Behavior, 2*.

Batty, M. (2013). Big data, smart cities and city planning. *Dialogues in Human Geography, 3*, 274–279.

Batty, M. (2018). Artificial intelligence and smart cities. *Environment and Planning B: Urban Analytics and City Science, 45*, 3–6.

Benrimoh, D., Chheda, F. D., & Margolese, H. C. (2022). The best predictor of the future-the metaverse, mental health, and lessons learned from current technologies. *JMIR Mental Health, 9*, E40410.

Bingöl, E. S. (2022). Citizen participation in smart sustainable cities. In E. A. Babaoğlu, & O. Kulaç (Eds.), *Research anthology on citizen engagement and activism for social change* IGI Global.

Bojic, L. (2022). Metaverse through the prism of power and addiction: What will happen when the virtual world becomes more attractive than reality? *European Journal of Futures Research*, *10*, 22.

Bosworth, A., & Gregg, N. (2021). *Building the metaverse responsibly* [online]. *Meta*. Available: https://About.Fb.Com/News/2021/09/Building-The-Metaverse-Responsibly/. (Accessed 22 April 2022).

Cheong, B. C. (2022). Avatars in the metaverse: Potential legal issues and remedies. *International Cybersecurity Law Review*, *3*, 467–494.

Debuire, D. (2022). *Terrorist use of the metaverse: New opportunities and new challenges* [online]. *Security Distillery*. Available: https://Thesecuritydistillery.Org/All-Articles/Terrorism-And-The-Metaverse-New-Opportunities-And-New-Challenges. (Accessed 30 May 2022).

Dwivedi, Y. K., Hughes, L., Baabdullah, A. M., Ribeiro-Navarrete, S., Giannakis, M., Al-Debei, M. M., Dennehy, D., Metri, B., Buhalis, D., Cheung, C. M. K., Conboy, K., Doyle, R., Dubey, R., Dutot, V., Felix, R., Goyal, D. P., Gustafsson, A., Hinsch, C., Jebabli, I., … Wamba, S. F. (2022). Metaverse beyond the hype: Multidisciplinary perspectives on emerging challenges, opportunities, and agenda for research, practice and policy. *International Journal of Information Management*, *66*, 102542.

Gadekallu, T., Huynh-The, T., Wang, W., Yenduri, G., Ranaweera, P., Pham, V., Costa, D. B., & Liyanage, M. (2022). *Blockchain for the metaverse: A review*.

Gartner. (2022). *Gartner predicts 25% of people will spend at least one hour per day in the metaverse by 2026* [online]. *Gartner*. Available: https://Www.Gartner.Com/En/Newsroom/Press-Releases/2022-02-07-Gartner-Predicts-25-Percent-Of-People-Will-Spend-At-Least-One-Hour-Per-Day-In-The-Metaverse-By-2026. (Accessed 4 June 2023).

George, A. S., Fernando, M., George, A. S., Baskar, D., & Pandey, D. (2021). Metaverse: The next stage of human culture and the internet. *International Journal of Advanced Research Trends in Engineering and Technology*, *8*, 1–10.

Gupta, A., Khan, H. U., Nazir, S., Shafiq, M., & Shabaz, M. (2023). Metaverse security: Issues, challenges and a viable ZTA model. *Electronics*, *12*, 391.

Hudson-Smith, A. (2022). Incoming metaverses: Digital mirrors for urban planning. *Urban Planning*, *7(2)*. https://doi.org/10.17645/Up.V7i2.5193. (2022): Gaming, Simulations, And Planning: Physical And Digital Technologies For Public Participation In Urban Planning.

Huynh-The, T., Gadekallu, T. R., Wang, W., Yenduri, G., Ranaweera, P., Pham, Q.-V., Da Costa, D. B., & Liyanage, M. (2023). Blockchain for the metaverse: A review. *Future Generation Computer Systems*, *143*, 401–419.

Kaji, S., Kolivand, H., Madani, R., Salehinia, M., & Shafaie, M. (2018). Augmented reality in smart cities: Applications and limitations. *Journal of Engineering Technology*, *6*, 18.

Kitchin, R. (2016). The ethics of smart cities and urban science. *Philosophical Transactions of the Royal Society A: Mathematical, Physical and Engineering Sciences*, *374*, 1–15.

KPMG. (2023). *Almost half of UK consumers think the metaverse will become widely used in the next 10 years* [online]. *KPMG*. Available: https://Kpmg.Com/Uk/En/Home/Media/Press-Releases/2023/05/Almost-Half-Of-Uk-Consumers-Think-The-Metaverse-Will-Become-Widely-Used-In-The-Next-10-Years.Html. (Accessed 4 June 2023).

Lee, Z. W. Y., Cheung, C. M. K., & Chan, T. K. H. (2021). Understanding massively multiplayer online role-playing game addiction: A hedonic management perspective. *Information Systems Journal*, *31*, 33–61.

Massally, K. N., Samuel, N., & Fukagawa, K. (2022). *Traversing the metaverse whilst managing risks with opportunities* [Online]. *Undp*. Available: https://www.Undp.Org/Blog/Traversing-Metaverse-Whilst-Managing-Risks-Opportunities. (Accessed 2 June 2023).

Multiverse. (2021). *Virtual agents are becoming major players in the expanding metaverse [online]*. Available: Multiverse.Ai https://www.Multiverse.Ai/Stories/Virtual-Agents-Are-Becoming-Major-Players-In-The-Expanding-Metaverse. (Accessed 5 June 2023).

Noble, S. U. (2018). *Algorithms of oppression: How search engines reinforce racism*. New York, NY: New York University Press.

Paiva, S., Ahad, M. A., Tripathi, G., Feroz, N., & Casalino, G. (2021). Enabling technologies for urban smart mobility: Recent trends, opportunities and challenges. *Sensors, 21*.

Patterson, C. (2019). *Anonymous hacker* [online]. *Unsplash*. Available: https://Unsplash.Com/Photos/Dyeufb8kqjk. (Accessed 29 June 2023).

Paulauskas, L., Paulauskas, A., Blažauskas, T., Damaševičius, R., & Maskeliūnas, R. (2023). Reconstruction of industrial and historical heritage for cultural enrichment using virtual and augmented reality. *Technologies [Online], 11*.

Pooyandeh, M., Han, K.-J., & Sohn, I. (2022). Cybersecurity in the AI-based metaverse: A survey. *12* (p. 12993).

Qi, W. (2022). The investment value of metaverse in the media and entertainment industry. *BCP Business & Management, 34*, 279–283.

Trunfio, M., & Rossi, S. (2022). Advances in metaverse investigation: Streams of research and future agenda. *Virtual Worlds [Online], 1*.

Wang, Y., & Lin, Y.-S. (2023). Public participation in urban design with augmented reality technology based on indicator evaluation. *Frontiers in Virtual Reality, 4*.

White, G., Zink, A., Codecá, L., & Clarke, S. (2021). A digital twin smart city for citizen feedback. *Cities, 110*, 103064.

Index

Note: Page numbers followed by *f* indicate figures, *t* indicate tables, and *b* indicate boxes.

A

Accessibility, 47, 95–96, 100, 106–107, 164–165, 197–198
Addiction, 24, 28–29, 39–40, 45, 64, 217
Adventure (game), 24–25
AI. *See* Artificial intelligence (AI)
AidChain, 161–162
Amsterdam Circular Innovation Program (ACIP), 62
Amsterdam city, 56–57, 62
AR. *See* Augmented reality (AR)
Architectural visualization, 142, 142*b*
Artificial intelligence (AI), 43–44, 65, 119–120, 122–123, 126–128, 144–145, 160, 179, 191, 209–211, 211*b*
Augmented reality (AR), 29–31, 43, 50, 85, 101, 103, 135–136, 136*t*, 157, 176, 195, 209–211
  for cultural experiences and diversity, 158–160
  in education, 30
  emergence, 29–31
  Pompeii Touch, 159–160, 159*f*
  in real estate development, 136, 142–144
  Streetmuseum, 160
  in transport sector, 123
Avatars, 8–9, 20, 26, 183

B

Barcelona city, 38–39, 42–43, 61, 61*f*, 77, 79, 86–87, 107
Bicycle land provision, in Paris, 197*f*
Big data, 179
Blockchain, 32, 32*f*, 43–44, 47, 65, 109, 128, 144, 151, 162, 176–177, 177*f*, 196, 198, 209–211
Blockchain-based decentralized finance tools, 8
Breach, data, 44–45, 50–51, 67, 146, 183
Burning Man Multiverse concept, 158
Buyers, 9, 129, 135–138, 142–143, 146, 148–149

C

Campus of the Future initiative, 150–151
Circular economy, 57, 62, 198–200, 199*f*
Citizen engagement, 107, 201
CityVR project, 102
Climate adaptation, 60, 108
Climate change, 1, 13–14, 31, 38, 57, 60, 108, 138, 150, 195
Cloudburst management plan, 60
Cocreation, 62, 110–111
Collaboration, 47, 110–111
Collaborative urban planning, 107
Colossal Cave Adventure (game), 24–25
Commercialization, 12, 183
Community building
  and social connections, 157–158
  virtual public spaces for, 123
Community engagement, 66, 76–77
Community moderation, 167–168
Community participation, 119, 122, 127
Congestion, 14, 96–97, 100, 129, 196
Copenhagen city, 60, 60*f*
The Country of the Blind, 22
COVID-19 pandemic, 31, 122–123, 196, 213
  impacts, 178–180
  metaverse's role during, 129–130
  real estate development during, 139
Creativity, 4, 43
Cryptovoxels, 149
Cultural diversity, 166
Cultural events, 106–108
Cultural Exchange Metaverse Initiative, 167
Cultural heritage, 159
Cultural sensitivity, 63–64, 109–110, 165–167
Cultural symbols, 166, 166*f*
Cultural tourism, 108
Curate app, 148–149
Cyberbullying, 213–214, 214*b*, 214*f*
Cybersecurity, 146

D

Data analytics, 160–161, 179, 191
Data breach, 44–45, 50–51, 67, 146, 183

223

Data computing, 179
Data-driven algorithms, 117
Data-driven decision-making, 62, 93–94, 98, 107, 145, 160–161
Data ownership, 109, 183–184
Data privacy, 50–51, 77, 102, 105–106, 122, 126*f*, 141, 143–144, 179, 210, 216
Data protection, 83–84, 145, 204, 210, 213
Dataveillance, 163
Decentraland, 10, 109, 140–141, 147–148
Decentralization, 65
Decision-making, 119–122, 126–127, 130, 143, 179, 195
Digital cities, 158
Digital City Testbed Center, Berlin, 129–130
Digital divide, 39–40, 48–49, 63, 82, 118, 126, 146–147, 164–165, 179, 181–182, 185, 193–194, 198, 201–202, 216–218
Digital equity, 104, 213
Digital Equity Initiative in Portland, 105
Digital interaction, 19–20
Digital land, 140, 149–150
Digital simulation, 122*b*
Digital twins (DT), 8–9, 8*b*, 26–27, 31, 56–57, 61, 119–120, 122, 127, 129, 135–136, 136*t*, 191, 210
Digitization, 135–136
DT. *See* Digital twins (DT)

E

Early virtual worlds, 24–26
Ecocities. *See* Sustainable cities
E-commerce, 5, 30, 39, 50, 123
Economic inequality, 174
Economics, 10–11, 32–33, 175–177
  challenges in traditional urban settings, 173–175
  ethical and legal implications, 183–184
  urban employment, 180–181
  urban planning and development, 178–179
Economic sustainability, 55–56
Education, 44, 212
  augmented reality (AR) in, 30
  early virtual worlds, impact of, 25–26
  metaverse-enabled work and, 80–82
Emergency management, 108
Energy consumption, 56–57
Energy efficiency, 191–194
Energy management, 76
Entertainment industry, 9, 23–24, 44, 175–176, 212
Environmental impact, 97, 104

Environmental monitoring and analysis, 194–196, 194*f*
Environmental sustainability, 203–204
Equity, 104, 182–183
Ethereum blockchain, 140–141, 147–150
Ethics, 46, 48–50, 64, 67, 108–110
eXistenZ (movie), 22–23

F

15-Minute City planning model, 38–39, 41–42, 56, 85–86, 178–179
Financing, 58–59
Fortnite (game), 37
Fourth Industrial Revolution, 122
Fragmentation, 155–157, 174
From the Earth to the Moon, 22
Future cities
  challenges and limitations, 82–84
  smart infrastructure, 75–77
  urban experience and engagement, 77–80
  work and education, 80–82

G

Gaming environments, 24–26
GDPR. *See* General Data Protection Regulation (GDPR)
General Data Protection Regulation (GDPR), 84, 105, 108–109, 163–164
Gini coefficient, 174
Global Commission on the Economy and Climate, 58–59
Global Nomads Group, 81
Greenhouse gas emission, 50, 55, 59, 138
Green spaces, 200–202
5G technology, 6–7, 10–11, 31, 42, 46, 62, 151, 160

H

Head-mounted display (HMD), 22
Heads-up display (HUD), 30
Healthcare industry, 9, 44, 161–162, 212, 217
Helsinki city, 56, 102
Heritage preservation, 108
High Line in New York City, 110–111
Holoporting, 10*b*
HVAC, 40–41, 40*b*

I

Iceberg, 161
Identity theft, 11, 163, 183, 210, 213

Immersive experiences, 20, 39, 48, 73–74, 77–78, 80
IMVU, 10
Inclusive cocreation, 110–111
Inclusivity, 104, 106–107, 164–165, 182–183, 197–198
Indigenous Metaverses Project, 167
Information and communication (ICT) system, 193–194
Innovative technologies, 62
Intellectual property rights, 46, 48, 183–186
Interactive graphics programs, 24–25
Interdisciplinary collaboration, 66, 106, 205, 212
Interdisciplinary research, 217
International Labor Organization (ILO), 173
International Renewable Energy Agency, 59
Internet, 5–6
Internet-in-a-Box project, 165
Internet of Things (IoT), 65, 77, 122–123, 144–145, 160, 191, 194, 197, 200
Invisible Cities, 160
IoT. *See* Internet of Things (IoT)

J
Job creation, 180, 216
Job displacement, 180–181
Journey to the Center of the Earth, 22

L
Land acquisition, 137–138
Land use, 178–179
Language, 110, 157, 165
La Rochele, France, 99*f*
The Lawnmower Man (movie), 29
Legal framework, 48
Legends of Future Past (game), 26
Loneliness, impacts of, 155, 156*f*
Louvre Museum, 102

M
Machine learning, 126–128, 179
Mana, 10
Massively multiplayer online games (MMOGS), 26–27, 27*b*
The Matrix (movie), 22–23, 28, 202
Maze War (game), 24–25
Melbourne city, 79, 108
Meshers, 10, 10*b*
Metaverse, 6–7, 6*b*, 73–74*b*, 93*b*
  challenges, 1–2, 12–13, 213–215
  concept, origins of, 22–24
  definition, 37*b*
  economy, 10–11
  environmental footprint, 49
  fears and critisms, 11–12
  foundational elements, 6–8
  future cities (*see* Future cities)
  future developments in, 210–212
  history, 2–3
  internet, 5–6
  limitations, 213–215
  perceived importance, 3–5
  pop culture, 28–29
  science fiction, 28–29
  smart cities, 13–14, 39–40, 45–46
  sustainable cities (*see* Sustainable cities)
  21st century, 31–33
  urban life (*see* Urban life)
  use cases, 8–9
Metaverse Seoul, 77
Microsoft, 150
Mobile apps, 41
Monetization, 12
Mori Building Digital Art Museum, 78
Multistakeholder collaboration, 62, 64
Multiuser Dungeon (MUD), 26
Museum of Other Realities, 102

N
Neom city, Saudi Arabia, 102
Neuromancer (novel), 28
New York City (NYC), 156–157
New York City Virtual Hub (NYCVH), 106–107
Nonfungible tokens (NFTs), 109, 147–148, 176, 176*b*
Nonplayer Characters (NPCs), 211

O
Online gaming industry, 8
Online harassment, 163
Open Metaverse Accessibility Initiative, 165
Ownership, of data, 183–184

P
Parallel digital universe, 22
Paris, bicycle land provision in, 197*f*
Participatory design, 84, 105, 109–110
Past View, 103
Polarization, 155–156

Policy
    and decision-makers, 217
    recommendations, 216–217
    and regulatory frameworks, 105–106
Policymakers, 151, 183–184, 215–216
Pompeii Touch, 159–160, 159*f*
Pop culture, 28–29
Portability of skills, 12
Privacy, 4–5, 24, 41–42, 44–45, 48, 77, 83–84, 104, 108–109, 162–164, 167–168, 183, 201–202, 204, 210
Privacy by Design principle, 163–164
Public engagement, 14, 62

Q

Quality of life, for urban residents, 98, 103, 106
Queen's Road Central, Hong Kong, 97*f*
QVerse, 21

R

Ready Player One (movie), 22–23, 28–29, 118–119, 139–140, 147, 158
Real estate
    benefits and challenges of metaverse in, 145–147
    cost implications, 137–138
    smart technologies in management, 144–145
    virtual, 139–141
    visualization, 139–141
Real estate development, 135–136
    case studies, 147–150
    challenges, 136–139
    during COVID-19 pandemic, 139
    limitations, 136–139
    real estate visualization, 139–141
    smart technologies in, 144–145
    traditional, 136–139
    virtual real estate, 139–141
Recycling, 199–200
Regulatory frameworks, 151, 183–186
Remote learning, 23
Remote sensing, 194
Remote work opportunities, 80
Renewable energy, 56–57, 192*b*, 193
Resource management, 191–194
Restoration, 201
Retail industry, 9, 30
Roblox, 31–32
Robust encryption, 146
Russia-Ukraine conflict, 173, 213

S

Sandbox, 140–141
Science fiction, 2, 28–29
Second Life (SL), 2, 20*b*, 25, 28–29, 31–32, 46–47
Security, 41–42, 44–45, 48, 77, 83–84, 108–109, 146, 183, 204, 210
Sensors, 40–41, 200
Seoul's Metaverse City Project, 107
Shanghai city, 47
Sidewalk Toronto project, 102
Singapore city, 38–39, 38*f*, 42–43, 47, 61, 75–76, 75*f*
6G technology, 10–11, 46, 74, 151, 160
Skill development, 80
Small Island Developing States (SIDS), 57, 195
Smart city, 1, 13–14, 19–20, 24, 38–43, 41*b*, 45–46, 98, 105, 120–121, 191, 210
Smart City Sandbox, 78–79
Smart City Vienna, 129
Smart contracts, 151
Smart Dubai initiative, 105
Smart economic zones, 179
Smart heat control device, 41*f*
Smart home monitoring device, 194, 194*f*
Smart infrastructure, 75–77
Smart Nation Initiative, 61
Smart technologies
    for efficient social service delivery, 160–162
    in real estate management, 144–145
Snow Crash, 19, 28, 37
Social cohesion, 94, 174–175
Social connections, community building and, 157–158
Social distancing, 123
Social implications, 46, 48–50, 108–110
Social interactions, 93–94, 100
    in urban environments, 155–157
Social isolation, 11, 45, 97–99, 155–157
Social media, 5, 123
Social service delivery, smart technologies for, 160–162
Social sustainability, 56
Societal expectations, 32–33
Socioeconomic inequality, 46, 174, 181
Sotheby's international realty, 148–149
Spirited conspiracy theory, 41–42
Stakeholders engagement, 119, 122, 129, 138, 194, 205, 215
Streetmuseum, 160
Structural inequality, 126–127
Superblocks project, 61, 61*f*

Supply chain disruption, 139
Sustainability, 118, 120–121
Sustainable behaviors, 202–203
Sustainable cities, 55, 57b
　challenges, 57–59
　economic benefits, 59
　environmental benefits, 59
　financing, 58–59
　opportunities, 57–59
Sustainable Development Goal 12 (SDG 12), 191–192, 192t, 202–203, 210
Sustainable lifestyles, 202–203
Sustainable mobility, 196–198
Sustainable transportation, 196–198
Sword of Damocles, 29–30

T

Targeted advertising, 163
Terrorism, 163
3D gaming environments, 24–25
3D graphics, 7–8, 8f
3D immersive simulations, 157
3D render of summer camp, 119, 120f
Tibetan Prayer Flag, 166f
TimeLooper, 103
Top-down decision-making approach, 121
Trade-offs, 200–201
Traditional real estate, 136–139
Traditional urban planning, 119–120
Traffic congestion, 14, 42–43, 96, 100, 129, 196
Traffic management, 196–197
Transformation, 111, 135, 139b, 150–151
TranslAide, 165
Transportation, 56, 58f, 75–76, 75f, 94, 196
Transport sector, VR and AR in, 123
Tron (movie), 28
Two-factor authentication, 146

U

Unemployment, 173, 185
United Kingdom, sustainable energy farm in, 193, 193f
Urban biodiversity, 200–202
Urban employment, 180–181
Urban farming, 201
Urbanization, 58, 138, 160
Urban life
　challenges, 95–99
　metaverse
　　applications, 99–103
　　benefits and challenges, 103–106
　case studies, 106–108
　collaboration and cocreation, 110–111
　ethical and social implications, 108–110
Urban livability, 38–41, 47
Urban planning, metaverse in, 13, 30–31, 38, 45, 56, 65–66, 74, 85, 93–94, 106–108, 212, 215
　applications, 122–123
　case studies, 129–130
　challenges, 124–127, 124–125t
　community engagement, 124–125t
　data privacy, risks of, 126, 126f
　developments, 127–128
　economic impact, 124–125t
　environmental impact, 124–125t
　equity and inclusivity, 124–125t, 126, 128
　limitations, 124–127
　opportunities and benefits, 119–122
　privacy and security, 124–125t, 126–127, 130
　regulatory compliance, 124–125t
　simulation fidelity, 124–125t
　technological and data-driven biases, 124–125t, 126–127, 130
　virtual and physical tool integration, 124–125t, 127
Urban resilience, 195
Urban services, 103
Use cases, 8–9

V

VirBELA, 161–162
Virtual Barcelona, 107
Virtual classrooms, 9, 81, 81f
Virtual collaboration, 60
Virtual concerts, 44, 44f
Virtual conferences, 20–21
Virtual currency, 176–177
Virtual environment, 94, 94f
Virtual Fixtures, 30
Virtual gardening, 201
Virtual Harlem project, 109–111
Virtual Helsinki, 79, 106–108
Virtual London, 108
Virtual meetings, 20–21
Virtual Melbourne, 108
Virtual real estate, 139–141, 175–176, 211
Virtual reality (VR), 2, 3f, 5, 6f, 22, 22b, 24, 43, 50, 65, 74, 85, 123, 135–136, 136t, 157, 176, 195, 209
　art exhibitions, 102
　emergence, 29–31

Virtual reality (VR) (*Continued*)
   headsets, 29–30, 30*f*, 118
   in real estate development, 129, 136, 142–144
   in transport sector, 123
Virtual replicas, of physical assets, 127
Virtual simulations, 119–120, 122, 127, 129–130, 178–179, 191, 199, 210
Virtual Singapore, 61, 74, 85, 101, 107, 129
Virtual staging, 143
Virtual tourism, 9
Virtual towns, 158
Virtual world, 24–26, 77, 86
VR. *See* Virtual reality (VR)
VRHealth, 161–162

W

Waste management, 57, 198–200
Water management, 76
WeWork, 149
Wonderland exhibition, 79
Work and commerce, 4
Work-from-home, 181, 196
Working from anywhere, 181
World of Warcraft (WoW), 2, 20*b*, 25, 31–32
World Wide Web, 5

Z

Zork (game), 24–25

Printed in the United States
by Baker & Taylor Publisher Services